IT Essentials:
PC Hardware and Software
Lab Manual
Fourth Edition

Cisco Networking Academy

Cisco Press

800 East 96th Street

Indianapolis, Indiana 46240 USA

IT Essentials: PC Hardware and Software Lab Manual, Fourth Edition

Cisco Networking Academy

Copyright© 2010 Cisco Systems, Inc.

Published by:
Cisco Press
800 East 96th Street
Indianapolis, IN 46240 USA

Printed in the United States of America

Second Printing June 2010

Library of Congress Cataloging-in-Publication Data available upon request.

ISBN-13: 978-1-58713-262-9

ISBN-10: 1-58713-262-1

Warning and Disclaimer

This book is designed to provide information about networking. Every effort has been made to make this book as complete and as accurate as possible, but no warranty or fitness is implied.

The information is provided on an "as is" basis. The authors, Cisco Press, and Cisco Systems, Inc. shall have neither liability nor responsibility to any person or entity with respect to any loss or damages arising from the information contained in this book or from the use of the discs or programs that may accompany it.

The opinions expressed in this book belong to the author and are not necessarily those of Cisco Systems, Inc.

Trademark Acknowledgments

All terms mentioned in this book that are known to be trademarks or service marks have been appropriately capitalized. Cisco Press or Cisco Systems, Inc., cannot attest to the accuracy of this information. Use of a term in this book should not be regarded as affecting the validity of any trademark or service mark.

This book is part of the Cisco Networking Academy® series from Cisco Press. The products in this series support and complement the Cisco Networking Academy curriculum. If you are using this book outside the Networking Academy, then you are not preparing with a Cisco trained and authorized Networking Academy provider.

For more information on the Cisco Networking Academy or to locate a Networking Academy, Please visit www.cisco.com/edu.

CISCO

Feedback Information

At Cisco Press, our goal is to create in-depth technical books of the highest quality and value. Each book is crafted with care and precision, undergoing rigorous development that involves the unique expertise of members from the professional technical community.

Readers' feedback is a natural continuation of this process. If you have any comments regarding how we could improve the quality of this book, or otherwise alter it to better suit your needs, you can contact us through email at feedback@ciscopress.com. Please make sure to include the book title and ISBN in your message.

We greatly appreciate your assistance.

Publisher	**Paul Boger**
Associate Publisher	**Dave Dusthimer**
Cisco Representative	**Erik Ullanderson**
Cisco Press Program Manager	**Anand Sundaram**
Executive Editor	**Mary Beth Ray**
Managing Editor	**Sandra Schroeder**
Senior Project Editor	**Tonya Simpson**
Editorial Assistant	**Vanessa Evans**
Cover Designer	**Sandra Schroeder**

Americas Headquarters
Cisco Systems, Inc.
170 West Tasman Drive
San Jose, CA 95134-1706
USA
www.cisco.com
Tel: 408 526-4000
800 553-NETS (6387)
Fax: 408 527-0683

Asia Pacific Headquarters
Cisco Systems, Inc.
168 Robinson Road
#28-01 Capital Tower
Singapore 068912
www.cisco.com
Tel: +65 6317 7777
Fax: +65 6317 7799

Europe Headquarters
Cisco Systems International BV
Haarlerbergpark
Haarlerbergweg 13-19
1101 CH Amsterdam
The Netherlands
www-europe.cisco.com
Tel: +31 0 800 020 0791
Fax: +31 0 20 357 1100

Cisco has more than 200 offices worldwide. Addresses, phone numbers, and fax numbers are listed on the Cisco Website at www.cisco.com/go/offices.

Contents

About This Lab Manual

The only authorized Lab Manual for the Cisco Networking Academy IT Essentials v4.1 course

IT Essentials: PC Hardware and Software Lab Manual, Fourth Edition is a supplemental book that helps the students in the Cisco Networking Academy course prepare to take the CompTIA A+ exams (based on the 2009 objectives). The hands-on labs, worksheets, and class discussions from the course are printed within this book to practice performing tasks that will help you become a successful PC technician. By reading and completing this book, you have the opportunity to review all key concepts that the CompTIA exams cover and reinforce those concepts with hands-on exercises.

Command Syntax Conventions

The conventions used to present command syntax in this book are the same conventions used in the IOS Command Reference. The Command Reference describes these conventions as follows:

∞ **Boldface** indicates commands and keywords that are entered literally as shown. In actual configuration examples and output (not general command syntax), boldface indicates commands that are manually input by the user (such as a **show** command).

∞ *Italic* indicates arguments for which you supply actual values.

∞ Vertical bars (|) separate alternative, mutually exclusive elements.

∞ Square brackets ([ ]) indicate an optional element.

∞ Braces ({ }) indicate a required choice.

∞ Braces within brackets ([{ }]) indicate a required choice within an optional element.

Chapter 1: Introduction to the Personal Computer

1.1.2 Worksheet: Job Opportunities

In this worksheet, you will use the Internet, magazines, or a local newspaper to gather information for jobs in the computer service and repair field. Be prepared to discuss your research in class.

1. Research three computer-related jobs. For each job, write the company name and the job title in the column on the left. Write the job details that are most important to you, as well as, the job qualifications in the column on the right. An example has been provided for you.

Company Name and Job Title	Details and Qualifications
Gentronics Flexible Solutions/ Field Service Representative	Company offers continuing education. Work with hardware and software. Work directly with customers. Local Travel. • A+ certification preferred • 1 year installation or repair experience of computer hardware and software required • Requires a valid driver's license • Must have reliable personal transportation • Mileage reimbursement • Ability to lift and carry up to 50 lbs

2. Based on your research, which job would you prefer? Be prepared to discuss your answer in class.

1.4.7 Worksheet: Research Computer Components

In this worksheet, you will use the Internet, a newspaper, or a local store to gather information about the components you will need to complete your customer's computer. Be prepared to discuss your selections.

Your customer already owns the **case** described in the table below.

Brand and Model Number	Features	Cost
Cooler Master CAC-T05-UW	ATX Mid Tower ATX, Micro ATX compatible form factor 2 External 5.25" drive bays 2 External 3.5" drive bay 2 Internal 5.25" drive bays 7 expansion slots USB, Firewire, Audio ports	

Search the Internet, a newspaper, or a local store to research a **power supply** compatible with the components that your customer owns. Enter the specifications in the table below.

Brand and Model Number	Features	Cost

Your customer already owns the **motherboard** described in the table below.

Brand and Model Number	Features	Cost
GIGABYTE GA-965P-DS3	LGA 775 DDR2 800 PCI Express x16 SATA 3.0Gb/s interface 1.8V-2.4V RAM voltage 1066/800/533MHz Front Side Bus 4 Memory Slots Dual Channel Memory Supported ATA100 connector RAID 0/1 4 USB 2.0 ports ATX Form Factor	

Search the Internet, a newspaper, or a local store to research a **CPU** compatible with the components that your customer owns. Enter the specifications in the table below.

Brand and Model Number	Features	Cost

Search the Internet, a newspaper, or a local store to research a **cooling device** compatible with the components that your customer owns. Enter the specifications in the table below.

Brand and Model Number	Features	Cost

Search the Internet, a newspaper, or a local store to research **RAM** compatible with the components that your customer owns. Enter the specifications in the table below.

Brand and Model Number	Features	Cost

Your customer already owns the **hard disk drive** described in the table below.

Brand and Model Number	Features	Cost
Seagate ST3400620AS	400 GB 7200 RPM 16 MB Cache SATA 3.0Gb/s interface	$119.99

Search the Internet, a newspaper, or a local store to research a **video adapter card** compatible with the components that your customer owns. Enter the specifications in the table below.

Brand and Model Number	Features	Cost

1. List three components that must have the same or compatible form factor.

2. List three components that must conform to the same socket type.

3. List two components that must utilize the same front side bus speed.

4. List three considerations when you choose memory.

5. What component must be compatible with every other component of the computer?

Chapter 2: Safe Lab Procedures and Tool Use

2.2.2 Worksheet: Diagnostic Software

In this worksheet, you will use the Internet, a newspaper, or a local store to gather information about a hard drive diagnostic program. Be prepared to discuss the diagnostic software you researched.

1. Based on your research, list at least two different hard drive manufacturers.

2. Based on your research, choose a hard drive manufacturer. Does this manufacturer offer hard drive diagnostic software to go with their products? If so, list the name and the features of the diagnostic software.

   Manufacturer:

   Software Name:

   File Name:

   File Size:

   Version:

   Publish Date:

   Description:

2.3.4 Lab: Computer Disassembly

In this lab you will disassemble a computer using safe lab procedures and the proper tools. Use extreme care and follow all safety procedures. Familiarize yourself with the tools you will be using in this lab.

NOTE: If you cannot locate or remove the correct component, ask your instructor for help.

Recommended Tools

Safety glasses or goggles	Part retriever (or tweezers or needle nose pliers)
Antistatic wrist strap	Thermal compound
Antistatic mat	Electronics cleaning solution
Flat head screwdrivers	Can of compressed air
Phillips head screwdrivers	Cable ties
Torx screwdrivers	Parts organizer
Hex driver	Computer with hard drive installed
Wire cutters	Plastic tub for storing computer parts
Plastic	Antistatic bags for electronic parts

Step 1

Turn off and disconnect the power to your computer.

Step 2

Locate all of the screws that secure the side panels to the back of the computer. Use the proper size and type of screwdriver to remove the side panel screws. Do not remove the screws that secure the power supply to the case. Put all of these screws in one place, such as a cup or a compartment in a parts organizer. Label the cup or compartment with a piece of masking tape on which you have written 'side panel screws'. Remove the side panels from the case.

What type of screwdriver did you use to remove the screws?

1st power supply
last: motherboard.

How many screws secured the side panels?

Step 3

Put on an antistatic wrist strap. One end of the conductor should be connected to the wrist strap. Clip the other end of the conductor to an unpainted, metal part of the case.

If you have an antistatic mat, place it on the work surface and put the computer case on top of it. Ground the antistatic mat to an unpainted, metal part of the case.

Step 4

Locate the hard drive. Carefully disconnect the power and data cable from the back of the hard drive.

Which type of data cable did you disconnect?

Step 5

Locate all of the screws that hold the hard drive in place. Use the proper size and type of screwdriver to remove the hard drive screws. Put all of these screws in one place and label them.

What type of screws secured the hard drive to the case?

How many screws secured the hard drive to the case?

Is the hard drive connected to a mounting bracket? If so, what type of screws secure the hard drive to the mounting bracket?

CAUTION: Do NOT remove the screws for the hard drive enclosure.

Step 6

Gently remove the hard drive from the case. Look for a jumper reference chart on the hard drive. If there is a jumper installed on the hard drive, use the jumper reference chart to see if the hard drive is set for a Master, Slave, or Cable Select (CS) drive. Place the hard drive in an antistatic bag.

Step 7

Locate the floppy disk drive. Carefully disconnect the power and data cable.

Step 8

Locate and remove all of the screws that secure the floppy drive to the case. Put all of these screws in one place and label them.

Place the floppy drive in an antistatic bag.

How many screws secured the floppy drive to the case?

Step 9

Locate the optical drive (CD-ROM, DVD, etc). Carefully disconnect the power and data cable from the optical drive. Remove the audio cable from the optical drive.

What kind of data cable did you disconnect?

Is there a jumper on the optical drive? What is the jumper setting?

Step 10

Locate and remove all of the screws that secure the optical drive to the case. Put all of these screws in one place and label them. Place the optical drive in an antistatic bag.

How many screws secured the optical drive to the case?

Step 11

Locate the power supply. Find the power connection(s) to the motherboard.

Gently remove the power connection(s) from the motherboard. How many pins are there in the motherboard connector? 20 pins

Does the power supply provide power to a CPU fan or case fan? If so, disconnect the power cable.

Does the power supply provide auxiliary power to the video card? If so, disconnect the power cable.

Step 12

Locate and remove all of the screws that secure the power supply to the case. Put all of these screws in one place and label them.

How many screws secure the power supply to the case?

Carefully remove the power supply from the case. Place the power supply with the other computer components.

Step 13

Locate any adapter cards that are installed in the computer, such as a video, NIC, or modem adapter.

Locate and remove the screw that secures the adapter card to the case. Put the adapter card screws in one place and label them.

Carefully remove the adapter card from the slot. Be sure to hold the adapter card by the mounting bracket or by the edges. Place the adapter card in an antistatic bag. Repeat this process for all of the adapter cards.

List the adapter cards and the slot types below.

Adapter Card	Slot Type
_____	_____
_____	_____
_____	_____

Step 14

Locate the memory modules on the motherboard.

What type of memory modules are installed on the motherboard?

How many memory modules are installed on the motherboard?

Remove the memory modules from the motherboard. Be sure to release any locking tabs that may be securing the memory module. Hold the memory module by the edges and gently lift out of the slot. Put the memory modules in an antistatic bag.

Step 15

Remove all data cables from the motherboard. Make sure to note the connection location of any cable you disconnect.

What types of cables were disconnected?

You have completed this lab. The computer case should contain the motherboard, the CPU, and any cooling devices. Do not remove any additional components from case.

Chapter 3: Computer Assembly—Step by Step

3.2 Lab: Install the Power Supply

Introduction

In this lab, you will install a power supply in a computer case.

Recommended Equipment

- Power supply with a compatible form factor to the computer case
- Computer case
- Tool kit
- Power supply screws

Step 1

Remove the screws from the side panels.

Remove the side panels from the computer case.

Step 2

Align the screw holes in the power supply with the screw holes in the case.

Secure the power supply to the case with the power supply screws.

Step 3

If the power supply has a voltage selection switch, set this switch to match the voltage in your area.

What is the voltage in your area?

How many screws secure the power supply in the case?

What is the total wattage of the power supply?

This lab is complete. Please have the instructor verify your work.

3.3.3 Lab: Install the Motherboard

Introduction

In this lab, you will install a CPU, a heat sink/fan assembly, and a RAM module on the motherboard. You will then install the motherboard in the computer case.

Recommended Equipment

- Computer case with power supply installed
- Motherboard
- CPU
- Heat sink/fan assembly
- Thermal compound
- RAM module(s)
- Motherboard standoffs and screws
- Antistatic wrist strap and antistatic mat
- Tool kit
- Motherboard manual

Step 1

Place the motherboard, the CPU, the heat sink/fan assembly and the RAM module on the antistatic mat.

Step 2

Put on your antistatic wrist strap and attach the grounding cable to the antistatic mat.

Locate Pin 1 on the CPU. Locate Pin 1 on the socket.

NOTE: The CPU may be damaged if it is installed incorrectly.

Align Pin 1 on the CPU with Pin 1 on the socket.

Place the CPU into the CPU socket.

Close the CPU load plate and secure it in place by closing the load lever and moving it under the load lever retention tab.

Step 3

Apply a small amount of thermal compound to the CPU and spread it evenly.

NOTE: Thermal compound is only necessary when not included on the heat sink. Follow all instructions provided by the manufacturer for specific application details.

Step 4

Align the heat sink/fan assembly retainers with the holes on the motherboard around the CPU socket.

Place the heat sink/fan assembly onto the CPU and the retainers through the holes on the motherboard.

Tighten the heat sink/fan assembly retainers to secure it.

Plug the fan connector into the motherboard. Refer to the motherboard manual to determine which set of fan header pins to use.

Step 5

Locate the RAM slots on the motherboard.

In what type of slot(s) will the RAM module(s) be installed?

How many notches are found on the bottom edge of the RAM module?

Align the notch(es) on the bottom edge of the RAM module to the notches in the slot.

Press down until the side tabs secure the RAM module.

Ensure that none of the RAM module contacts are visible. Reseat the RAM module if necessary.

Check the latches to verify that the RAM module is secure.

Install any additional RAM modules using the same procedures.

Step 6

Install the motherboard standoffs.

Align the connectors on the back of the motherboard with the openings in the back of the computer case.

Place the motherboard into the case and align the holes for the screws and the stand-offs. You may need to adjust the motherboard to line up the holes for the screws.

Attach the motherboard to the case using the appropriate screws.

Step 7

Connect the wires from the case link lights and buttons to the motherboard connectors.

This lab is complete. Please have the instructor verify your work.

3.5.2 Lab: Install the Drives

Introduction

In this lab, you will install the hard disk drive, the optical drive, and the floppy drive.

Recommended Equipment

- Computer case with power supply and motherboard installed
- Antistatic wrist strap and antistatic mat
- Tool kit
- Hard disk drive
- Hard disk drive screws
- Floppy drive
- Floppy drive screws
- Optical drive
- Optical drive screws
- Motherboard manual

Step 1

Align the hard disk drive with the 3.5 inch drive bay.

Slide the hard disk drive into the bay from the inside of the case until the screw holes line up with the holes in the 3.5 inch drive bay.

Secure the hard disk drive to the case using the proper screws.

Step 2

NOTE: Remove the 5.25 inch cover from one of the 5.25 inch external drive bays if necessary.

Align the optical drive with the 5.25 inch drive bay.

Insert the optical drive into the drive bay from the front of the case until the screw holes line up with the holes in the 5.25 inch drive bay and the front of the optical drive is flush with the front of the case.

Secure the optical drive to the case using the proper screws.

Step 3

NOTE: Remove the 3.5 inch cover from one of the 3.5 inch external drive bays if necessary.

Align the floppy drive with the 3.5 inch drive bay.

Insert the floppy drive into the drive bay from the front of the case until the screw holes line up with the holes in the 3.5 inch drive bay and the front of the floppy drive is flush with the front of the case.

Secure the floppy drive to the case using the proper screws.

This lab is complete. Please have the instructor verify your work.

3.6.3 Lab: Install Adapter Cards

Introduction
In this lab, you will install a NIC, a wireless NIC, and a video adapter card.

Recommended Equipment
- Computer with power supply, motherboard, and drives installed
- NIC
- Wireless NIC
- Video Adapter Card
- Adapter card screws
- Antistatic wrist strap and antistatic mat
- Tool kit
- Motherboard manual

Step 1
What type of expansion slot is compatible with the NIC?

Locate a compatible expansion slot for the NIC on the motherboard.

Remove the slot cover from the back of the case, if necessary.

Align the NIC to the expansion slot.

Press down gently on the NIC until the card is fully seated.

Secure the NIC by attaching the PC mounting bracket to the case with a screw.

Step 2

What type of expansion slot is compatible with the wireless NIC?

Locate a compatible expansion slot for the wireless NIC on the motherboard.

Remove the slot cover from the back of the case, if necessary.

Align the wireless NIC to the expansion slot.

Press down gently on the wireless NIC until the card is fully seated.

Secure the wireless NIC by attaching the PC mounting bracket to the case with a screw.

Step 3

What type of expansion slot is compatible with the video adapter card?

Locate a compatible expansion slot for the video adapter card on the motherboard.

Remove the slot cover from the back of the case, if necessary.

Align the video adapter card to the expansion slot.

Press down gently on the video adapter card until the card is fully seated.

Secure the video adapter card by attaching the PC mounting bracket to the case with a screw.

This lab is complete. Please have the instructor verify your work.

3.7.2 Lab: Install Internal Cables

Introduction

In this lab, install the internal power and data cables in the computer.

Recommended Equipment

- Computer with power supply, motherboard, drives, and adapter cards installed
- Hard disk drive data cable
- Optical drive data cable
- Floppy drive data cable
- Antistatic wrist strap and antistatic mat
- Tool kit
- Motherboard manual

Step 1

Align the motherboard power supply connector to the socket on the motherboard.

Gently press down on the connector until the clip clicks into place.

Step 2

NOTE: This step is necessary only if your computer has an auxiliary power connector.

Align the auxiliary power connector to the auxiliary power socket on the motherboard.

Gently press down on the connector until the clip clicks into place.

Step 3

Plug a power connector into the hard disk drive, optical drive, and floppy drive. Ensure that the floppy drive power connector is inserted right side up.

Step 4

NOTE: This step is necessary only if your computer has a fan power connector.

Connect the fan power connector into the appropriate fan header on the motherboard.

Step 5

NOTE: Pin 1 on a PATA cable must align with Pin 1 on the motherboard connector and the hard disk drive connector.

Align and plug the hard disk drive data cable into the motherboard connector.

Align and plug the other end of the hard disk drive data cable into the hard disk drive connector.

Step 6

NOTE: Pin 1 on a PATA cable must align with Pin 1 on the motherboard connector and the optical drive connector.

Align and plug the optical drive data cable into the motherboard connector.

Align and plug the other end of the optical drive data cable into the optical drive connector.

Step 7

NOTE: Pin 1 on a floppy drive cable must align with Pin 1 on the motherboard connector and the floppy drive connector.

Align and plug the floppy drive data cable into the motherboard connector.

Align and plug the other end of the floppy drive data cable into the floppy drive connector.

This lab is complete. Please have the instructor verify your work

3.8.2 Lab: Complete the Computer Assembly

Introduction

In this lab, you will install the side panels and the external cables on the computer.

Recommended Equipment

- Computer with power supply, motherboard, drives, and adapter cards installed, and internal cables connected
- Monitor cable (DVI or VGA)
- Keyboard
- Mouse
- USB cable for the USB hub
- USB cable for the USB printer
- Network cable
- Wireless antenna
- Power cable
- Tool kit
- Motherboard manual

Step 1

Attach the side panels to the computer case.

Secure the side panels to the computer using the panel screws.

Step 2

Attach the monitor cable to the video port.

Secure the cable by tightening the screws on the connector.

Step 3

Plug the keyboard cable into the PS/2 keyboard port.

Step 4

Plug the mouse cable into the PS/2 mouse port.

Step 5

Plug the hub USB cable into any USB port.

Step 6

Plug the printer USB cable into a USB port in the hub.

Step 7

Plug the Ethernet cable into the Ethernet port.

Step 8

Connect the wireless antenna to the antenna connector.

Step 9

Plug the power cable into the power socket of the power supply.

3.9.2 Lab: Boot the Computer

Introduction

In this lab, you will boot the computer for the first time, explore the BIOS setup program, and change the boot order sequence.

Recommended Equipment

- Assembled computer without an operating system installed
- Motherboard manual

Step 1

Plug the power supply cable into an AC wall outlet.

Turn on the computer.

NOTE: If the computer beeps more than once, or if the power does not come on, notify your instructor.

Step 2

During POST, press the BIOS setup key or key combination.

The BIOS setup program screen will appear.

What is the key or combination of keys used to enter the BIOS setup program?

Who manufactures the BIOS for your computer?

What is the BIOS version?

What menu options are available?

Step 3

Navigate through each screen to find the boot order sequence.

What is the first boot device in the boot order sequence?

How many additional devices can be assigned in the boot order sequence?

Step 4

Ensure that the first boot order device is the optical drive.

Ensure that the second boot order device is the hard disk drive.

Why would you change the first boot device to the optical drive?

What happens when the computer boots and the optical drive does not contain bootable media?

Step 5

Navigate through each screen to find the power management setup screen, or ACPI screen.

What power management settings are available?

Step 6

Navigate through each screen to find the PnP settings.

What PnP settings are available?

Step 7

Save the new BIOS settings and exit the BIOS setup program.

Step 8

The computer will restart.

An operating system can be installed at this time.

This lab is complete. Please have the instructor verify your work.

Chapter 4: Basics of Preventive Maintenance and Troubleshooting

There are no labs in this chapter.

Chapter 5: Fundamental Operating Systems

5.2.2 Worksheet: NOS Certifications and Jobs

In this worksheet, you will use the Internet, a newspaper, or magazines to gather information about network operating system certifications and jobs that require these certifications.

1. Use the Internet to research three different network operating system certifications. Based on your research, complete the table below.

	Network Operating System (s) Covered	Certification(s) Title	Courses/Training Required for Certification

2. Use the Internet, a newspaper, or a magazine to find at least two network jobs available in your area. Describe the network jobs and the required certifications needed for the position.

3. Which job would you prefer? List reasons for your selection.

5.3.2 Worksheet: Upgrade Hardware Components

In this worksheet, you will use the Internet, a newspaper, or a local store to gather information about hardware components. Your customer's computer currently has 1 Module of 256 MB of RAM, a 40 GB hard disk drive, and an AGP video adapter card with 32 MB of RAM. Your customer wants to be able to play advanced video games.

1. Shop around, and in the table below list the brand, model number, features and cost for two different 1 GB Modules of DDR400 (PC3200).

Brand and Model Number	Features	Cost

2. Based on your research, which RAM would you select? Be prepared to discuss your decisions regarding the RAM you select.

3. Shop around, and in the table below list the brand, model number, features and cost for two different 500 GB 7200 rpm IDE hard disk drives.

Brand and Model Number	Features	Cost

4. Based on your research, which hard disk drive would you select? Be prepared to discuss your decisions regarding the hard disk drive you select.

5. Shop around, and in the table below list the brand, model number, features and cost for two different 8x AGP video adapter cards with 256 MB RAM.

Brand and Model Number	Features	Cost

6. Based on your research, which video adapter card would you select? Be prepared to discuss your decisions regarding the video adapter card you select.

5.4.2 Lab: Install Windows XP

Introduction

In this lab, you will install the Windows XP Professional operating system.

Recommended Equipment

The following equipment is required for this exercise:

- A computer with a blank hard disk drive.
- Windows XP Professional installation CD.

Step 1

Insert the Windows XP installation CD into the CD-ROM drive.

When the system starts up, watch for the message "Press any key to boot from CD..".

If the message appears, press any key on the keyboard to boot the system from the CD. The system will now begin inspecting the hardware configuration. If the message does not appear, the hard drive is empty and the system will now begin inspecting the hardware configuration.

Step 2

The Windows XP Professional Setup screen appears. During this part of setup, the mouse will not work, so you must use the keyboard. On the Welcome to Setup page, press **Enter** to continue.

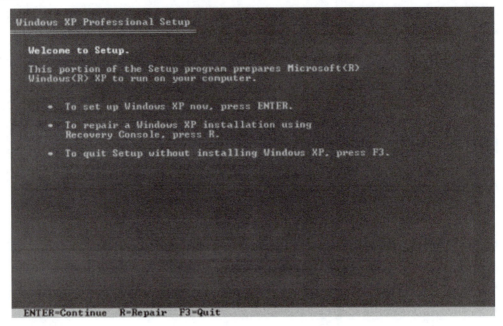

Step 3

The "Windows XP Licensing Agreement" page appears. Press the **Page Down** key to scroll to the bottom of the license agreement. Press the **F8** key to agree to the license.

Step 4

Select the hard drive or partition on which Windows XP will be installed.

Press **Enter** to select "Unpartitioned space", which is the default setting.

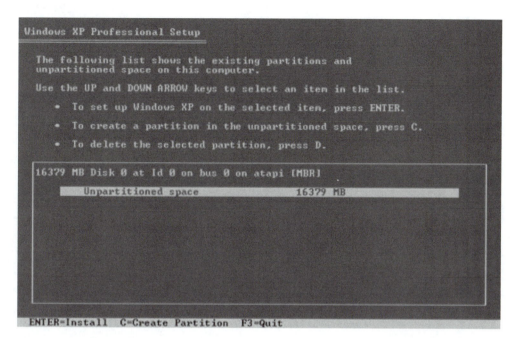

Step 5

Press **Enter** again to select "Format the partition using the NTFS file system", which is the default setting.

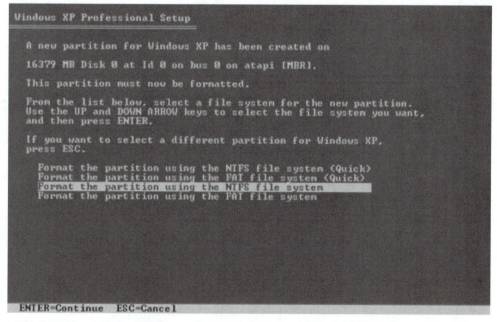

Windows XP Professional Setup erases the hard disk drive, formats the hard disk drive, and copies the setup files from the installation CD to the hard disk drive. This process should take between 20 and 30 minutes to complete.

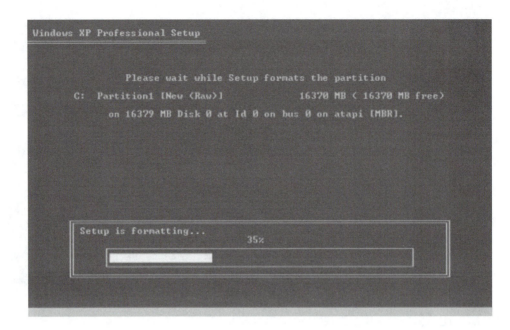

Step 6

After the formatting process, Windows XP restarts and continues with the installation process. At this point, the mouse can be used to make selections. The "Regional and Language Options" page appears. Click **Next** to accept the default settings. Regional and language options can be configured after setup is complete.

The "Personalize Your Software" page appears. Type the name and the organization name provided by your instructor. Click **Next**.

Step 7

The "Your Product Key" page appears. On this page, type your product key as it appears on your Windows XP CD case. Click **Next**.

On the "Computer Name and Administrator Password screen", type the computer name provided by your instructor. Type the Administrator password provided by your instructor, and retype it in the Confirm password section. Click **Next**.

Step 8

On the "Date and Time Settings" screen, configure the computer clock to match your local date, time, and time zone. Click **Next**.

Step 9

On the "Networking Settings" page, click **Next** to accept "Typical settings". "Custom settings" can be configured after setup is complete.

Step 10

On the "Workgroup or Computer Domain" page, accept the default settings and click **Next**.

Step 11

Windows XP Professional Setup may take about 25 minutes to configure your computer. Your computer will automatically restart when the setup program is complete. When the "Display Settings" dialog box appears, click **OK**.

Step 12

When the "Monitor Settings" dialog box appears, click **OK**.

Step 13

The final phase of Windows XP Professional Setup begins. On the "Welcome to Microsoft Windows" page, click **Next**.

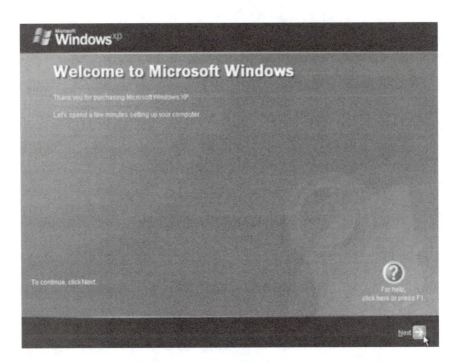

Step 14

On the "Help protect your PC screen", select "Help protect my PC by turning on Automatic Updates now". Click **Next**.

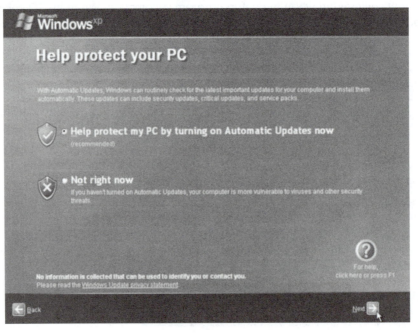

Step 15

Windows XP will now check to make sure that you are connected to the Internet. If you are already connected to the Internet, select the choice that represents your network connection. If you are unsure of the connection type, accept the default selection, and click **Next**.

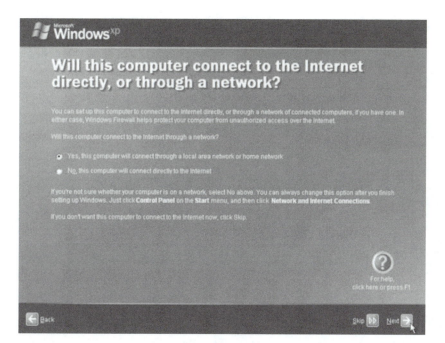

Step 16

If you use dial-up Internet access, or if Windows XP Professional Setup cannot connect to the Internet, you can connect to the Internet after setup is complete. Click **Skip** to continue.

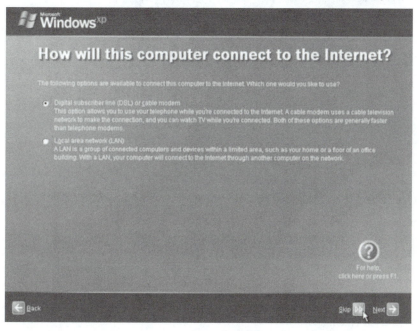

Step 17

Windows XP Professional Setup displays the "Ready to activate Windows?" screen.

If you are already connected to the Internet, click **Yes**, and then click **Next**.

If you are not yet connected to the Internet, click **No**, and then click **Next**.

After setup is complete, Windows XP setup program will remind you to activate and register your copy of Windows XP.

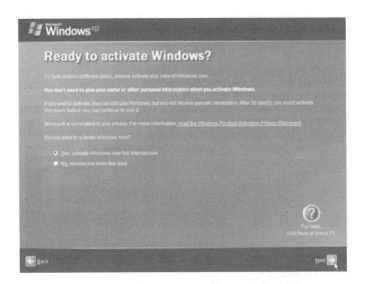

Step 18

If you have an Internet connection, click "Yes, I'd like to register with Microsoft now".

If you do not have an Internet connection, click "No, not at this time".

Click **Next**.

Step 19

On the "Collecting Registration Information screen", fill in the fields using the information provided by your instructor and click **Next**.

Step 20

On the "Who will use this computer?" screen, enter the information provided by your instructor. Click **Next**.

Step 21

On the "Thank you!" screen, click **Finish** to complete the installation.

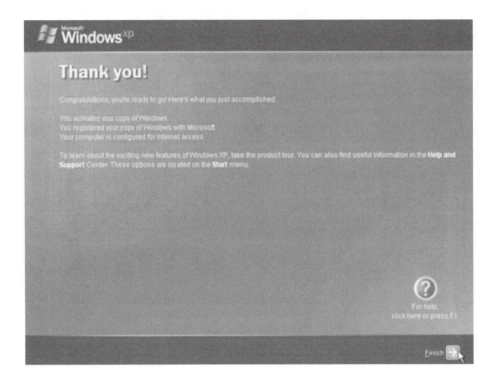

5.4.2 Optional Lab: Install Windows Vista

Introduction

In this lab, you will install the Windows Vista operating system.

Recommended Equipment

The following equipment is required for this exercise:

- A computer with a blank hard disk drive.
- Windows Vista installation DVD.

Step 1

Insert the Windows Vista installation DVD into the DVD-ROM drive.

When the system starts up, watch for the message "Press any key to boot from CD or DVD.".

If the message appears, press any key on the keyboard to boot the system from the DVD. If the press any key message does not appear, the computer automatically starts loading files from the DVD.

The computer starts loading files from the DVD.

Step 2

The Windows Vista boot screen appears.

Step 3

The Install Windows screen appears. Press Next unless you need to change the defaults.

Step 4

Press **Install now** to continue.

Step 5

The Collecting information section of the installation begins.

The "Type your product key for activation" page appears. On this page, type your product key as it appears on your Windows Vista DVD case. Click **Next**.

NOTE: If you entered your product key, Setup will determine the Vista product edition to install and will not display the next two screens.

Because you have left the product key field blank, the "Do you want to enter your product key now?" window appears. If you were instructed not to enter a product key, click **No**.

Setup now prompts you to select the Vista version you purchased. In general, you should choose the version you purchased, but note that you can install any Vista version listed and experiment with it for a limited time before product activation requires you to activate.

NOTE: Your product key will only activate the version of Vista you purchased.

Select the Windows Vista version that will be installed, check the item title "I have selected the edition of Windows that I purchased," and then click **Next**.

Step 6

The "Please read the license terms" page appears. Read and confirm that you accept the license by selecting the box "I accept the license terms". Click **Next**.

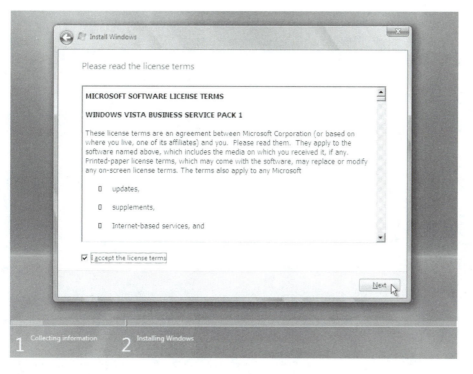

Step 7

The "Which type of installation do you want?" page appears. Click **Custom (advanced)**.

Step 8

The "Where do you want to install Windows?" page appears. Select the hard drive or partition on which Windows Vista will be installed.

Click **Next** to select "Disk 0 Unallocated Space", which is the default setting.

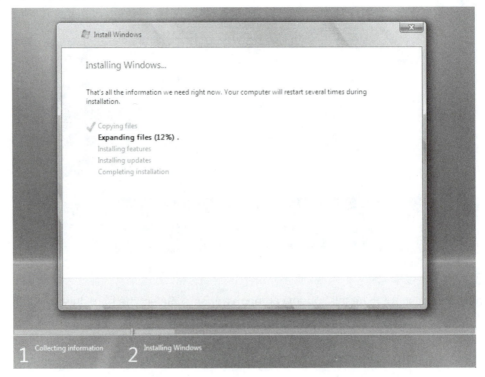

The Collecting information section of the installation ends.

Step 9

The Installing Windows section begins.

The "Installing Windows …" page appears. Windows Vista Setup may take about 50 minutes to configure your computer.

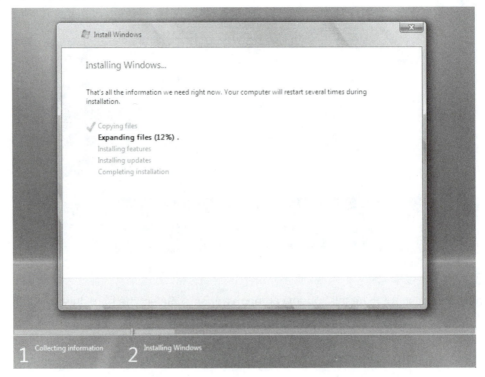

Step 10

The "Windows needs to restart to continue" page appears. Your computer will automatically restart or you can click **Restart now**.

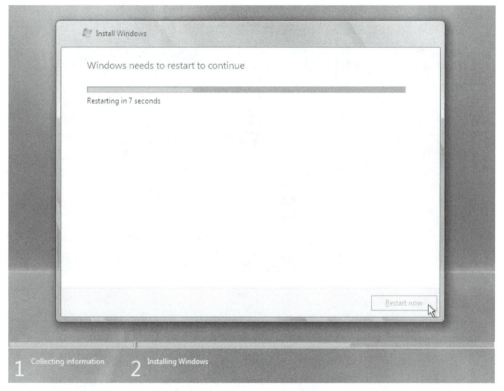

If you get the message "Press any key to boot from CD or DVD", **do not press any key** and Windows will boot from the hard disk to continue the installation.

Step 11

The "please wait while windows continues setting up your computer ..." page appears.

Step 12

The "Installing Windows …" page appears again. Windows may reboot a few more times. This may take several minutes.

The Installing Windows section of the installation is completed.

Step 13

The Set Up Windows section begins.

The "Choose a user name and picture" page appears. Type the name provided by your instructor. Type the Administrator password provided by your instructor. When you type in a password, two new fields will appear. Retype the password and the password hint. Click **Next**.

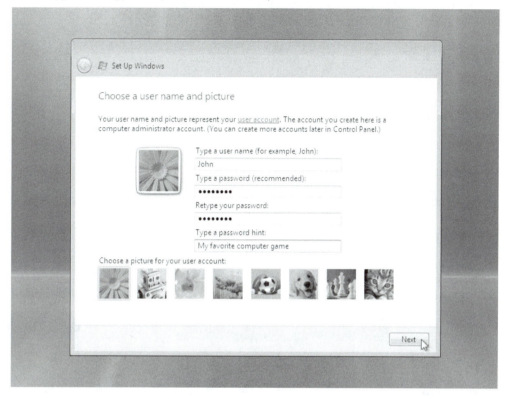

Step 14

The "Type a computer name and choose a desktop background" page appears. Type the computer name provided by your instructor. Click **Next**.

Step 15

On the "Help protect Windows automatically" screen, click **Use recommended setting**.

Step 16

On the "Review your time and date settings" screen, configure the computer clock to match your local date, time, and time zone. Click **Next**.

Step 17

The "Select your computer's current location" page appears. Select the option provided by your instructor.

NOTE: This screen will not show up if the installation did not correctly install drivers for the network card.

Step 18

On the "Thank you" screen, click **Start**.

The Set Up Windows section is completed.

Step 19

The "Please wait while Windows checks your computer's performance" page appears.

Please wait while Windows checks your computer's performance.

Step 20

Windows Vista boots for the first time.

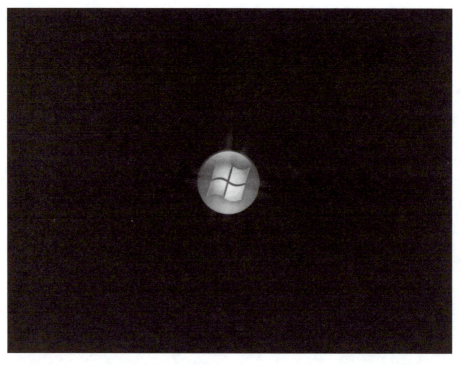

Step 21

The login window appears. Enter the password that you used during the install process and click the **blue arrow** to login.

Step 22

The "Preparing your desktop ..." window appears. Your account profile is created and configured.

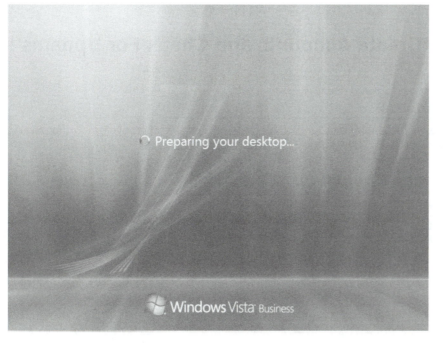

Step 23

The "Welcome" screen appears. Windows Vista is now installed.

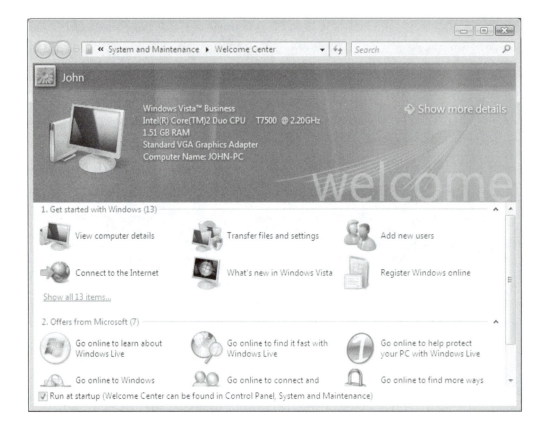

5.4.5 Lab: Create Accounts and Check For Updates in Windows XP

Introduction

In this lab, you will create user accounts and configure the operating system for automatic updates after the Windows XP Professional installation process.

Recommended Equipment

The following equipment is required for this exercise:

*   A computer with a new installation of Windows XP Professional

Step 1

Boot the computer. Navigate to the "Control Panel" window by clicking **Start > Control Panel.**

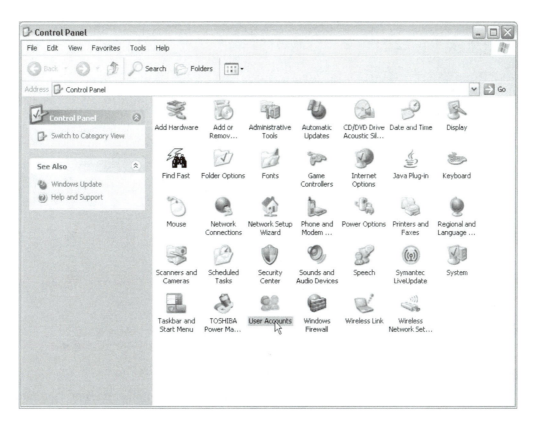

Step 2

Double-click the **User Accounts** icon.

The "User Accounts" window appears. Click **Create a new account**.

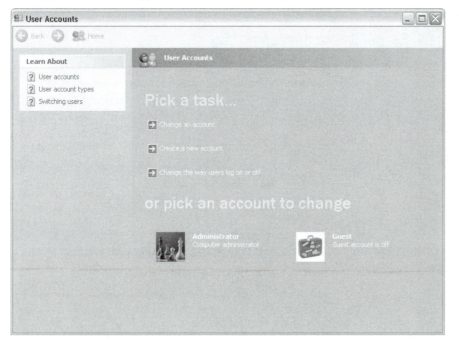

Step 3

At "Name the new account", type your name in the field and then click **Next**.

Step 4

At "Pick an account type", leave the default setting of Computer administrator and click **Create Account**.

You have now finished creating a new account. Log off the computer and log back on as yourself. Leave the password field blank.

Step 5

Return to the "User Accounts" window of the control panel.

Click your account.

Click **Create a password**.

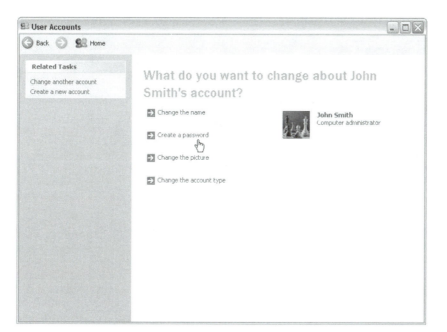

Step 6

On the "Create a password for your account" page, type your first initial and your last name in the "Type a new password:" field. Example: jsmith

Type the same password in the "Type the new password again to confirm:" field.

Type **fi last name** in the "Type a word or phrase to use as a password hint:" field.

Click **Create Password**.

Step 7

Click the red **X** in the upper-right corner of the "User Accounts" window to close the window.

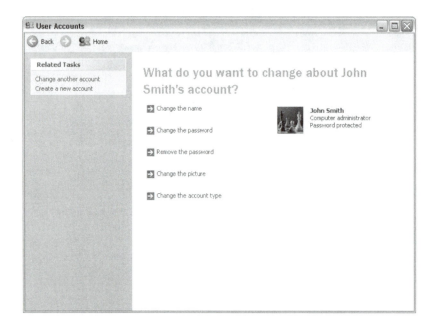

Step 8

Click **Start** > **Control Panel**.

Double-click the **Automatic Updates** icon.

Step 9

The "Automatic Updates" dialog box appears.

Click the **Automatic (recommended)** radio button.

Click **OK** to accept the change and close the dialog box.

5.4.5 Optional Lab: Create Accounts and Check For Updates in Windows Vista

Introduction

Print and complete this lab.

In this lab, you will create user accounts and configure the operating system for automatic updates after the Windows Vista installation process.

Recommended Equipment

The following equipment is required for this exercise:

- A computer with a new installation of Windows Vista

Step 1

Boot the computer. Navigate to the "Control Panel" window by clicking **Start > Control Panel.**

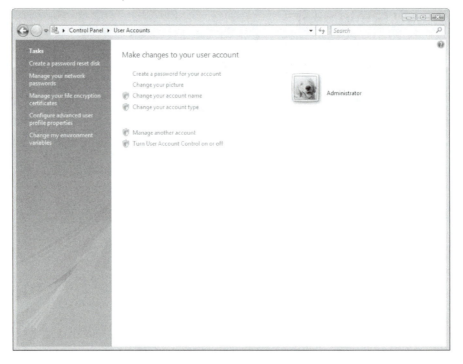

Step 2

Double-click the **User Accounts** icon.

The "User Accounts" window appears. Click **Manage another account**.

Click **Continue** if asked for permission.

The "Manage Accounts" window appears. Click **Create a new account**.

Step 3

At "Name the account and choose an account type", type your name in the field, select Administrator as the account type and then click **Create Account**.

You have now finished creating a new account. Log off the computer and log back in as yourself. Leave the password field blank.

Step 4

Return to the "User Accounts" window of the control panel.

Click **Create a password for your account**.

Step 5

On the "Create a password for your account" page, type your first initial and your last name in the "Type a new password:" field. Example: jsmith

Type the same password in the "Type the new password again to confirm:" field.

Type **fi last name** in the "Type a word or phrase to use as a password hint:" field.

Click **Create Password**.

Step 6

Click the **X** in the Close box in the upper-right corner of the "User Accounts" window to close the window.

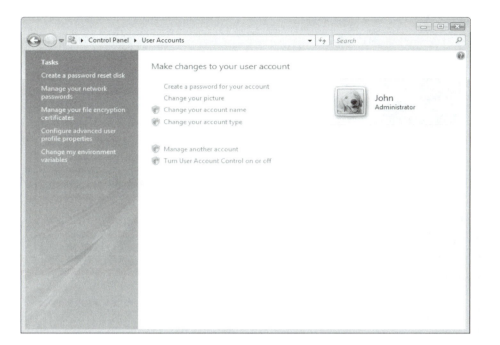

Step 7

Click Start > Control Panel.

Double-click the Windows Updates icon.

Step 8

The "Windows Updates" dialog box appears.

Click **Change settings**.

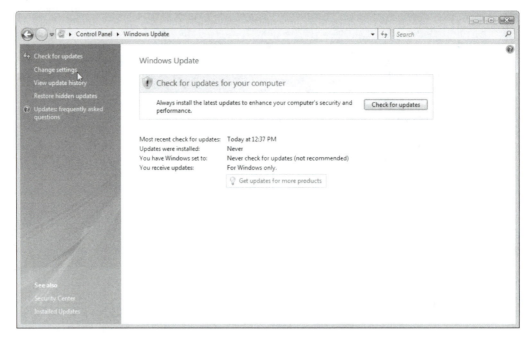

The "Choose how Windows can install updates" dialog box appears.

Click the **Install updates automatic (recommended)** radio button.

Click **OK** to accept the change.

Click **Continue** if asked for permission and close the dialog box.

5.4.8 Lab: Managing System Files with Built-in Utilities in Windows XP

Introduction

In this lab, you will use Windows built-in utilities to gather information about the system and to troubleshoot system resources. You will also learn how to export and import registry setting.

Recommended Equipment

The following equipment is required for this exercise:

- A computer running Windows XP Professional

Step 1

Log on to the computer as an administrator.

Open the command prompt by clicking **Start > Run >** type **cmd >** click **OK**.

What is the drive path shown? Answers may vary.

Type **help** and press **Enter**.

What is the command to change directory?

What is the command to display the contnets in a directory?

Type **cd ..** and press **Enter**.

What is the drive path shown? Answers may vary.

Change back to original drive path.

Example: Type **cd John** and press **Enter**.

What is the drive path shown? Answers may vary

Type **dir /?** and press **Enter**.

If asked, Press any key to continue.

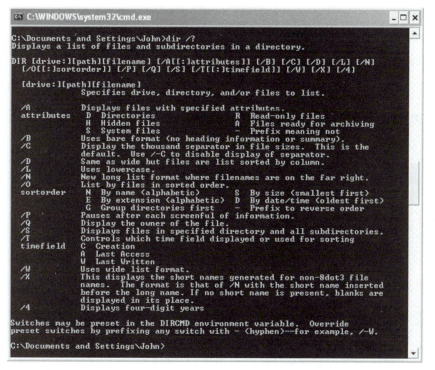

Which switch displays a wide list format?

Type **dir** and press **Enter**.

Type **dir /w** and press **Enter**.

What is the difference between these two commands?

Type **VOL**.

What volume is drive C in? Answers may vary.

Close the Command prompt window.

Step 2

Open System Information by clicking **Start > Run >** type **msinfo32 >** click **OK**.

Click the **plus sign** next to Hardware Resources, Components, and Software Environment. Expand the window so you can see all the content.

Under the System Summary heading locate and list the following:

Processor:

BIOS Version/Date:

Total Physical Memory:

Under the Hardware Resources heading locate and list the following:

DMA channels and the device using the resources.

I/O address range for these devices.

Printer Port (LPT1):

Communications Port (COM1):

Communications Port (COM2):

IRQ address for these devices.

System timer:

Communications Port (COM1):

Communications Port (COM2):

Under the Components heading and Software heading look around to see what information is provided in these areas.

Close the System Information window.

Step 3

Open System Configuration Utility by clicking **Start > Run >** type **msconfig >** click **OK**.

NOTE: It is very important that you do not make any changes in this utility without instructor permission.

Click the **General** tab if not already active.

What are the startup options?

Click the **SYSTEM.INI**, **WIN.INI** and **BOOT.INI** tabs. These tab are for modifying these files.

Click the **Service** tab. This tab lists the computers services and there status.

Can you enable and disable services at this tab?

Click the **Startup** tab. This tab lists the programs that are automatically loaded every time you turn on your computer.

Click **Cancel** to close the System Configuration Utility window.

Step 4

Open DirectX Diagnostic Tool by clicking **Start > Run >** type **dxdiag >** click **OK**.

If you are asked to have DirectX check driver signatures click **No**.

NOTE: When DirectX Diagnostic Tool first opens it may take a minute to load all information. Your DirectX Diagnostic Tool may not appear exactly as shown in this lab.

Make sure the System tab is active.

What does this tool report?

Click **Next Page** until you are at the DirectX Files tab.

A list of DirectX files is listed.

Click **Next Page** until you are at the Display tab.

Click **Test DirectDraw**.

Follow the rest of the instruction as the test progresses.

Place a check mark next to every test that your computer passes.

alternating black and white rectangles   _____

bouncing white box in a black box   _____

fullscreen bouncing white box   _____

Click **Test Direct3D**.

Follow the rest of the instruction as the test progresses.

DirectX 7 interface test: what did you see?

DirectX 8 interface test: what did you see?

DirectX 9 interface test: what did you see?

Click **Next Page** until you are at the Sound tab.

If you have a headphones click **Test DirextSound**. If you have no headphones move to the next instruction.

Did you hear the sound effects in the audio test?

Click **Next Page** until you are at the Music tab.

If you have a headphones click **Test DirextMusic**. If you have no headphones move to the next instruction.

Did you hear music playing?

Click **Next Page** until you are on the Input tab.

What information is listed on this page?

Click **Next Page** until you are on the Network tab.

What information is listed on this page?

Click **Next Page** until you are on the More Help tab.

Click on the various buttons to see what is provided.

What tools are provided on this page?

Click **Exit**.

Step 5

Open the Desktop tab in Display Properties by right clicking the **desktop > Properties > Desktop** tab.

What is the Background picture?

Set the background image to (None). If the **Color** dropdown button is not blue, click the **Color** dropdown button, select **blue**.

Click **OK**.

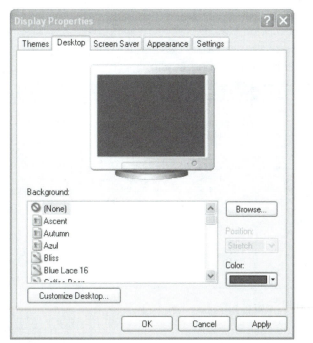

The computer screen should now have a blue background. If not ask the instructor for assistance.

Step 6

Open Registry Editor by clicking **Start > Run >** type **regedit >** click **OK**.

NOTE: Do make any changes in the Registry Editor without instructor permission.

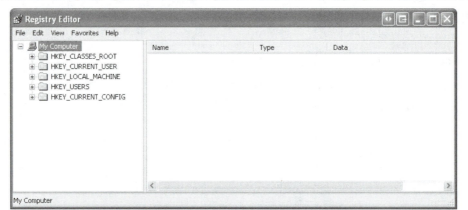

Click the **HKEY_Current_User** icon. To search for the desktop Background key **click Edit > Find >** type **Background >** click **Find Next**.

The Background value is located. Leave this window open.

In which folder is the Background located?

What is the data value of the Background (hint – it has three number that corresponds to red, green blue)? Answers may vary based on the shade of red selected in Display Properties.

Step 7

We will now export the **HKEY_CURRENT_USER\Control Panel\Colors** folder.

In the left pane click the **Colors** folder.

Click **File** > **Export**. Save the file to the Desktop. File name: **BlueBKG**.

At the desktop right click the **BlueBKG.reg** icon > **Edit**.

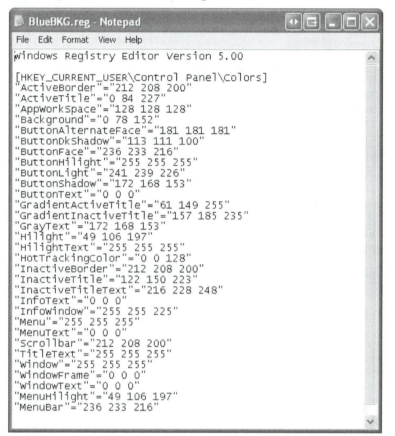

What is the data value of the Background? Answers may vary based on the shade of blue selected in Display Properties.

Close **BlueBKG.reg – Notepad** window.

Step 8

Open the Desktop tab in Display Properties by right clicking the **desktop > Properties > Desktop** tab.

Set the **Color** dropdown button is not red, click the **Color** dropdown button, select **red**.

Click **OK**.

In a few second the desktop will turn to red.

Click the Registry Editor window so it is activated.

On your keyboard press F5 to refresh the Registry Editor window.

What is the data value of the Background? Answers may vary based on the shade of red selected in Display Properties.

Step 9

We will now import the **BlueBKG.reg** file.

Click the Registry Editor window so it is activated.

Click **File > Import**. Locate and click the **BlueBKG.reg** icon then click **Open**. Click OK.

Click the Registry Editor window so it is activated.

What is the data value of the Background? Answers may vary based on the shade of red selected in Display Properties.

What is the color of the desktop?

Restart the computer.

What is the color of the desktop?

Reset Display Properties Background to the original settings (hint – see step 5).

5.4.8 Optional Lab: Managing System Files with Built-in Utilities in Windows Vista

Introduction

In this lab, you will use Windows built-in utilities to gather information about the system and to troubleshoot system resources. You will also learn how to export and import registry setting.

Recommended Equipment

The following equipment is required for this exercise:

- A computer running Windows Vista

Step 1

Log on to the computer as an administrator.

To add Run to the Start menu right click **Start > Properties**. Select **Start Menu** tab then click **Customize ....**

Scroll down until you see the Run command. Click in the box next to Run command. Click **OK**.

Click **Apply > OK** to close the "Taskbar and Start Menu Properties" window.

Open the command prompt by clicking **Start > Run >** type **cmd >** click **OK**.

What is the drive path shown?

Type **help** and press **Enter**.

What is the command to change directory?

What is the command to display the contnets in a directory?

Type **cd ..** and press **Enter**.

What is the drive path shown?

Change back to original drive path.

Example: Type **cd John** and press **Enter**.

What is the drive path shown?

Type **dir /?** and press **Enter**.

If asked, Press any key to continue.

```
C:\Windows\system32\cmd.exe                                        _ □ ×

C:\Users\John>dir /?
Displays a list of files and subdirectories in a directory.

DIR [drive:][path][filename] [/A[[:]attributes]] [/B] [/C] [/D] [/L] [/N]
  [/O[[:]sortorder]] [/P] [/Q] [/R] [/S] [/T[[:]timefield]] [/W] [/X] [/4]

  [drive:][path][filename]
              Specifies drive, directory, and/or files to list.

  /A          Displays files with specified attributes.
  attributes   D  Directories                R  Read-only files
               H  Hidden files               A  Files ready for archiving
               S  System files               I  Not content indexed files
               L  Reparse Points             -  Prefix meaning not
  /B          Uses bare format (no heading information or summary).
  /C          Display the thousand separator in file sizes.  This is the
              default.  Use /-C to disable display of separator.
  /D          Same as wide but files are list sorted by column.
  /L          Uses lowercase.
  /N          New long list format where filenames are on the far right.
  /O          List by files in sorted order.
  sortorder    N  By name (alphabetic)       S  By size (smallest first)
               E  By extension (alphabetic)  D  By date/time (oldest first)
               G  Group directories first    -  Prefix to reverse order
  /P          Pauses after each screenful of information.
  /Q          Display the owner of the file.
  /R          Display alternate data streams of the file.
  /S          Displays files in specified directory and all subdirectories.
  /T          Controls which time field displayed or used for sorting
  timefield    C  Creation
               A  Last Access
               W  Last Written
  /W          Uses wide list format.
  /X          This displays the short names generated for non-8dot3 file
              names.  The format is that of /N with the short name inserted
              before the long name. If no short name is present, blanks are
              displayed in its place.
  /4          Displays four-digit years

Switches may be preset in the DIRCMD environment variable.  Override
preset switches by prefixing any switch with - (hyphen)--for example, /-W.

C:\Users\John>
```

Which switch displays a wide list format?

Type **dir** and press **Enter**.

Type **dir /w** and press **Enter**.

```
C:\Windows\system32\cmd.exe                                        _ □ ×

C:\Users\John>dir
 Volume in drive C has no label.
 Volume Serial Number is 2031-2964

 Directory of C:\Users\John

07/20/2009  11:59 AM    <DIR>          .
07/20/2009  11:59 AM    <DIR>          ..
07/18/2009  12:59 PM    <DIR>          Contacts
07/22/2009  04:32 PM    <DIR>          Desktop
07/20/2009  12:00 PM    <DIR>          Documents
07/20/2009  09:12 AM    <DIR>          Downloads
07/18/2009  12:59 PM    <DIR>          Favorites
07/18/2009  12:59 PM    <DIR>          Links
07/18/2009  12:59 PM    <DIR>          Music
07/18/2009  12:59 PM    <DIR>          Pictures
07/18/2009  12:59 PM    <DIR>          Saved Games
07/18/2009  12:59 PM    <DIR>          Searches
07/18/2009  12:59 PM    <DIR>          Videos
               0 File(s)              0 bytes
              13 Dir(s)   6,152,069,120 bytes free

C:\Users\John>dir /w
 Volume in drive C has no label.
 Volume Serial Number is 2031-2964

 Directory of C:\Users\John

[.]           [..]          [Contacts]    [Desktop]     [Documents]
[Downloads]   [Favorites]   [Links]       [Music]       [Pictures]
[Saved Games] [Searches]    [Videos]
               0 File(s)              0 bytes
              13 Dir(s)   6,151,995,392 bytes free

C:\Users\John>
```

What is the difference between these two commands?

Type **VOL**.

What volume is drive C in? Answers may vary.

Close the Command prompt window.

Step 2

Open System Information by clicking **Start > Run >** type **msinfo32 >** click **OK**.

Click the **plus sign** next to Hardware Resources, Components, and Software Environment. Expand the window so you can see all the content.

Under the System Summary heading locate and list the following:

Processor:

BIOS Version/Date:

Total Physical Memory:

Under the Hardware Resources heading locate and list the following:

DMA channels and the device using the resources.

I/O address range for these devices.

Printer Port (LPT1):

Communications Port (COM1):

Communications Port (COM2):

IRQ address for these devices.

System timer:

Communications Port (COM1):

Communications Port (COM2):

Under the Components heading and Software heading look around to see what information is provided in these areas.

Close the System Information window.

Step 3

Open System Configuration by clicking **Start > Run >** type **msconfig >** click **OK**.

If the "User Account Control" window appears click **Continue**.

NOTE: It is very important that you do not make any changes in this utility without instructor permission.

Click the **General** tab if not all ready active.

What are the startup options?

Click the **BOOT** tabs. This tab is for modifying boot options.

Click the **Service** tab. This tab lists the computers services and there status.

Can you enable and disable services at this tab?

Click the **Startup** tab. This tab lists the programs that are automatically loaded every time you turn on your computer.

Click the **Tools** tab.

What can you do in this tab?

Click **Cancel** to close the "System Configuration" window.

Step 4

Open DirectX Diagnostic Tool by clicking **Start > Run >** type **dxdiag >** click **OK**.

If you are asked to have DirectX check driver signatures click **No**.

NOTE: When DirectX Diagnostic Tool first opens it may take a minute to load all information. Your DirectX Diagnostic Tool may not appear exactly as shown in this lab.

Make sure the System tab is active.

What does this tool report?

Click **Next Page** until you are at the Display tab.

What information is listed on this page?

Click **Next Page** until you are at the Sound tab.

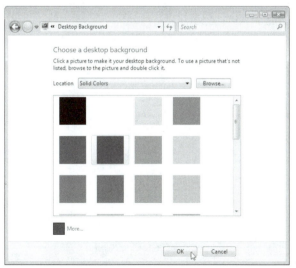

What information is listed on this page?

Click **Next Page** until you are on the Input tab.

What information is listed on this page?

Click **Exit**.

Step 5

Open the "Choose a desktop background" page in Personalize appearance and sounds by right clicking the **desktop > Personalize > Desktop Background**.

What is the Background picture?

Click the Location dropdown button and select **Solid Colors**. Select a **blue** color.

Click **OK**.

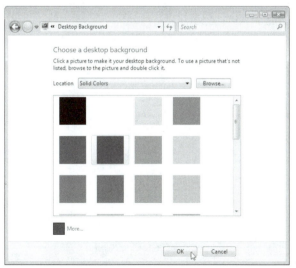

The computer screen should now have a blue background. If not ask the instructor for assistance.

Step 6

Open Registry Editor by clicking **Start > Run >** type **regedit >** click **OK**.

If the "User Account Control" window appears click **Continue**.

NOTE: Do make any changes in the Registry Editor without instructor permission.

Click the **HKEY_Current_User** icon. To search for the desktop Background key **click Edit > Find >** type **Background >** click **Find Next**.

The Background value is located. Leave this window open.

In which folder is the Background located?

What is the data value of the Background (hint – it has three number that corresponds to red, green blue)? Answers may vary based on the shade of blue selected in Choose a desktop background.

Step 7

We will now export **HKEY_CURRENT_USER\Control Panel\Colors** folder.

In the left pane click the **Colors** folder.

Click **File** > **Export**. Save the file to the Desktop. File name: **BlueBKG**.

At the desktop right click the **BlueBKG.reg** icon > **Edit**.

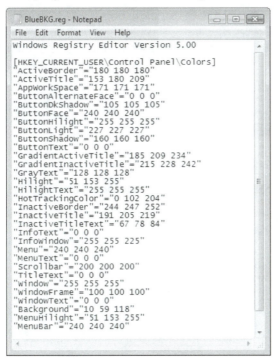

What is the data value of the Background? Answers may vary based on the shade of blue selected in Display Properties.

Close **BlueBKG.reg – Notepad** window.

Step 8

Open the "Choose a desktop background" page in Personalize appearance and sounds by right clicking the **desktop > Personalize > Desktop Background**.

Click the **Location** dropdown button and select **Solid Colors**. Select a **red** color.

Click **OK**.

In a few second the desktop will turn to red.

Click the Registry Editor window so it is activated.

On your keyboard press F5 to refresh the Registry Editor window.

What is the data value of the Background? Answers may vary based on the shade of red selected in Display Properties.

Step 9

We will now import **BlueBKG.reg** file.

Click the Registry Editor window so it is activated.

Click **File > Import**. Locate and click the **BlueBKG.reg** icon then click **Open**.

Click **OK**.

Click the Registry Editor window so it is activated.

What is the data value of the Background? Answers may vary based on the shade of blue selected in Display Properties.

What is the color of the desktop?

Restart the computer.

What is the color of the desktop?

Reset Display Properties Background to the original settings (hint – see step 5).

5.4.9 Worksheet: Answer NTFS and FAT32 Questions

Hard disk drives can be formatted using different file systems. NTFS and FAT32 are file systems used by the Windows XP operating system and provide different file system features.

Answer the following questions about the NTFS and FAT32 file systems.

1. What is the default cluster size setting when formatting a Windows NTFS partition on a hard disk drive larger than 2 GB?

2. What is the command used to change a FAT32 partition to an NTFS partition?

3. What is the Master File Table (MFT) and what does it contain?

4. What is NTFS journaling?

5. How does journaling help an operating system recover from system failures?

6. Why is an NTFS partition more secure than FAT32?

5.5.1 Lab: Run Commands in Windows XP

Introduction

In this lab, you will open the same program by using the Windows Explorer and the "Run…" command.

Recommended Equipment

The following equipment is required for this exercise:

* A computer system running Windows XP

Step 1

Boot the computer and log on as yourself.

Right-click the **Start** button and then click **Explore**.

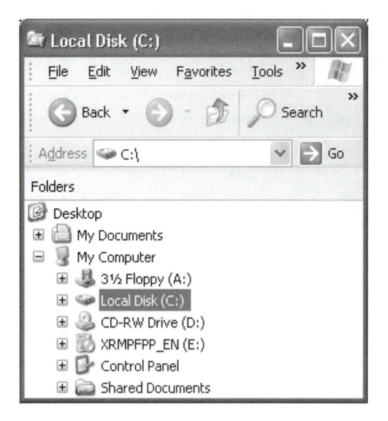

Step 2

Right-click the **Local Disk(C:)** hard disk drive.

Click **Properties** and then click the **Disk Cleanup** button.

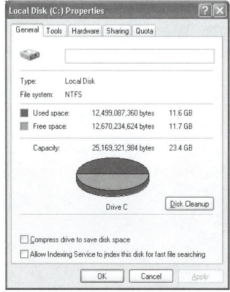

The Disk Cleanup for (C:) window appears.

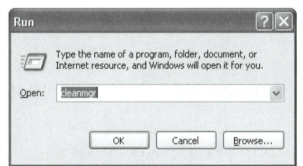

Windows calculates the amount of space used by unnecessary files.

Click **Cancel**.

Step 3

Open the Run dialog box by clicking **Start > Run...**.

Type **cleanmgr** in the "Open:" field.

Click **OK**.

The "Disk Cleanup for (C:)" window opens.

Step 3

Click the **OK** button.

    1.   Why should disk cleanup be performed regularly?

5.5.1 Optional Lab: Run Commands in Windows Vista

Introduction

In this lab, you will open the same program by using the Windows Explorer and the "Run..." command.

Recommended Equipment

The following equipment is required for this exercise:

- A computer system running Windows Vista

Step 1

Boot the computer and log on as yourself.

Right-click the **Start** button and then click **Explore**.

Navigate to the Local Disk (C:) hard drive disk

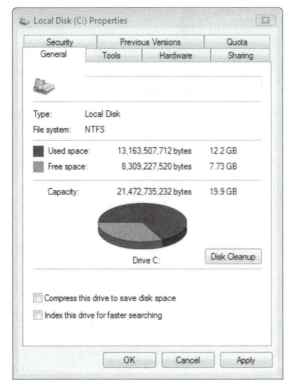

Step 2

Right-click the **Local Disk(C:)** hard disk drive.

Click **Properties** and then click the **Disk Cleanup** button.

The **Disk Cleanup Options** window appears.

Click **My files only**.

NOTE: Clicking **Files from all users on this computer** will display the **User Account Control** window to ask for permission.

The Disk Cleanup for (C:) window appears.

Windows calculates the amount of space used by unnecessary files.

Click **Cancel**.

Step 3

Open the Run dialog box by clicking **Start >** in the Start Search box, type **Run**.

Type **cleanmgr** in the "Open:" field.

Click **OK**.

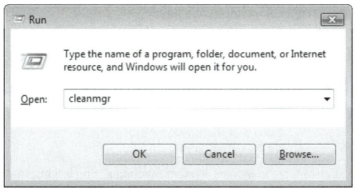

The **Disk Cleanup Options** window appears.

Click **My files only**.

NOTE: Clicking **Files from all users on this computer** will display the **User Account Control** window to ask for permission.

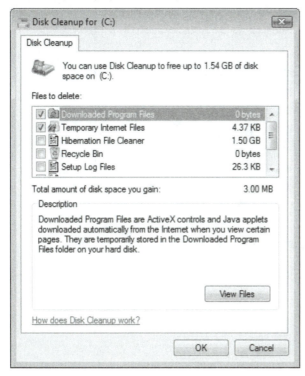

The "Disk Cleanup for (C:)" window opens.

Step 4
Click the **OK** button.

1. Why should disk cleanup be performed regularly?

5.5.3 Lab: Managing Administrative Settings and Snap-ins in Windows XP

Introduction

In this lab, you will use administrative tools to monitor system resources. You will also build a custom console to manage storage devices.

Recommended Equipment

The following equipment is required for this exercise:

- A computer running Windows XP Professional
- Internet access

Step 1

Log on to the computer as an administrator.

Navigate to the "Control Panel" window by clicking **Start > Control Panel.** Double-click the **Network Connections** icon.

Reduce the size of the "Network Connections" window. Leave this window open.

Step 2

Once again navigate to the "Control Panel" window by clicking **Start > Control Panel.** Double-click the **Administrative Tools** icon.

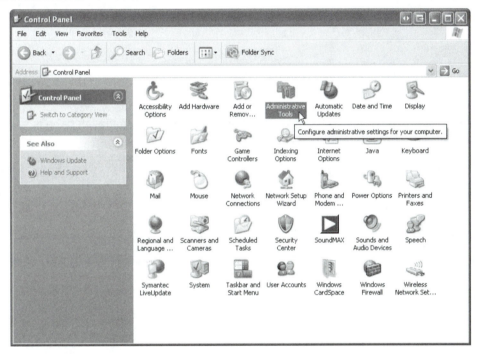

Double-click the **Performance** icon.

Step 3

The "Performance" window appears. Make sure the System Monitor in the left pane is highlighted. Click the **Freeze Display** icon to stop the recording.

Click the **Clear Display** icon to clear the graph. Leave this window open.

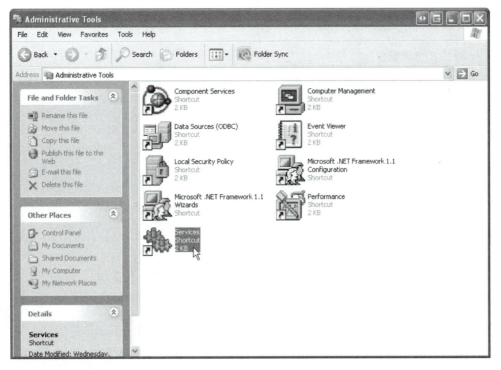

Step 4

Navigate to the "Administrative Tools" window by clicking **Start > Control Panel > Administrative Tools.** Double-click the **Services** icon.

Step 5

Expand the width of the "Services" window so you have a clear view of the content. Scroll down in the right pane until you see the service Routing and Remote Access. Double click **Routing and Remote Access**.

The "Routing and Remote Access Properties (Local Computer)" windows appears. In the Startup type select **Manual**. Click **Apply**.

The Start button is now active; do not click the button yet. Leave this window open.

Step 6

Position the following three windows so you can clearly see them at the same time for steps 7 to 14: Network Connections, Routing and Remote Access Properties (Local Computer), and Performance.

Step 7

Click the "Performance" window so it is activated. Click the **Freeze Display** icon to start the recording.

Step 8

Click the "Routing and Remote Access Properties (Local Computer)" window so it is activated. To start the Service click **Start**.

A window with a progress bar appears.

Service Control

Windows is attempting to start the following service on Local Computer...

Routing and Remote Access

Close

The "Routing and Remote Access Properties (Local Computer)" window now shows the Stop and Pause button active. Leave this window open.

Routing and Remote Access Properties (Local Computer)

General | Log On | Recovery | Dependencies

Service name: RemoteAccess

Display name: Routing and Remote Access

Description: Offers routing services to businesses in local area and wide area network environments.

Path to executable:
C:\WINDOWS\system32\svchost.exe -k netsvcs

Startup type: Manual

Service status: Started

Start | Stop | Pause | Resume

You can specify the start parameters that apply when you start the service from here.

Start parameters:

OK | Cancel | Apply

Step 9

Click the "Network Connections" window so it is activated.

1. What changes appear in the right pane, after starting the Routing and Remote Access service?

Step 10

Click the "Routing and Remote Access Properties (Local Computer)" window so it is activated. Click **Stop**.

Step 11

Click the "Network Connections" window so it is activated.

2. What changes appear in the right pane, after stopping the Routing and Remote Access service?

Step 12

Click the "Performance" window so it is activated. Click the **Freeze Display** icon to stop the recording.

3. Which Counter is being recorded the most in the graph (hint: look at the graph color and Counter color)?

Click the **View Report** icon.

4.   List the values of the three counters.

Step 13

Click the "Routing and Remote Access Properties (Local Computer)" window so it is activated. In the Startup type select **Disabled**. Click **OK**.

Click the "Service" window so it is activated.

5.   What is the Status and Startup Type for Routing and Remote Access?

Step 14

Click the "Performance" window so it is activated. Click the **Freeze Display** icon to start the recording.

Step 15

Close all open windows.

Step 16

Navigate to the "Control Panel" window by clicking **Start > Control Panel.** Double-click the **Computer Management** icon.

Step 17

The "Computer Management" window appears. Expand the three categories by clicking on the **plus sign** next to: System Tools, Storage and Services, and Applications.

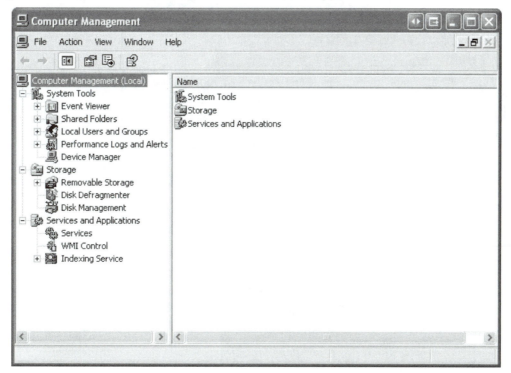

Step 18

Click the **plus sign** next to Event Viewer. Then click on **System**.

Double click the first event in the window.

The "Event Properties" window appears for the event. Click the down arrow key to locate an event for Routing and Remote Access.

Step 19

You should find four events that describe the order for starting and stopping the Routing and Remote access service.

Write down the description for each of the four events. Do not include any URL information.

Event Properties

Event

Date:	7/22/2009	Source:	Service Control Manager
Time:	9:31:42 AM	Category:	None
Type:	Information	Event ID:	7035
User:	JOHN-DESKTOP\John		
Computer:	JOHN-DESKTOP		

Description:

The Routing and Remote Access service was successfully sent a start control.

For more information, see Help and Support Center at http://go.microsoft.com/fwlink/events.asp.

Data: ● Bytes ○ Words

OK   Cancel   Apply

Event Properties

Event

Date:	7/22/2009	Source:	Service Control Manager
Time:	9:31:42 AM	Category:	None
Type:	Information	Event ID:	7036
User:	N/A		
Computer:	JOHN-DESKTOP		

Description:

The Routing and Remote Access service entered the running state.

For more information, see Help and Support Center at http://go.microsoft.com/fwlink/events.asp.

Data: ● Bytes ○ Words

OK   Cancel   Apply

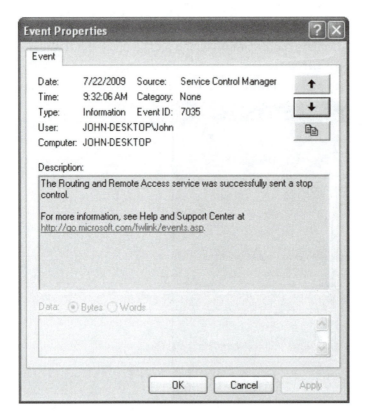

Step 20

Close all open windows.

Step 21

Navigate to the "Run" window by clicking **Start > Run**. Type **MMC** and click **OK**.

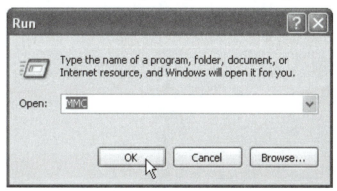

Step 22

The "Console1" (console number may vary) window and the Console Root window appear.

Step 23

To build your own custom console click **File > Add/Remove Snap-in**. The "Add/Remove Snap-in" window appears.

To add a snap-in click **Add**.

The "Add Standalone Snap-in" window appears. To add a folder snap-in so that you can organize all your snap-ins, scroll down until you see the Folder snap-in. Select **Folder >** click **Add**.

To add the "Link to Web Address" snap-in, scroll down until you see the snap-in. Select **Link to Web Address** > click **Add**. The "Link to Web Address" wizard opens. In the Target box type **http://www.cisco.com/**. Click **Next**.

In the "Select a name for the URL reference" box type **Cisco**. Click **Finish**.

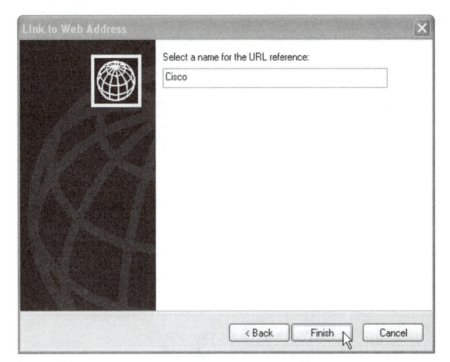

To close the "Add Standalone Snap-in" window, click **Close**.

Step 24

Click the "Add/Remove Snap-in" window so it is activated. In the "Snap-ins added to" box select **Folder**. Click **Add**.

Add these snap-ins: Disk Defragmenter, Disk Management, and Removable Storage Management.

NOTE: When asked what computer the snap-in will manage; select the default by clicking **Finish**.

To close the "Add Standalone Snap-in" window, click **Close**.

Click the "Add/Remove Snap-in" window so it is activated. Click **OK**.

Step 25

The "Console1" window appears. Right click the Folder icon and select Rename. Change the name of the folder to Storage Tools.

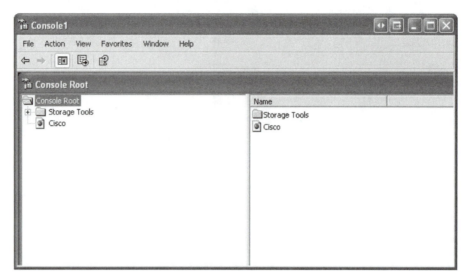

To save the custom console click **File > Save As**. Change the file name to your name. Example: **John's Console**. Change the "Save in" box to **Desktop**. Click **Save**.

Step 26

Close all open windows.

On the desktop double click the **Console** icon to re-open the console with your snap-ins.

5.5.3 Optional Lab: Managing Administrative Settings and Snap-ins in Windows Vista

Introduction

In this lab, you will use administrative tools to monitor system resources. You will also build a custom console to manage storage devices.

Recommended Equipment

The following equipment is required for this exercise:

- A computer running Windows Vista
- Internet access

Step 1

Log on to the computer as an administrator.

Navigate to the "Network and Sharing Center" window by clicking **Start > Network > Network and Sharing Center.** Click **Manage network connections** in the left pane below Tasks.

Reduce the size of the "Network Connections" window. Leave this window open.

Step 2

Navigate to the "Control Panel" window by clicking **Start > Control Panel.** If not in Classic View select this interface. Double-click the **Administrative Tools** icon.

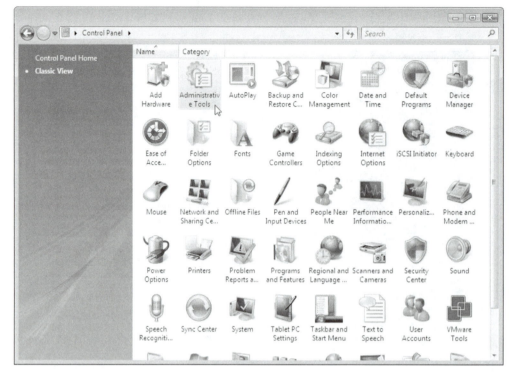

Double-click the Reliability and Performance Monitor icon.

If the "User Account Control" window appears, click Continue.

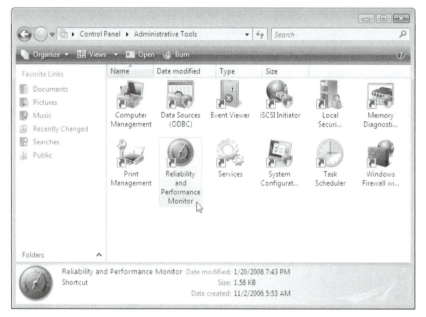

Step 3

The "Reliability and Performance Monitor" window appears. Make sure the Performance Monitor in the left pane is highlighted. Click the **Freeze Display** icon to stop the recording.

Right click the Performance Monitor menu bar, select **Clear** to clear the graph. Leave this window open.

Step 4

Navigate to the "Administrative Tools" window by clicking **Start > Control Panel > Administrative Tools.** Double-click the **Services** icon.

If the "User Account Control" window appears, click **Continue**.

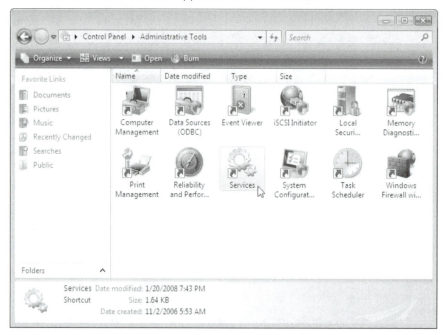

Step 5

Expand the width of the "Services" window so you have a clear view of the content. Scroll down in the right pane until you see the service Routing and Remote Access. Double click **Routing and Remote Access**.

The "Routing and Remote Access Properties (Local Computer)" windows appears. In the Startup type select **Manual**. Click **Apply**.

The Start button is now active; do not click the button yet. Leave this window open.

Step 6

Position the following three windows so you can clearly see them at the same time for steps 7 to 14: Network Connections, Routing and Remote Access Properties (Local Computer), and Reliability and Performance Monitor.

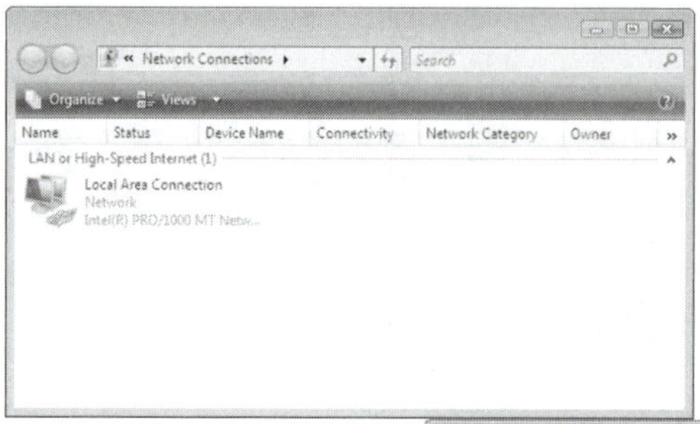
Network Connections
Search
Organize
Views
Name
Status
Device Name
Connectivity
Network Category
Owner
LAN or High-Speed Internet (1)
Local Area Connection
Network
Intel(R) PRO/1000 MT Netw...

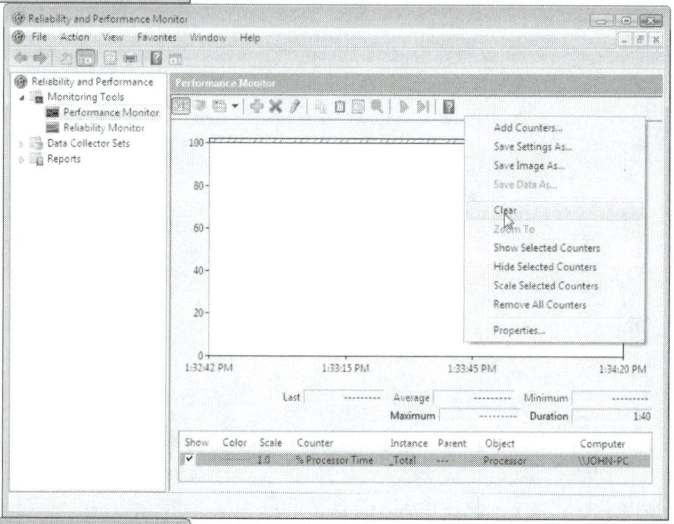
Reliability and Performance Monitor
File
Action
View
Favorites
Window
Help
Reliability and Performance
Monitoring Tools
Performance Monitor
Reliability Monitor
Data Collector Sets
Reports
Performance Monitor
Add Counters...
Save Settings As...
Save Image As...
Save Data As...
Clear
Zoom To
Show Selected Counters
Hide Selected Counters
Scale Selected Counters
Remove All Counters
Properties...
100
80
60
40
20
0
1:32:42 PM
1:33:15 PM
1:33:45 PM
1:34:20 PM
Last
Average
Minimum
Maximum
Duration
1:40
Show
Color
Scale
Counter
Instance
Parent
Object
Computer
1.0
% Processor Time
_Total
Processor
\\JOHN-PC

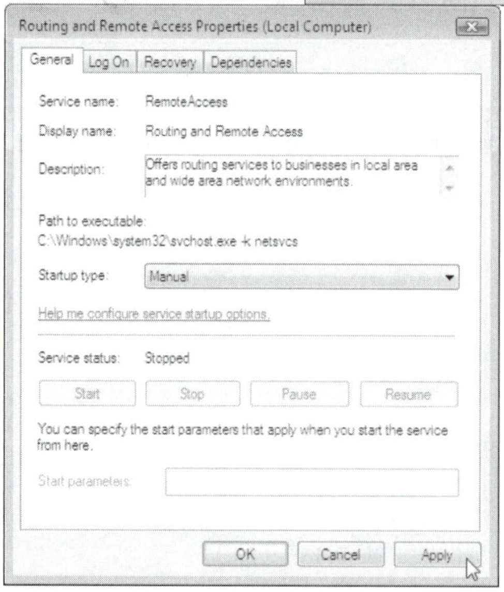
Routing and Remote Access Properties (Local Computer)
General
Log On
Recovery
Dependencies
Service name:
RemoteAccess
Display name:
Routing and Remote Access
Description:
Offers routing services to businesses in local area and wide area network environments.
Path to executable:
C:\Windows\system32\svchost.exe -k netsvcs
Startup type:
Manual
Help me configure service startup options.
Service status:
Stopped
Start
Stop
Pause
Resume
You can specify the start parameters that apply when you start the service from here.
Start parameters:
OK
Cancel
Apply

Step 7

Click the "Performance" window so it is activated. Click the **Unfreeze Display** icon to start the recording.

Step 8

Click the "Routing and Remote Access Properties (Local Computer)" window so it is activated. To start the Service click **Start**.

A window with a progress bar appears.

The "Routing and Remote Access Properties (Local Computer)" window now shows the Stop and Pause button active. Leave this window open.

Routing and Remote Access Properties (Local Computer)

General | Log On | Recovery | Dependencies

Service name: RemoteAccess

Display name: Routing and Remote Access

Description: Offers routing services to businesses in local area
                   and wide area network environments.

Path to executable:
C:\Windows\system32\svchost.exe -k netsvcs

Startup type: Manual

Help me configure service startup options.

Service status: Started

| Start | Stop | Pause | Resume |

You can specify the start parameters that apply when you start the service
from here.

Start parameters:

| OK | Cancel | Apply |

Step 9

Click the "Network Connections" window so it is activated. Press function key **F5** to refresh the content.

« Network Connections ▸   ▾ | ↻ | Search

Organize ▾   Views ▾

| Name | Status | Device Name | Connectivity | Network Category | Owner | » |

Incoming (1)

Incoming Connections
No clients connected

LAN or High-Speed Internet (1)

Local Area Connection
Network
Intel(R) PRO/1000 MT Netw...

1. What changes appear in the right pane, after starting the Routing and Remote Access service?

Step 10

Click the "Routing and Remote Access Properties (Local Computer)" window so it is activated.
Click **Stop**.

Step 11

Click the "Network Connections" window so it is activated.

2. What changes appear in the right pane, after stopping the Routing and Remote Access service?

Step 12

Click the "Performance" window so it is activated. Click the **Freeze Display** icon to stop the recording.

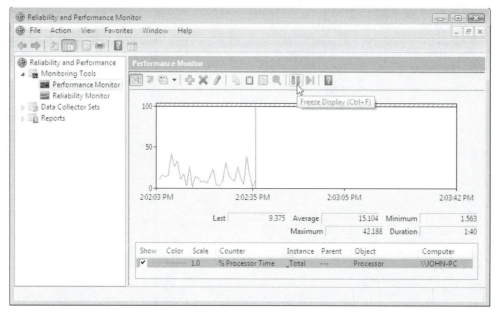

3. Which Counter is being recorded the most in the graph (hint: look at the graph color and Counter color)?

Click the Change graph type drop down menu, select **Report**.

The display changes to report view.

4. List the values of the counter.

Step 13

Click the "Routing and Remote Access Properties (Local Computer)" window so it is activated. In the Startup type select **Disabled**. Click **OK**.

Click the "Service" window so it is activated.

5. What is the Status and Startup Type for Routing and Remote Access?

Step 14

Click the "Performance" window so it is activated. Click the **Unfreeze Display** icon to start the recording.

Step 15

Close all open windows.

Step 16

Navigate to the "Administrative Tools" window by clicking **Start > Control Panel > Administrative Tools.** Double-click the **Computer Management** icon.

If the "User Account Control" window appears, click **Continue**.

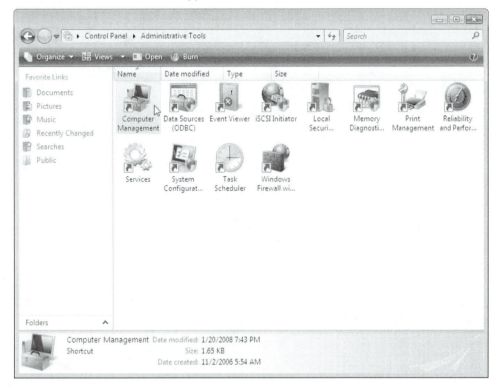

Step 17

The "Computer Management" window appears. Expand the three categories by clicking on the **arrow** next to: System Tools, Storage, and Services and Applications.

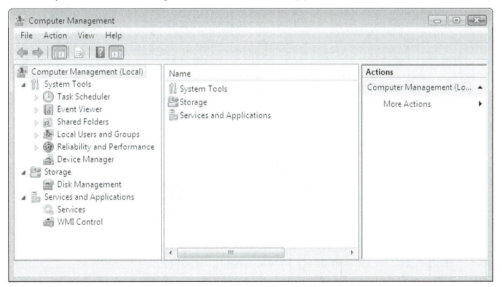

Step 18

Click the **arrow** next to Event Viewer then click the **arrow** next to Windows Logs. Click **System.**

Double click the first event in the window.

The "Event Properties" window appears for the event. Click the down arrow key to locate an event for Routing and Remote Access.

Step 19

You should find four events that describe the order for starting and stopping the Routing and Remote access service.

Write down the description for each of the four events.

Event Properties - Event 7036, Service Control Manager Eventlog Provider

General | Details

The Routing and Remote Access service entered the running state.

Log Name:	System		
Source:	Service Control Manager Eve	Logged:	7/28/2009 2:33:13 PM
Event ID:	7036	Task Category:	None
Level:	Information	Keywords:	Classic
User:	N/A	Computer:	John-PC
OpCode:	Info		
More Information:	Event Log Online Help		

Copy   Close

Event Properties - Event 7036, Service Control Manager Eventlog Provider

General | Details

The Routing and Remote Access service entered the stopped state.

Log Name:	System		
Source:	Service Control Manager Eve	Logged:	7/28/2009 2:34:06 PM
Event ID:	7036	Task Category:	None
Level:	Information	Keywords:	Classic
User:	N/A	Computer:	John-PC
OpCode:	Info		
More Information:	Event Log Online Help		

Copy   Close

Event Properties - Event 7040, Service Control Manager Eventlog Provider

General | Details

The start type of the Routing and Remote Access service was changed from demand start to disabled.

Log Name:	System		
Source:	Service Control Manager Eve	Logged:	7/28/2009 2:34:18 PM
Event ID:	7040	Task Category:	None
Level:	Information	Keywords:	Classic
User:	John-PC\John	Computer:	John-PC
OpCode:	Info		
More Information:	Event Log Online Help		

Copy | Close

Step 20

Close all open windows.

Step 21

Navigate to the "Run" window by clicking **Start > Run**. Type **MMC** and click **OK**.

If the "User Account Control" window appears, click **Continue**.

Run

Type the name of a program, folder, document, or Internet resource, and Windows will open it for you.

Open: mmc

OK | Cancel | Browse...

Step 22

The "Console1 [Console Root]" (console number may vary) window appears.

Step 23

To build your own custom console click **File > Add/Remove Snap-in**. The "Add or Remove Snap-in" window appears.

To add a folder snap-in so that you can organize all your snap-ins, scroll down until you see the Folder snap-in. Select **Folder >** click **Add**.

To add the "Link to Web Address" snap-in, scroll down until you see the snap-in. Select **Link to Web Address >** click **Add**. The "Link to Web Address" wizard opens. In the Target box type **http://www.cisco.com/**. Click **Next**.

In the "Friendly name for the Link to Web Address snap-in" box type **Cisco**. Click **Finish**.

Step 24

To add snap-ins to the folder snap-in, click **Advanced**.

Click in the **box** next to Allow changing the parent snap-in. Click **OK**.

A dropdown menu appears for "Parent snap-in". In the "Parent snap-in" box select **Folder**.

Add these snap-ins: Computer Management, Device Manager, and Disk Management.

NOTE: When asked what computer the snap-in will manage; select the default by clicking **Finish**.

Click **OK** to accept all changes.

Step 25

The "Console1" window appears. Right click the Folder icon and select Rename. Change the name of the folder to ManagementTools.

To save the custom console click **File > Save As**. Change the file name to your name. Example: **John's Console**. Change the "Save in" box to **Desktop**. Click **Save**.

Step 26

Close all open windows.

On the desktop double click the **Console** icon to re-open the console with your snap-ins.

5.5.4 Lab: Install Third-Party Software in Windows XP

Introduction

In this lab, you will install and remove a third party software application by using the Microsoft Windows XP Professional Installation CD. The student will install the CITRIX ICA 32-bit Windows Client application.

Recommended Equipment

The following equipment is required for this exercise:

- A computer system that is using Windows XP
- A Microsoft Windows XP installation CD

Step 1

Log on to the computer with the Administrator account.

Place the Windows XP Professional installation CD into the CD drive. Use Windows Explorer to navigate to the following folder:

D:\VALUEADD\3RDPARTY\MGMT\CITRIX

Locate the ICA32.exe application in the folder. Click the ICA32 icon to start the installation process of the Citrix application. You may need to double-click the icon to start the installation.

Step 2

Click Next when the InstallShield Wizard window opens.

A window opens displaying the file extraction progress.

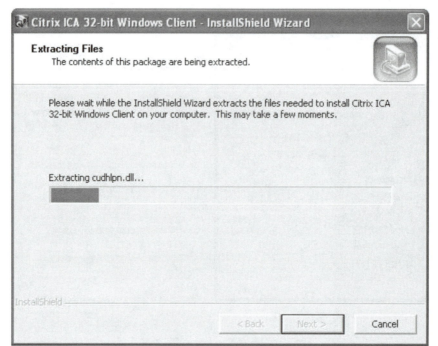

After the files have been extracted, the ICA Client Setup program begins. Click **Next** to begin the installation.

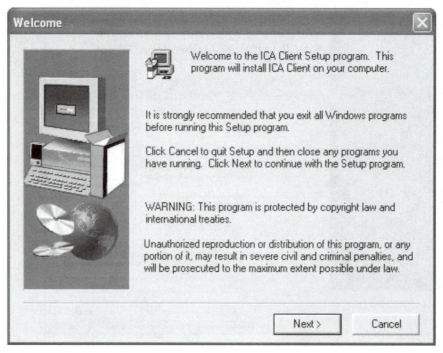

Click **Yes** on the License agreement.

Use the default location. Click **Next**.

Use the default location. Click **Next**.

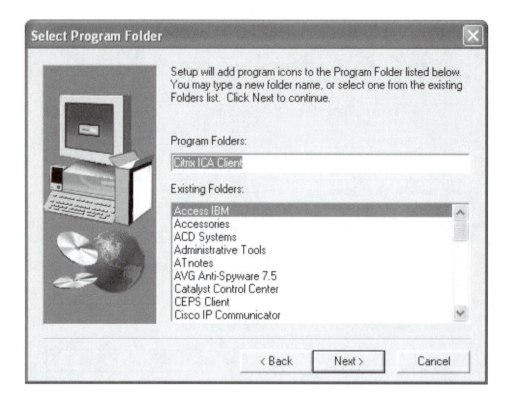

Enter "student" as the ClientName. Click **Next**.

In the Select Desired Features window, leave the default choice of **No**. Click **Next**.

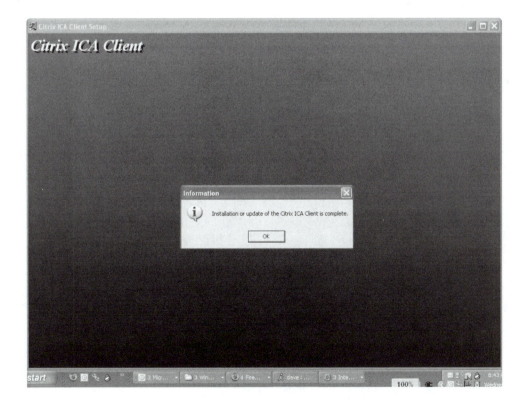

You have successfully installed the Citrix program.

Step 3

To uninstall a program, choose **Start > Control Panel > Add or Remove Programs**. Click the Citrix ICA Client in the list. Click **Change/Remove**.

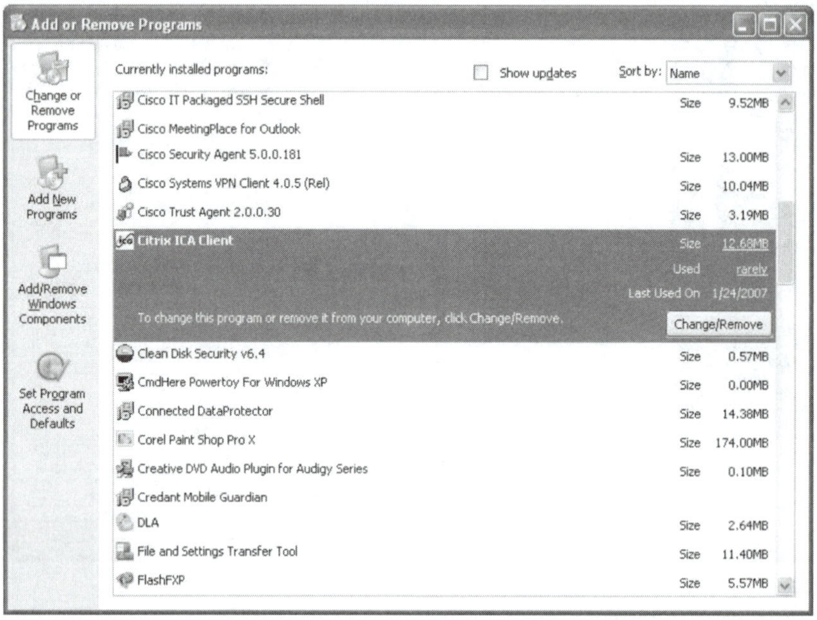

Click **Yes** to confirm the removal.

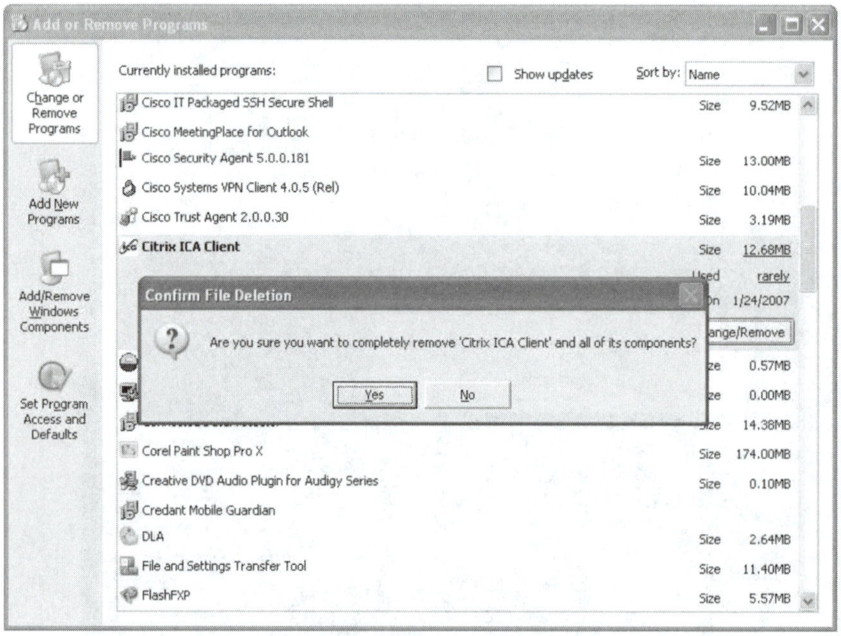

The following screen will appear displaying the removal progress:

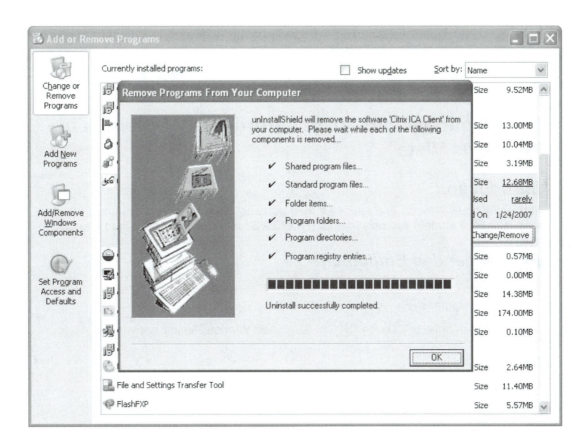

After the application removal process, the Add or Remove Programs window no longer shows the Citrix ICA Client in the list.

1. Why does Microsoft recommend using Add/Remove Programs to remove an installed application?

5.5.4 Optional Lab: Install Third-Party Software in Windows Vista

Introduction

In this lab, you will install and remove a third party software application supplied by your instructor. The student will install the CITRIX ICA 32-bit Windows Web Client application.

Recommended Equipment

The following equipment is required for this exercise:

- A computer system that is using Windows Vista
- A flash drive or CD with CITRIX ICA 32-bit Windows install package

Step 1

Log on to the computer with the Administrator account.

Use Windows Explorer to navigate to the CITRIX folder.

If installing from a CD, place the CD into the CD drive.

Navigate to D: \CITRIX.

If installing from a flash drive, place the flash drive into a USB port.

Navigate to E: \CITRIX.

Locate the Ica32pkg.msi application in the CD or flash drive. Click the Ica32pkg icon to start the installation process of the Citrix application. You may need to double-click the icon to start the installation.

Step 2

When the Select Language window opens, select a language and click **OK**.

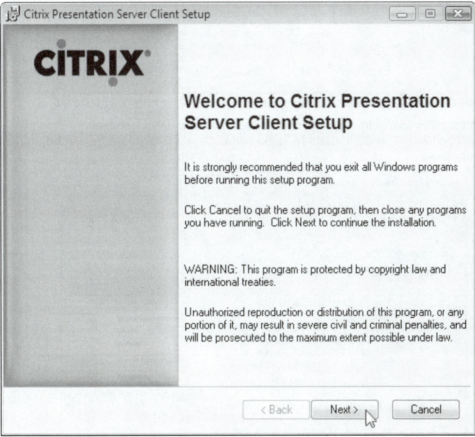

Click **Next** when the Citrix Presentation Server Client Setup program window opens.

Select "I accept the license agreement". Click **Next**.

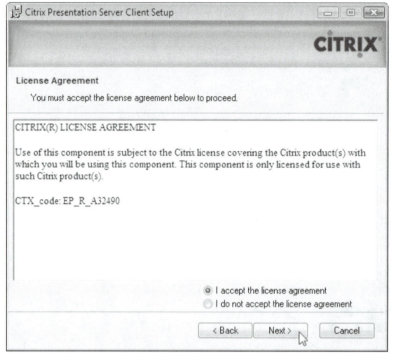

The "Select Client" page appears. Only the Web Client will be installed in this lab.

To stop the other clients from being installed click the **hard drive** icon next to "Program Neighborhood Agent" and "Program Neighborhood". Select **Entire feature will be unavailable**, for both of these.

How can you tell if a program will not be installed?

Click **Next**.

The "Client Name" page appears. Leave the default choice and click **Next**.

In the "Use Locale Name and Password" page, leave the default choice of **No**.

Click **Next**.

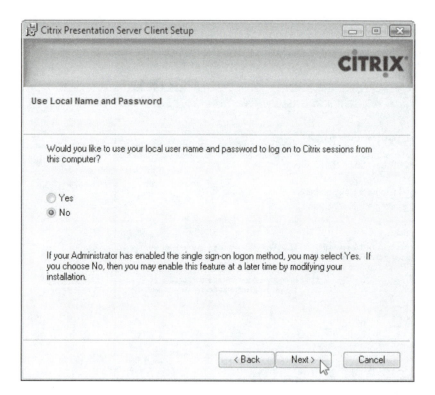

On the "Ready to install" page, click **Next** to install the application.

Click **Continue** if asked for permission.

A window opens displaying the file installation progress.

When the "Citrix Presentation Sever Client has been successfully installed" page appears, click **Finish**.

Step 3

To uninstall a program, choose **Start > Control Panel > Programs and Features**. Click the Citrix Presentation Server Client in the list.

Click **Uninstall**.

Click **Yes** to confirm the removal.

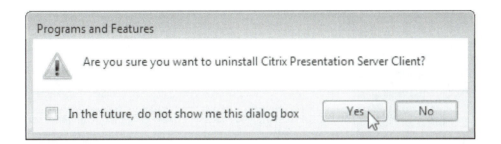

The following screen will appear displaying the removal progress:

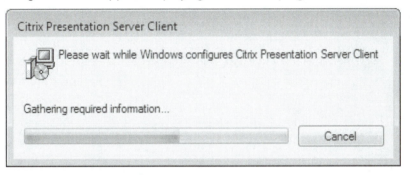

If the "An unidentified program wants access to your computer" appears, click **Allow**.

User Account Control

An unidentified program wants access to your computer

Don't run the program unless you know where it's from or you've used it before.

Unidentified Publisher

→ Cancel
I don't know where this program is from or what it's for.

→ Allow
I trust this program. I know where it's from or I've used it before.

⌄ Details

User Account Control helps stop unauthorized changes to your computer.

After the application removal process, the Uninstall or change a program window no longer shows the Citrix Presentation Server Client in the list.

1. Why does Microsoft recommend using Uninstall or change a program to remove an installed application?

5.6.2 Lab: Restore Points in Windows XP

Introduction

In this lab, you will create a restore point and return your computer back to that point in time.

Recommended Equipment

The following equipment is required for this exercise:

- A computer system running Windows XP
- The Windows XP installation CD

Step 1

Click **Start** > **All Programs** > **Accessories** > **System Tools** > **System Restore**.

Click the **Create a restore point** radio button.

Click **Next**.

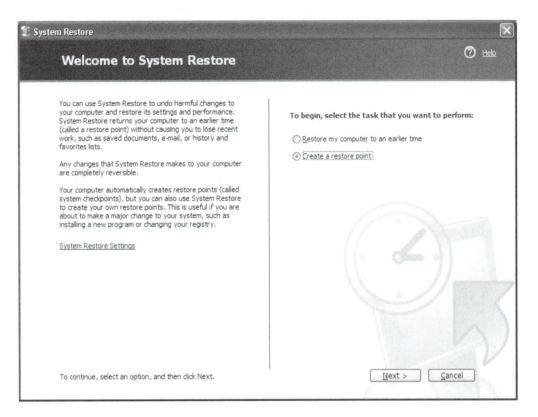

Step 2

In the "Restore point description" field, type **Application Installed**.

Click **Create**.

Step 3

The "Restore Point Created" window appears.

Click **Close**.

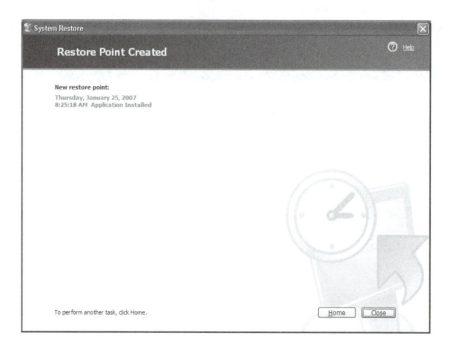

Step 4

Click **Start > Control Panel > Add or Remove Programs**.

Click the **Add or Remove Programs** icon.

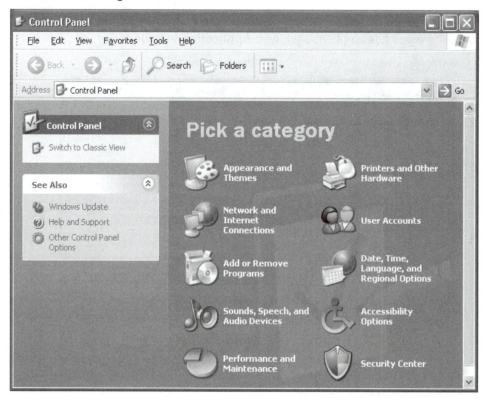

Step 5

Click **Add/Remove Windows Components**.

Step 6

Click the **Internet Information Services (IIS)** checkbox.

Click **Next**.

Step 7

Place the Windows XP installation CD into the optical drive.

Click **OK**.

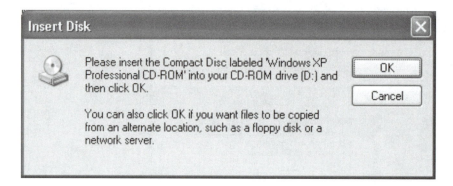

Step 8

The "Files Needed" window appears.

Click **OK**.

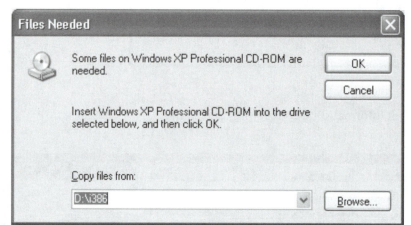

The "Configuring Components" progress window appears.

Step 9

The "Completing the Windows Components Wizard" window appears.

Click **Finish**.

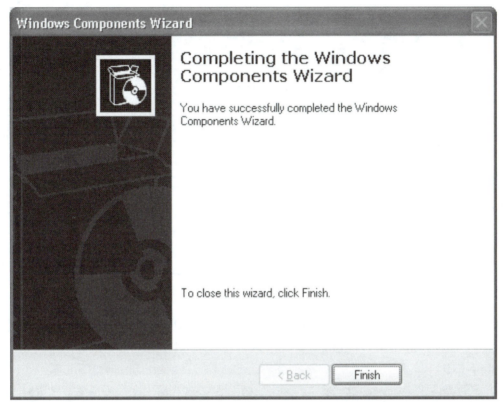

Step 10

The "System Settings Change" dialog box appears.

Remove the Windows XP installation disk from the optical drive.

Click **Yes**.

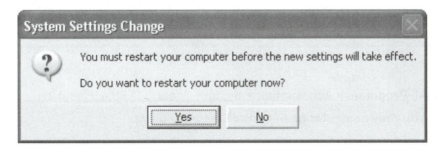

Step 11

Log on to Windows as yourself.

Open the Notepad application by clicking **Start > All Programs > Accessories > Notepad**.

Type **This is a test of the Restore Points** in the Notepad application.

Click **File > Save As…**.

Click **My Documents.**

Type **Restore Point Test file** in the "File Name:" field.

Click **Save.**

Click **File > Exit**.

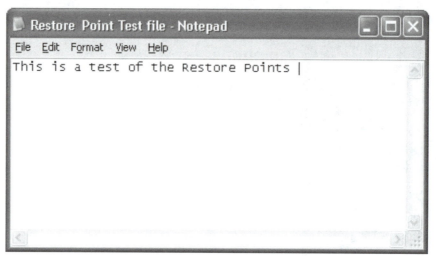

Step 12

Open IIS to confirm that you have successfully installed this service.

Click **Start > All Programs > Administrative Tools > Internet Information Services**.

Click **File > Exit**.

Step 13

Click **Start > All Programs > Accessories > System Tools > System Restore**.

Select the **Restore my computer to an earlier time** radio button.

Click **Next**.

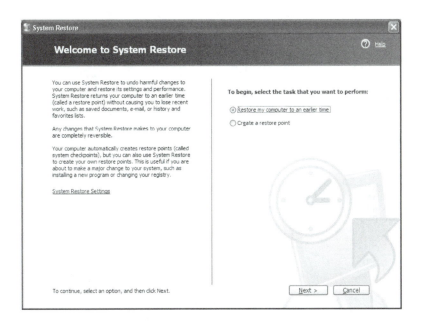

Step 14

Select today's date from the calendar on the left.

Select **Application Installed** from the list on the right.

Click **Next**.

Step 15

The "Confirm Restore Point Selection" window appears.

NOTE: When you click Next, Windows will restart the computer. Close all applications before you click Next.

Click **Next**.

The operating system restores to the point before the IIS application was installed.

Step 16

The "Restoration Complete" window appears. Click **OK**.

Step 17

Click **Start > All Programs > Administrative Tools**.

Is the Internet Information Services application listed?

Step 18

Navigate to the "My Documents" folder.

Open the "Restore Point Test file.txt" file.

Are the contents the same?

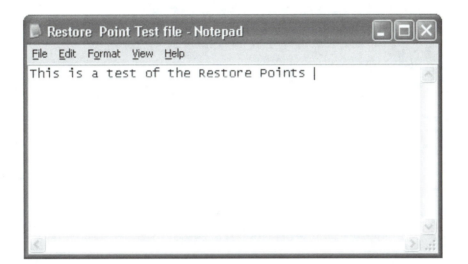

5.6.2 Optional Lab: Restore Points in Windows Vista

Introduction

In this lab, you will create a restore point and return your computer back to that point in time.

Recommended Equipment

The following equipment is required for this exercise:

- A computer system running Windows Vista

Step 1

Click **Start > All Programs > Accessories > System Tools > System Restore**.

Click **Continue** if asked for permission.

The "System Restore" window appears.

To create a restore point, click **open System Protection**.

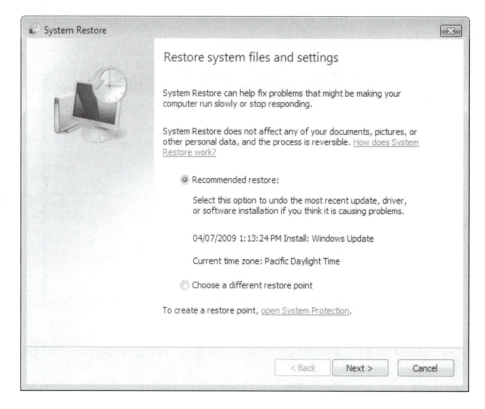

Step 2

The "System Properties" window appears.

In the "System Protection" tab, click **Create**.

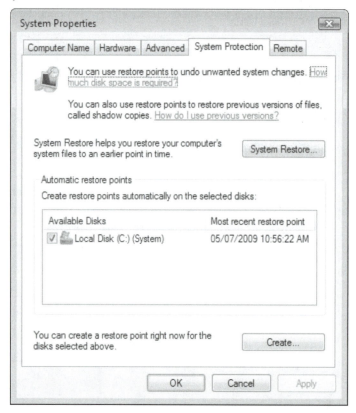

Step 3

In the "Create a restore point" description field, type **Application Installed**.

Click **Create**.

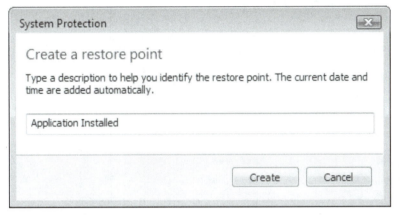

Step 4

After a period of time, a "The restore point was created successfully" message appears.

Click **OK**.

Step 5

The "System Properties" window with the "System Protection" tab selected appears. Notice in "Available Disks" area the new date below "Most recent restore point".

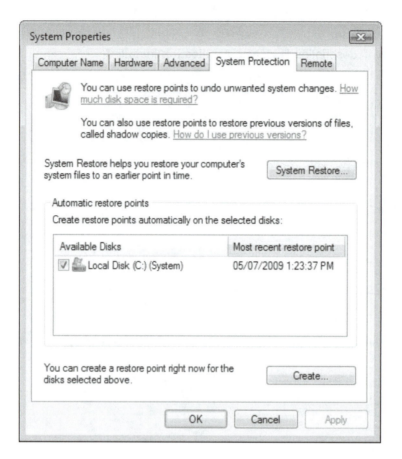

Click **OK**.

Close all open windows.

Step 6

Click **Start > Control Panel > Programs and Features**.

Click the **Turn Windows features on or off** link.

Click **Continue** if asked for permission.

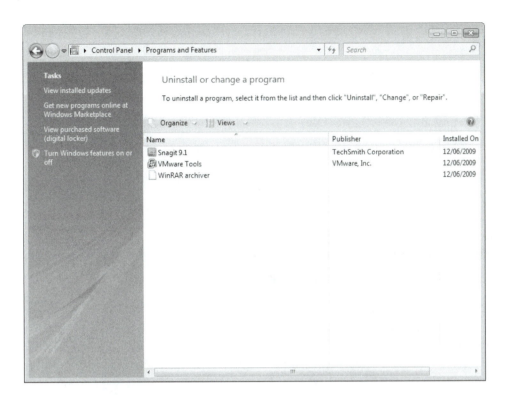

Step 7

The "Windows Features" window appears.

Click the **Internet Information Services** checkbox.

Click **OK**.

Step 8

The configuring features progress window appears.

The progress windows will close on its own when the configuration is completed.

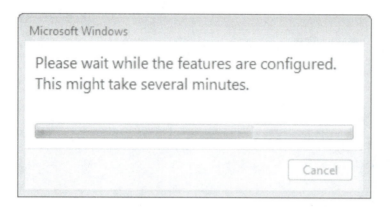

Step 9

When you navigate in a browser to localhost, you will see the new IIS default page.

Click **Start >** in **Start Search** type **http://localhost**.

Close the browser.

Step 10

Open the Notepad application by clicking **Start > All Programs > Accessories > Notepad**.

Type **This is a test of the Restore Points** in the Notepad application.

Click **File > Save As...**.

Click **Documents**.

Type **Restore Point Test file** in the "File Name:" field.

Click **Save**.

Click **File > Exit**.

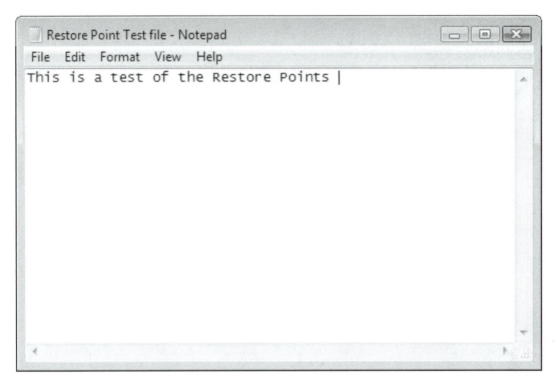

Step 11

Open IIS to confirm that you have successfully installed this service.

Click **Start > All Programs > Administrative Tools > IIS Manager**.

Click **Continue** if asked for permission.

Click **File > Exit**.

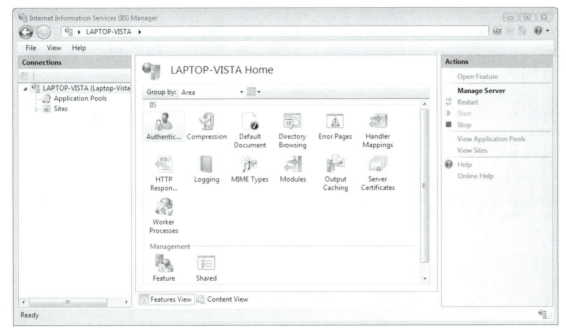

Step 12

Click **Start > All Programs > Accessories > System Tools > System Restore**.

Click **Continue** if asked for permission.

Select the **Recommended Restore** radio button.

Click **Next**.

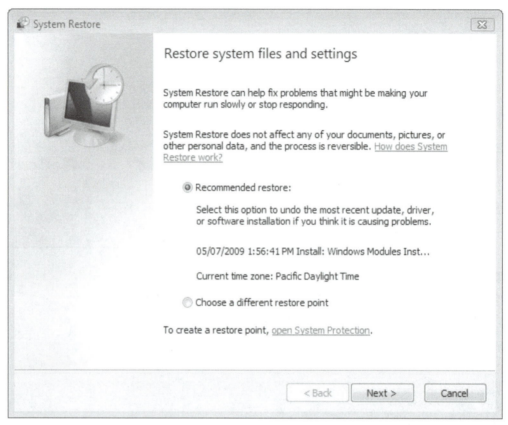

Step 13

The "Confirm your restore point" window appears.

NOTE: When you click Finish, Windows will restart the computer. Close all applications before you click Finish.

Click **Finish**.

Click **Yes** to confirm "System Restore".

The operating system restores to the point before the IIS application was installed. This can take several minutes to complete.

Step 14

The "Restoration Complete" window appears. Click **Close**.

Step 15

Click **Start > Control Panel > Administrative Tools**.

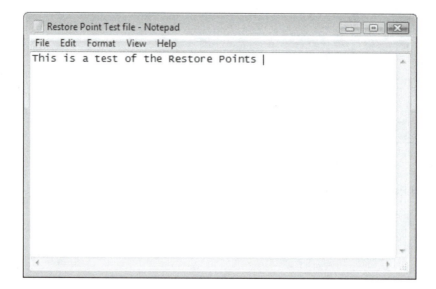

Is the IIS Manager application listed?

Step 16

Navigate to the "Documents" folder.

Open the "Restore Point Test file.txt" file.

Are the contents the same?

5.6.3 Lab: Registry Backup and Recovery in Windows XP

Introduction

In this lab, you will back up a computer registry. You will also perform a recovery of a computer registry. The registry is also called System State data.

Recommended Equipment

The following equipment is required for this exercise:

- A computer system running Windows XP is required for this exercise.

Step 1

Log on to the computer as yourself.

Click **Start > Run**.

Type **ntbackup** and then click **OK**. The "Backup or Restore Wizard" window appears.

Step 2

Click **Advanced Mode**.

The Backup Utility window appears.

Step 3

Click **Backup Wizard**.

The "Welcome to the Backup Wizard" window appears.

Step 4

Click **Next**.

Click the **Only back up the System State data** radio button.

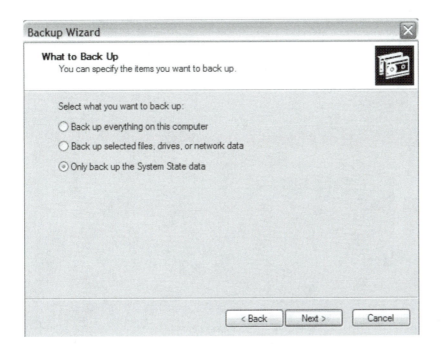

Step 5

Click **Next**.

The "Backup Type, Destination, and Name" window appears.

Step 6

Click **Browse…**.

If you are asked to insert a disk into the floppy disk drive, click **Cancel**.

The "Save As" dialog box appears.

Step 7

Click the **My Documents** icon on the left side of the "Save As" dialog box.

Click **Save**.

The "Backup Type, Destination, and Name" window re-appears.

Step 8

Click **Next**.

The "Completing the Backup Wizard" window appears.

Step 9

Click **Advanced…**.

The "Type Of Backup" window appears.

The default backup type is "Normal". If available, make sure that "Backup Migrated Remote Storage Data" is not checked.

Step 10

Click **Next**.

The "How To Backup" window appears.

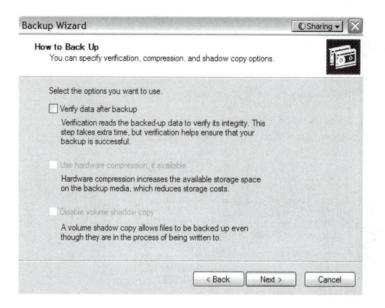

Step 11

Click the **Verify Data After Backup** check box, and then click **Next**.

The "Backup Options" window appears.

Step 12

Click **Replace the existing backups**, and then click Next.

The "When to Back Up" window appears.

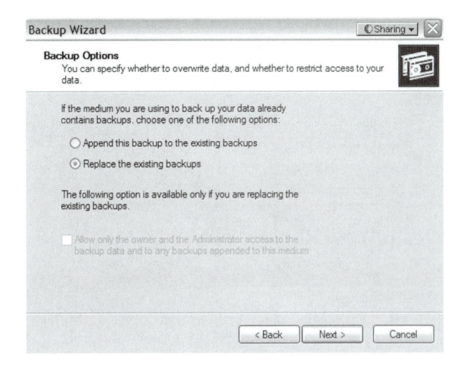

Step 13

At the "When To Back Up" window, click **Now** and then click **Next**.

The "Completing the Backup Wizard" window appears.

Step 14

Click **Finish**.

The "Backup Progress" window appears.

The "Backup Progress" window indicates that the backup is complete.

Step 15

Click **Report**.

The Notepad application window appears containing the report.

Close Notepad.

In the Backup Progress dialog box, click **Close**.

Close the Backup Utility.

Step 16

Click **Start > Run…**.

Type **regedit** in the "open:" field. The Registry Editor window appears.

Step 17

Expand the **HKEY_CURRENT_USER** Registry Key.

Expand the **Control Panel** Registry Key.

Expand the **PowerCfg** Registry Key.

Right-Click the **Screen Saver.Stars** Registry Key.

Click **Delete**.

Click **File > Exit** in the Registry Editor window.

Browse to the "My Documents" folder and locate the "backup.bkf" file.

Double-click the backup file to bring up the Backup Utility Wizard.

Click **Next**.

Step 18

Click the **Restore files and settings** radio button and then click **Next**.

The "What to Restore" window appears.

Step 19

Expand the file.

Expand the backup.bkf file.

Click the **System State** check box.

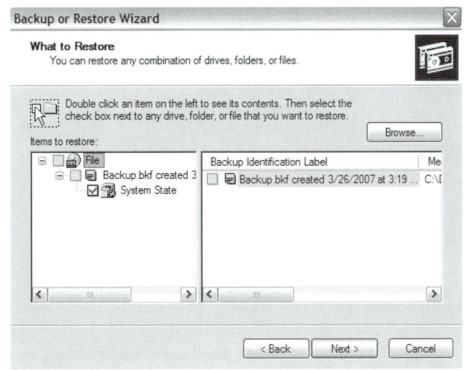

Step 20

Click **Next**.

The "Completing the Backup or Restore Wizard" window appears.

Step 21

Click **Advanced**.

The "Where to Restore" window appears.

Step 22

The default restoration location is "Original location".

Click **Next**.

The "Restoring System State will always overwrite current System State unless restoring to an alternate location." Warning window appears.

Click **OK**.

Step 23

Click the **Replace existing files if they are older than the backup files** radio button.

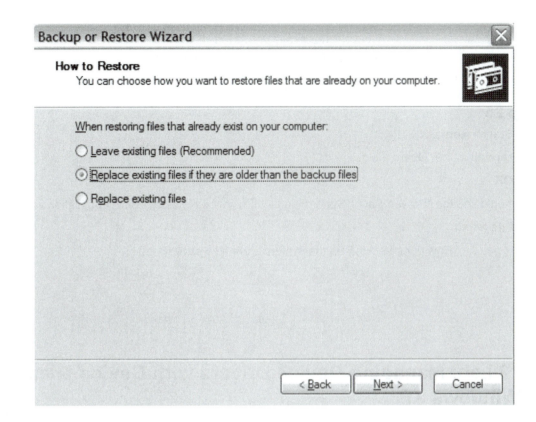

Step 24

Click **Next**.

The "Advanced Restore Options" window appears.

Be sure that all three check boxes are selected, and then click **Next**.

Click **Finish**.

The system recovery begins by copying the files back to the computer.

When prompted to restart the computer, click **Yes**. The computer will restart.

Step 25
Click **Start > Run…**.

Type **regedit** in the "Open:" field.

Click **OK**.

You should see the "Screen Saver.Stars" Registry key in the Registry Editor application window.

Click **File > Exit**.

1. How does backing up the system state files save time?

5.7.2 Lab: Managing Device Drivers with Device Manager in Windows XP

Introduction
In this lab, you will use Windows Device Manager to gather information about different drivers and learn how Device Manager manages drivers.

Recommended Equipment
The following equipment is required for this exercise:

- A computer running Windows XP Professional

Step 1
Log on to the computer as an administrator.

Navigate to the "Control Panel" by clicking **Start > Settings > Control Panel**. Double-click the **System** icon.

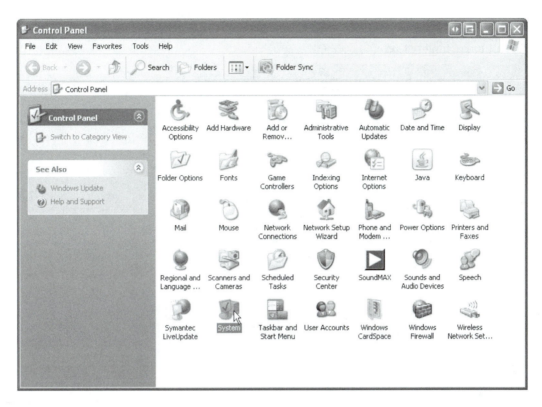

Step 2

The "System Properties" window appears. Open "Driver Signing Options" by clicking **Hardware** tab > **Driver Signing** button.

Accept the default setting and click **OK**.

Step 3

Click the **Device Manager** button.

Step 4

Click the **plus sign** next to Display adapter. Right click the adapter name and select **Properties**.

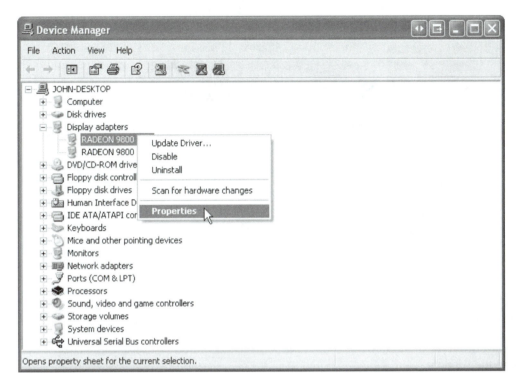

Step 5

The "Display adapters Properties" window appears.

What information is displayed under the General tab?

Click the **Troubleshoot ...** button.

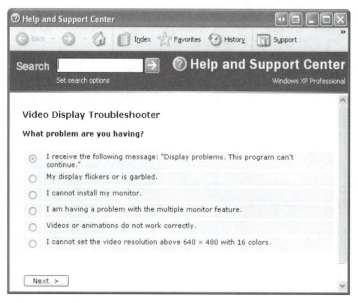

What window opens?

Close the window.

Step 6

Click the **Driver** tab.

What functions can you accomplish from this page?

Step 7

Click the **Detail** tab. This tab provides more details about the hardware.

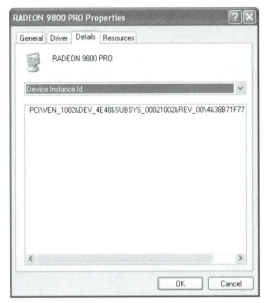

Step 8

Click the **Resource** tab.

What information is displayed under the Resource tab?

Close the "Display adapters Properties" windows, click **Cancel**.

Step 9

Navigate to the "Network adapter Properties" window" by clicking the **plus sign** next to Network adapter > right click the adapter name > select **Properties**.

Which tabs are available?

Are there any extra tabs?

What is the purpose of the extra tabs?

Close the "Network adapters Properties" windows, click **Cancel**.

Close all windows and log off.

5.7.2 Optional Lab: Managing Device Drivers with Device Manager in Windows Vista

Introduction

In this lab, you will use Windows Device Manager to gather information about different drivers and learn how Device Manager manages drivers.

Recommended Equipment

The following equipment is required for this exercise:

- A computer running Windows Vista

Step 1

Log on to the computer as an administrator.

Navigate to the "Control Panel" by clicking **Start > Control Panel**. Double-click the **System** icon.

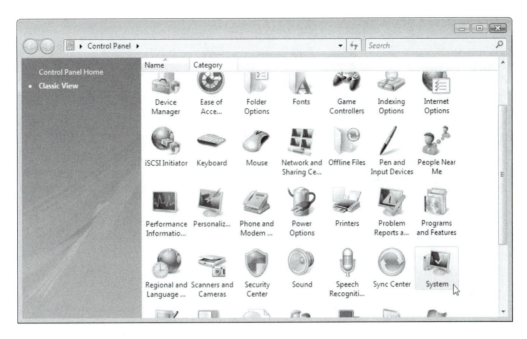

Step 2

The "System" window appears. At the left pane click **Advanced system settings**.

If User Account Control appears, click **Continue**.

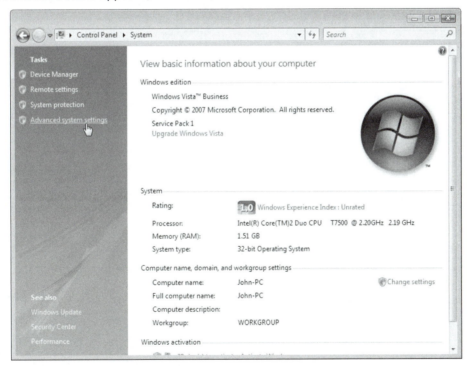

The "System Properties" window appears. Open "Windows Update Driver Settings" by clicking **Hardware** tab > **Windows Update Driver Settings** button.

Accept the default setting and click **OK**.

Step 3

Click the **Device Manager** button.

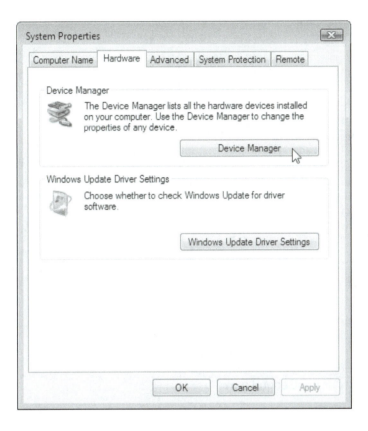

Step 4

Click the **plus sign** next to Display adapters. Right click the adapter name and select **Properties**.

Step 5

The "Display adapters Properties" window appears.

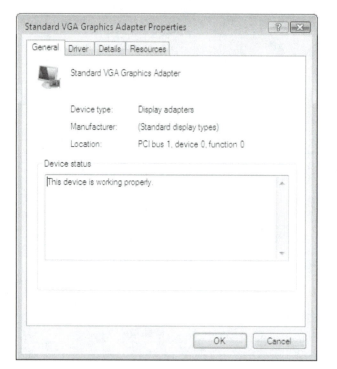

What information is displayed under the General tab?

Step 6

Click the **Driver** tab.

What functions can you accomplish from this page?

Step 7

Click the **Detail** tab. This tab provides more details about the hardware.

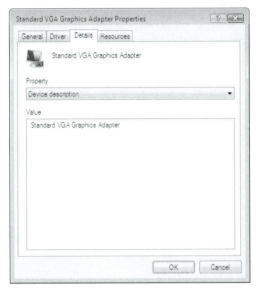

Step 8

Click the **Resource** tab.

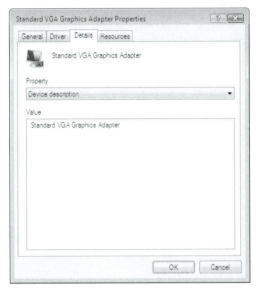

What information is displayed under the Resource tab?

Close the "Display adapters Properties" windows, click **Cancel**.

Step 9

Navigate to the "Network adapter Properties" window" by clicking the **plus sign** next to Network adapters **>** right click the adapter name **>** select **Properties**.

Which tabs are available?

Are there any extra tabs?

What is the purpose of the extra tabs?

Close the "Network adapters Properties" windows, click **Cancel**.

Close all windows and log off.

Chapter 6: Fundamental Laptops and Portable Devices

6.1.2 Worksheet: Research Laptops, Smartphones, and PDAs

In this worksheet, you will use the Internet, a newspaper, or a local store to gather information, and then enter the specifications for a laptop, smartphone, and PDA onto this worksheet. What type of equipment do you want? What features are important to you?

For example, you may want a laptop that has an 80 GB hard drive and plays DVDs or has built-in wireless capability. You may need a smartphone with Internet access or a PDA that takes pictures.

Shop around, and in the table below list the features and cost for a laptop, smartphone, and PDA.

Equipment	Features	Cost
Laptop Computer		
Smartphone		

PDA		

6.2.3 Worksheet: Complete Docking Stations True or False Questions

True or False?

	Docking stations are usually smaller than port replicators and do not have speakers or PCI slots.
	The exhaust vent is an outlet through which the fan expels hot air from the interior of the docking station.
	A laptop can be secured to a docking station with a key lock.
	The RJ-11 modem port connects a laptop to a cabled local area network.
	The Ethernet port uses an RJ-45 socket to connect a laptop to a standard telephone line.
	The DVI port is a 15-pin socket that allows output to external displays and projectors.
	The Line In connector is a socket used to attach an audio source.
	The eject button releases the peripherals from the docking station.
	The parallel port is a socket used to connect a device such as a printer or a scanner.

6.3.4 Worksheet: Answer Laptop Expansion Questions

1. List three types of PC Cards and the thickness of each.

Type	Thickness

2. Are PC ExpressCards interchangeable with PC cards?

3. What does APM use to control power management?

4. What does ACPI use to control power management?

5. Can you add desktop RAM to a laptop motherboard?

6. Does a desktop processor use more or less power than a laptop processor of the same speed?

7. Does a laptop processor generate more or less heat than a desktop processor?

6.4.1 Worksheet: Match ACPI Standards

Enter the ACPI standard next to the matching power management state description.

S0   S1   S2   S3   S4   S5

ACPI Standard	Power Management States
	The CPU is off, but the RAM is refreshed to maintain the contents.
	The CPU and RAM are off. The contents of RAM have been saved to a temporary file on the hard disk.
	The CPU is not executing instructions; however the CPU and RAM are still receiving power.
	The CPU is off, and the RAM is set to a slow refresh rate.
	The computer is off and any content that has not been saved will be lost.
	The computer is on and all devices are operating at full power.

6.7.2 Worksheet: Research Laptop Problems

Laptops often use proprietary parts. To find information about the replacement parts, you may have to research the web site of the laptop manufacturer.

Before you begin this worksheet, you need to know some information about the laptop.

Your instructor will provide you with the following information:

Laptop manufacturer:

Laptop model number:

Amount of RAM:

Size of the hard drive:

Use the Internet to locate the web site for the laptop manufacturer. What is the URL for the web site?

Locate the service section of the web site and look for links that focus on your laptop. It is common for web site to allow you to search by the model number. The list below shows common links that you might find:

- FAQs
- WIKIs
- Service notices
- White papers
- Blogs

List the links you found specific to the laptop and include a brief description of the information in that link.

Briefly describe any service notices you found on the web site. A service notice example is a driver update, a hardware issue, or a recall notice for a laptop component.

Open forums may exist for your laptop. Use an Internet search engine to locate any open forums that focus on your laptop by typing in the name and model of the laptop. Briefly describe the web sites (other than the manufacturer website) that you located.

Chapter 7: Fundamental Printers and Scanners

7.4.2 Lab: Install All-in-One Device and Software

Introduction

In this lab, you will install an all-in-one device. You will find, download, and update the driver and the software for the all-in-one device.

Recommended Equipment

- A Computer running Window XP Professional
- Internet connection
- All-in-one device

Step 1

If you are installing an all-in-one device that connects to a parallel port, shut down the computer and connect the cable to the all-in-one device and computer using a parallel cable. Plug the all-in-one device power cord into an AC outlet and unlock the all-in-one device if necessary. Restart your computer.

If you are installing a USB all-in-one device, plug the all-in-one device into the computer using a USB cable. Plug the all-in-one device power cord into an AC outlet if necessary. Unlock the all-in-one device if it is locked.

Step 2

Windows detects the new hardware.

The "Found New Hardware Wizard" window appears.

Click the **Yes, this time only** radio button, and then click **Next**.

The second screen of the Found New Hardware Wizard appears.

The default is "Install the software automatically (Recommended)".

Click **Next**.

The "Please wait while the wizard searches…" window appears.

The "Cannot Install this Hardware" window may appear.

If this happens, click **Finish**.

Step 3

If the computer does not detect the all-in-one device, right-click **My Computer**, then choose **Manage > Device Manager**.

Under "Other Devices", double-click the all-in-one device you are trying to install.

Step 4

The "Properties" window for the all-in-one device appears.

The "Device Status" area shows that "The drivers for this device are not installed. (Code 28)".

Do not click "Reinstall Driver..." at this time.

Click **Cancel**.

All-in-One Device Properties

General | Driver | Details

All-in-One Device

Device type: Other devices
Manufacturer: Unknown
Location: Location 0 (CanoScan)

Device status

The drivers for this device are not installed. (Code 28)

To reinstall the drivers for this device, click Reinstall Driver.

Reinstall Driver...

Device usage:

Use this device (enable)

OK | Cancel

Step 5

Find the manufacturer and the model number of the all-in-one device.

Visit the manufacturer's web site and navigate to the product downloads or support page. Download the most recent driver and software for the model of all-in-one device that you have installed. The software and driver must be compatible with your operating system.

Download the driver to a temporary folder on your desktop.

Double-click the installation file that you downloaded.

WinZip Self-Extractor - SetupSG.exe

All-in-One Device Setup

Setup
Cancel
About

Step 6

Unplug the all-in-one device, and plug it back in.

The Windows XP operating system detects the new device and installs the new drivers.

To verify, right-click **My Computer**, and then choose **Manage > Device Manager**. You should now see the all-in-one device installed under "Imaging devices" on the right side of the window.

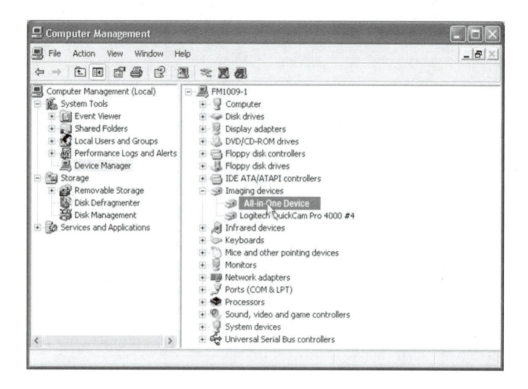

Chapter 8: Fundamental Networks

8.3.2 Worksheet: Identify IP Address Classes

In this worksheet, your instructor will write several IP addresses with their appropriate subnet masks on the board. You will copy the IP address and Subnet Mask. You will write which IP Address Class is appropriate in the IP Address Class column in the chart below. An example has been provided for you.

Be prepared to discuss the IP Address Class you select.

IP Address	Subnet Mask	IP Address Class
10.0.0.0	255.0.0.0	A

8.9.1 Worksheet: Internet Search for NIC Drivers

In this worksheet, you will search the Internet for the latest NIC drivers for a network card.

Complete the table below. An example has been provided for you. Drivers are routinely updated. Manufacturers often move driver files to different areas of their web sites. Version numbers change frequently. The driver in the example was found by visiting the manufacturer's (www.intel.com) web site. A search for the full name of the NIC was used to find the driver download file.

NIC	URL Driver Location and Latest Version Number
Intel PRO/1000 PT Desktop Adapter	http://downloadcenter.intel.com/Detail_Desc.aspx?agr=Y&ProdId=2247&DwnldID=12197&lang=eng Ver. # 14.7

3COM 905CX-TXM	
Linksys WMP54GX4	

8.9.2 Lab: Configure an Ethernet NIC to use DHCP in Windows XP

Introduction

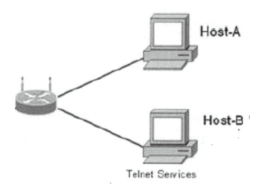

In this lab, you will configure an Ethernet NIC to use DHCP to obtain an IP address, test connectivity and establish a telnet connection between 2 computers.

NOTE: The instructor will have a Telnet server configured on Host B.

Recommended Equipment

- Linksys 300N router
- Two Computers running Window XP Professional
- Ethernet patch cable

Step 1

For Host A, plug one end of the Ethernet patch cable into "Port 1" on the back of the router.

For Host A, plug the other end of the Ethernet patch cable into the network port on the NIC in your computer.

For Host B, plug one end of the Ethernet patch cable into "Port 2" on the back of the router.

For Host B, plug the other end of the Ethernet patch cable into the network port on the NIC in your computer.

Plug in the power cable of the router if it is not already plugged in.

Turn on both computers and log on to Windows in Host A as an administrator.

Click **Start**.

Right-click **My Network Places**, and then choose **Properties**.

The "Network Connections" window appears.

Step 2

Right-click **Local Area Connection**, and then choose **Properties**.

The "Local Area Connection Properties" window appears.

What is the name and model number of the NIC in the "Connect using:" field?

What are the items listed in the "This connection uses the following items:" field?

Step 3

Choose **Internet Protocol (TCP/IP)**.

Click **Properties**.

The "Internet Protocol (TCP/IP) Properties" window appears.

What is the IP address, Subnet mask, and Default gateway listed in the fields of the "Use the following IP address:" area?

Click the **Obtain an IP address automatically** radio button.

Click **OK**.

The "Internet Protocol (TCP/IP) Properties" window closes.

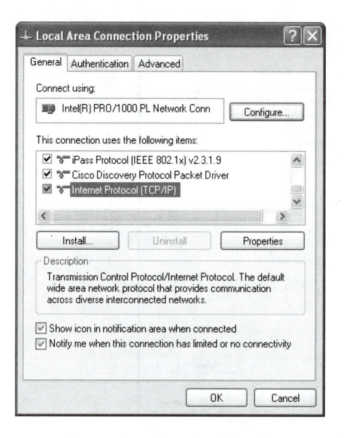

Click **OK.**

Restart your computer.

Step 4

Log onto Windows as an administrator.

Check the lights on the back of the NIC. These lights will blink when there is network activity.

Choose **Start > Run....**

Type **cmd** and click **OK.**

Type **ipconfig/all**, and then press the **Enter** key.

```
C:\WINDOWS\system32\cmd.exe                                    _ □ X

Microsoft Windows XP [Version 5.1.2600]
(C) Copyright 1985-2001 Microsoft Corp.

C:\Documents and Settings\glambeth>ipconfig /all

Windows IP Configuration

        Host Name . . . . . . . . . . . . : glamb
        Primary Dns Suffix  . . . . . . . : amer.cisco.com
        Node Type . . . . . . . . . . . . : Hybrid
        IP Routing Enabled. . . . . . . . : No
        WINS Proxy Enabled. . . . . . . . : No
        DNS Suffix Search List. . . . . . : cisco.com

Ethernet adapter Wireless Network Connection:

        Connection-specific DNS Suffix  . : cisco.com
        Description . . . . . . . . . . . : Intel(R) PRO/Wireless 3945ABG Networ
k Connection
        Physical Address. . . . . . . . . : 00-13-02-AD-BB-BB
        Dhcp Enabled. . . . . . . . . . . : Yes
        Autoconfiguration Enabled . . . . : Yes
        IP Address. . . . . . . . . . . . : 64.101.114.1
        Subnet Mask . . . . . . . . . . . : 255.255.255.0
        Default Gateway . . . . . . . . . : 64.101.114.1
        DHCP Server . . . . . . . . . . . : 171.68.10.6
        DNS Servers . . . . . . . . . . . : 68.2.16.3
                                            68.1.208.3
        Primary WINS Server . . . . . . . : 171.69.2.8
        Secondary WINS Server . . . . . . : 171.68.235.2
        Lease Obtained. . . . . . . . . . : Friday, February 02, 2007 1:16:25 PM

        Lease Expires . . . . . . . . . . : Saturday, February 03, 2007 7:00:53
AM
```

What is the IP address and subnet mask of the "Ethernet Adapter Local Area Network Connection"?

What is the IP address of the DHCP server?

On what date was the Lease Obtained?

On what date does the Lease Expire?

Step 5

Type **ping** and your IP address. For example, **ping 192.168.1.103**

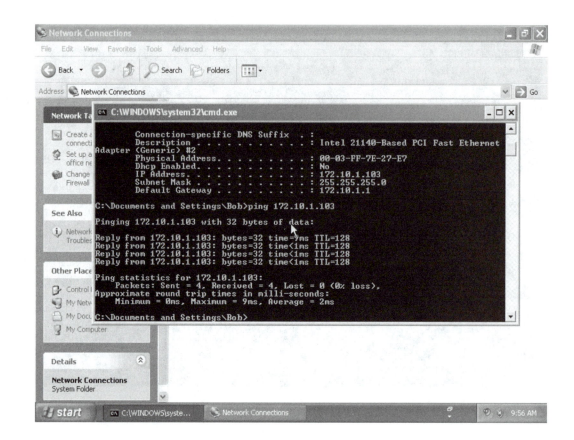

Write one of the replies of your ping command.

_____

Ask the instructor for the IP address for Host B or login to Host B and obtain the IP address by typing **ipconfig** in the command window.

What is the IP address for Host B?

Type **ping** and the IP address for Host B.

If the ping was not successful, troubleshoot.

Type **exit,** and then press **Enter.**

Step 6

Log in to Host A as an administrator, if not already done.

Choose **Start > Run....**

Type **telnet** and click **OK**.

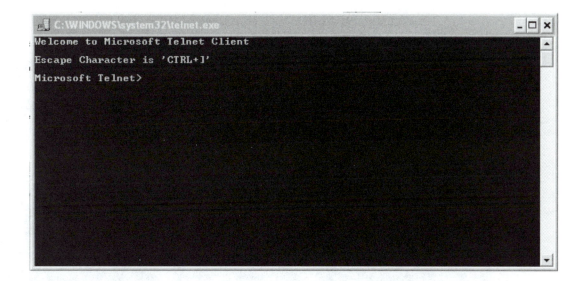

Type **help**.

List each of Windows telnet supported commands and descriptions.

At the Microsoft Telnet> prompt type: **o hostname** (IP address of Host B).

Log in to the telnet server (Host B).

Ask the instructor for account username and password.

Username:

Password:

What message is displayed on the telnet server to indicate you are connected?

What directory are you connected to?

Type **exit** to disconnect from the telnet server.

Press any key to continue.

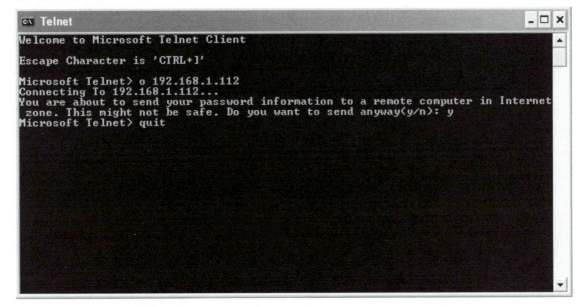

Type the proper command to exit the telnet session.

Close all windows and properly log off both computers.

8.9.2 Optional Lab: Configure an Ethernet NIC to use DHCP in Windows Vista

Introduction

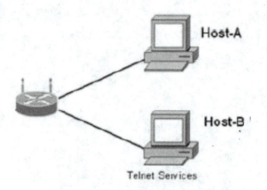

In this lab, you will configure an Ethernet NIC to use DHCP to obtain an IP address, test connectivity and establish a telnet connection between 2 computers.

NOTE: The instructor will have a Telnet server configured on Host B.

Recommended Equipment

- Linksys 300N router
- Two Computers running Window Vista
- Ethernet patch cable

Step 1

For Host A, plug one end of the Ethernet patch cable into "Port 1" on the back of the router.

For Host A, plug the other end of the Ethernet patch cable into the network port on the NIC in your computer.

For Host B, plug one end of the Ethernet patch cable into "Port 2" on the back of the router.

For Host B, plug the other end of the Ethernet patch cable into the network port on the NIC in your computer.

Plug in the power cable of the router if it is not already plugged in.

Turn on both computers and log on to Windows in Host A as an administrator.

Click **Start.**

Right-click **Network**, and then choose **Properties**.

The "Network and Sharing Center" window appears.

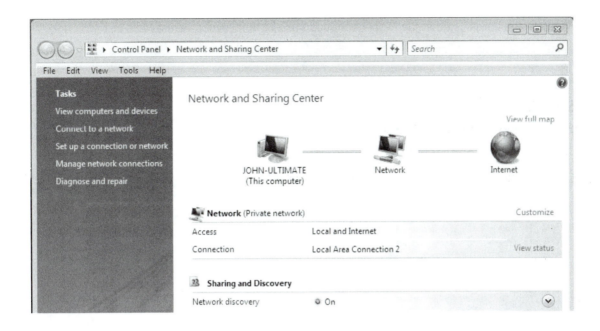

Step 2

Click View Status, and then choose **Properties > Continue** if asked.

The "Local Area Connection Status" window appears.

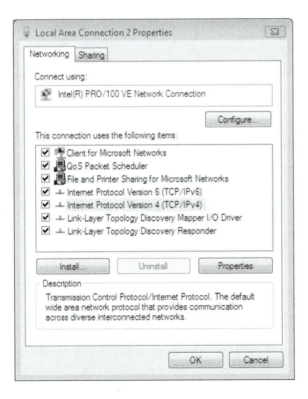

What is the name and model number of the NIC in the "Connect using:" field?

What are the items listed in the "This connection uses the following items:" field?

Step 3

Choose **Internet Protocol (TCP/IP)**.

Click **Properties**.

The "Internet Protocol (TCP/IP) Properties" window appears.

What is the IP address, Subnet mask, and Default gateway listed in the fields of the "Use the following IP address:" area?

Click the **Obtain an IP address automatically** radio button.

Click **OK** for the next two windows.

The "Internet Protocol (TCP/IP) Properties" window closes.

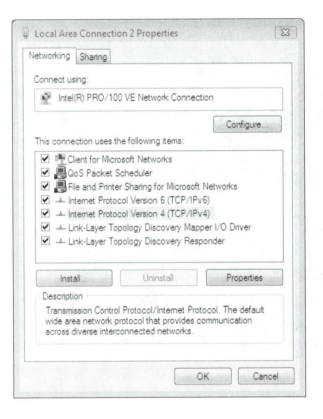

Click **Close.**

Restart your computer.

Step 4

Log onto Windows as an administrator.

Check the lights on the back of the NIC. These lights will blink when there is network activity.

Choose **Start**.

In **Start Search** type **cmd** and press **Enter**.

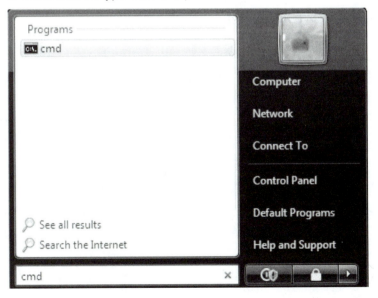

Type **ipconfig /all**, and then press the **Enter** key.

```
C:\Windows\system32\cmd.exe                                          _ □ x

Microsoft Windows [Version 6.0.6000]
Copyright (c) 2006 Microsoft Corporation.  All rights reserved.

C:\Users\John>ipconfig /all

Windows IP Configuration

   Host Name . . . . . . . . . . . . : John-Ultimate
   Primary Dns Suffix  . . . . . . . :
   Node Type . . . . . . . . . . . . : Hybrid
   IP Routing Enabled. . . . . . . . : No
   WINS Proxy Enabled. . . . . . . . : No
   DNS Suffix Search List. . . . . . : va.shawcable.net

Ethernet adapter Local Area Connection 2:

   Connection-specific DNS Suffix  . : va.shawcable.net
   Description . . . . . . . . . . . : Intel(R) PRO/100 VE Network Connection
   Physical Address. . . . . . . . . : 00-03-47-C1-EA-5D
   DHCP Enabled. . . . . . . . . . . : Yes
   Autoconfiguration Enabled . . . . : Yes
   Link-local IPv6 Address . . . . . : fe80::7cb1:a08a:7079:435d%9(Preferred)
   IPv4 Address. . . . . . . . . . . : 192.168.1.113(Preferred)
   Subnet Mask . . . . . . . . . . . : 255.255.255.0
   Lease Obtained. . . . . . . . . . : June-07-09 1:31:46 PM
   Lease Expires . . . . . . . . . . : June-08-09 1:31:46 PM
   Default Gateway . . . . . . . . . : 192.168.1.1
   DHCP Server . . . . . . . . . . . : 192.168.1.1
   DHCPv6 IAID . . . . . . . . . . . : 234881863
   DNS Servers . . . . . . . . . . . : 64.59.144.18
                                       64.59.144.19
   NetBIOS over Tcpip. . . . . . . . : Enabled
```

What is the IP address and subnet mask of the "Ethernet Adapter Local Area Network Connection"?

What is the IP address of the DHCP server?

On what date was the Lease Obtained?

On what date does the Lease Expire?

Step 5

Type **ping** and your IP address. For example, **ping 192.168.1.113**

Write one of the replies of your ping command.

Step 6

To install Telnet Client, log in to Host A as an administrator, if not already done.

Click **Start > Control Panel > Programs and Features**.

Click **Turn Windows features on or off** > if asked click **Continue.**

In the **Windows Features** list, select **Telnet Client**, and then click **OK.**

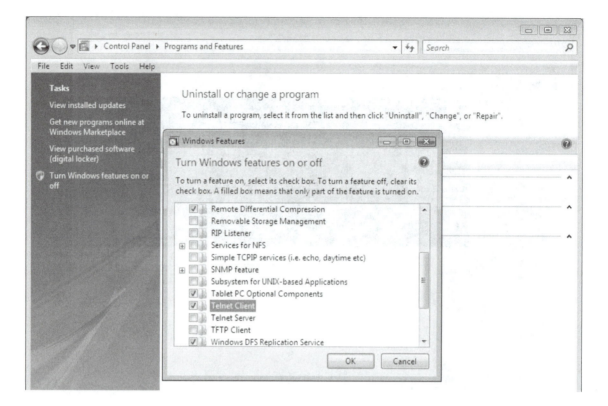

Close all windows.

Choose **Start > Command Prompt**

Type **telnet** and press **Enter**.

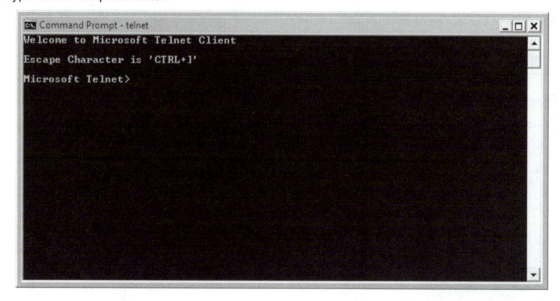

Type **help**.

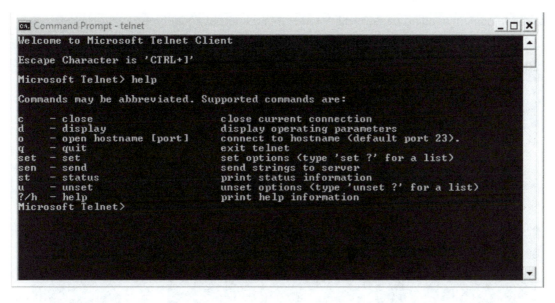

List each of the Windows telnet supported commands and descriptions.

At the Microsoft Telnet> prompt type: **o hostname** (IP address of Host B).

Log in to the telnet server (Host B).

Ask instructor for account username and password.

Username:

Password:

If asked to confirm sending password information in a Internet zone, type _____

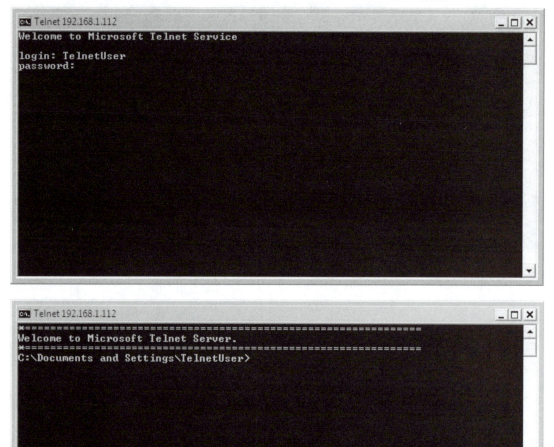

What message is displayed on the telnet server to indicate you are connected?

What directory are you connected to?

Type **exit** to disconnect from the telnet server.

Press any key to continue…

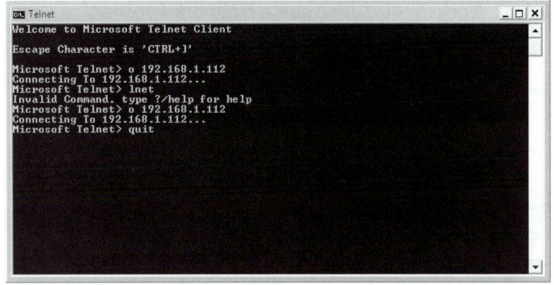

Type the proper command to exit the telnet session.

Close all windows and properly log off both computers.

8.10.3 Worksheet: Answer Broadband Questions

1. Which types of signals are carried over a DSL cable?

2. What is the typical upload speed of a satellite broadband connection?

3. Which type of broadband technology is referred to as CATV?

4. Which cable type is used by a CATV broadband connection?

5. ISDN uses existing telephone copper wires to send and receive which types of signals?

6. Which technology is usually an alternative when cable or DSL are not available?

7. What is the 16 Kbps digital line used for in an ISDN connection?

8. What is the typical download speed of a satellite broadband connection?

9. What is the maximum data rate for ISDN BRI?

10. Which device on a DSL connection requires a filter?

8.12.2 Worksheet: Diagnose a Network Problem

(Student Technician Sheet)

Gather data from the customer to begin the troubleshooting process. Document the customer's problem in the work order below.

Work Order

Company Name: Handford Insurance_____

Contact: J. Halle_____

Company Address: 1671 N. 52nd Ave._____

Company Phone: 555-9991_____

Generating a New Ticket

Category Network_____Closure Code___Status Open_____

Type_____Escalated_____Pending_____

Item _____ Pending Until Date_____

Business Impacting? X Yes   O No

Summary The customer is not able to connect to the network. Customer is not able to send or receive email. _____

_____

Case ID#_____   Connection Type_____

Priority_____   Environment_____

User Platform Windows XP____

Problem Description Customer cannot access network folders. Customer cannot send or receive e-mail. Customer was able to access the network yesterday.

_____

_____

Problem Solution:_____

_____

_____

8.12.2 Worksheet: Diagnose a Network Problem

(Student Customer Sheet)

Use the contact information and problem description below to report the following information to a level-one technician:

Contact Information

Company Name: Handford Insurance

Contact: J. Halle

Company Address: 1671 N. 52nd Ave.

Company Phone: 555-9991

Problem Description

I am not able to connect to the network. I can log onto Windows, but I cannot get to my folders on the network. I cannot get to the Internet either. Everything was fine yesterday because Johnny was using my computer while I was at home sick, but now it does not work. In fact, my e-mail does not work either. I tried to send e-mail, but it did not go anywhere. It just sits in my Outbox. My friend said she sent me some e-mail this morning, but I do not have it. It just is not there. What am I going to do? I have to get started on my work. My boss is going to be very upset. Can you help me get to the network? And my files? And my e-mail?

(NOTE: Once you have given the level-one tech the problem description, use the Additional Information to answer any follow up questions the technician may ask.)

Additional Information

- I am using Windows XP Pro.
- Cable connects me to the Internet.
- I am using a desktop computer.
- Everybody else in the office can access their files.
- Everybody else in the office can use e-mail.

Chapter 9: Fundamental Security

9.1 Worksheet: Security Attacks

Print and complete this activity.

In this activity, you will use the Internet, a newspaper, or magazines to gather information to help you become familiar with computer crime and security attacks in your area. Be prepared to discuss your research with the class.

1. Briefly describe one article dealing with computer crime or a security attack.

2. Based on your research, could this incident have been prevented? List the precautions that might have prevented this attack.

9.2.1 Worksheet: Third-Party Anti-Virus Software

Print and complete this activity.

In this activity, you will use the Internet, a newspaper, or a local store to gather information about third-party anti-virus software.

1. Using the Internet, research 2 different anti-virus software applications. Based on your research, complete the table below.

Company/Software Name Website URL	Software Features Subscription Length (Month/Year/Lifetime) Cost

2. Which anti-virus software would you purchase? List reasons for your selection.

9.4.2 Worksheet: Operating System Updates

In this activity, you will use the Internet to research operating system updates. Be prepared to discuss your research with the class.

1. Which operating system (OS) is installed on your computer?

2. List the configuration options available for updating the OS.

3. Which configuration option would you use to update the OS? List the reason for choosing a particular option.

4. If the instructor gives you permission, begin the update process for the OS. List all security updates available.

9.5.2 Worksheet: Gather Information from the Customer

(Student Technician Sheet)

Print and complete this activity.

Gather data from the customer to begin the troubleshooting process. Document the customer's problem in the work order below.

Work Order

Company Name: _____

Contact: _____

Company Address: _____

Company Phone: _____

Generating a New Ticket

Category _____Closure Code_____   Status_____

Type_____   Escalated_____   Pending_____

Item_____   Pending Until Date_____

Business Impacting? O Yes O No

Summary_____

_____

Case ID#_____   Connection Type_____

Priority_____   Environment_____

User Platform_____

Problem Description: _____

_____

_____

_____

Problem Solution: _____

_____

_____

_____

(Student Customer Sheet)

Use the contact information and problem description below to report the following information to a level-one technician:

Contact Information

Company Name: Organization of Associated Chartered Federations, Inc.

Contact: Henry Jones

Company Address: 123 E. Main Street

Company Phone:480-555-1234

Category: Security

Problem Description

I am not able to login. I was able to login yesterday and all days previously. I tried to login with a different computer but was unsuccessful there also. I received an e-mail last week about changing my password, but I have not changed my password yet.

(NOTE: Once you have given the level-one tech the problem description, use the Computer Configuration to answer any follow up questions the technician may ask.)

Computer Configuration

- Windows XP Pro
- I do not know when it was last updated.
- There is some kind of anti-virus program that used to run when I started the computer, but I haven't seen it recently.

Chapter 10: Communication Skills

10.1 Worksheet: Technician Resources

In this worksheet, you will use the Internet to find online resources for a specific computer component. Search online for resources that can help you troubleshoot the component. In the table below list a least one website for each of the following types of resources: online FAQs, online manuals, online troubleshooting/help site, and blogs. Give a brief description of the content on the site. Be prepared to discuss the usefulness of the resources you found.

Component to research: _____

Type of Resources	Website Address

10.2.2 Class Discussion: Controlling the Call

In this activity, the class will discuss positive ways to tell customers negative things. There are four scenarios.

1. Demonstrate a positive way to tell a customer that you cannot fix the component and that the customer will have to purchase a new component. The customer's name is Fred. You have been helping him conduct a variety of tests on his computer. After attempting several different solutions, it has become apparent that his hard drive is beyond repair.

2. Demonstrate a positive way to tell a customer that you cannot fix a computer component, because it falls outside the scope of that customer's SLA with your company. The customer's name is Barney.

3. Demonstrate how you would put a customer on hold. You have forgotten one of the steps for setting up a user account for Windows XP and need to ask a fellow worker the instructions for that step. The customer's name is Wilma.

4. Demonstrate how you would transfer a customer to another technician. You have not learned how to configure the security feature on the wireless router used by the customer (Betty) and need to transfer the call to a knowledgeable technician.

10.2.3 Class Discussion: Identifying Difficult Customer Types

In this activity, the class will identify difficult customer types.

Try to choose only one customer type for each scenario:

- Rude Customer
- Very Knowledgeable Customer
- Inexperienced Customer
- Angry Customer
- Talkative Customer

Scenario 1: The customer asks you to repeat the last three steps you just gave. When you do the customer says that you did not say the same thing and asks if you know how to fix the problem. The customer then goes into an explanation of what he thinks you should know and asks if you have ever done this before.

Scenario 2: When you ask the customer to explain the problem, they start off by telling you how the computer is acting up and that it happened after their grandson was over for a visit last weekend. They go on to explain that their grandson is taking computer courses and knows a lot about computers. They ask what computer courses you have taken and from where. When asked a close-ended question the customer gives a quick yes and goes on to explain how wet and cold the weather is where he lives.

Scenario 3: The customer tells you how frustrated he is about the internet not working. When the customer is asked if the computer is on, he replies with "nothing shows when I click on the little picture on the TV. When the technician restates the question, "is the computer plugged in to the wall." The customer's reply is "not all of the cables, there are too many for me to know where they all go." The customer then informs you that a friend set everything up.

Scenario 4: The customer tells you how frustrated he is about the new color printer not working. He explains that he was told that he only needed to plug in two different cords and that everything would work. You ask the customer to check some obvious issues with the printer. He responds by asking how long this will take and tells you that the only reason he bought the printer was because he was told it was the easiest printer on the market to install.

Scenario 5: When the customer is asked to explain the problem they go into great technical detail about how the new external hard drive is not showing up in the Device Manager. You ask him to click on **Start > My Computer** to see if it is showing up there. Instead of doing as you ask, the customer provides details of all the different settings and configurations and updates he has tried.

10.3 Class Discussion: Customer Privacy

In this activity, the class will discuss the importance of respecting customer privacy.

1. You are working on a customer's computer and you need to logoff as the administrator and logon as the customer. You have not talked with the customer about her own access to the computer. You see a note with the customer's access information. Do you logon as the customer to test the system and logoff, and why or why not?

2. You are out on a office call. When you leave the customer's office, which is in an open public area, you leave your briefcase behind. It contains work order forms from all the customers you serviced that day. When you contact the office where the briefcase was left, you are told that no one has seen it. What should you do to protect you customers and why?

3. A new customer calls you with concerns about privacy regarding using a computer and the Internet. List several security concerns you should discuss.

Chapter 11: Advanced Personal Computers

11.1 Worksheet: Job Opportunities

In this activity, you will use the Internet, magazines, or a local newspaper to gather information for jobs in the computer service and repair field. Try to find jobs that require the same types of courses that you are presently taking. Be prepared to discuss your research in class.

1. Research three computer-related jobs. For each job, write the company name and the job title in the column on the left. Write the job details that are most important to you, as well as, the job qualifications in the column on the right. An example has been provided for you.

Company Name and Job Title	Details and Qualifications
Getronics Flexible Solutions/ Field Service Representative	Company offers continuing education. Work with hardware and software. Work directly with customers. Local Travel. • A+ certification preferred • Installation or repair experience of computer hardware and software not required • Requires a valid driver license • Reliable personal transportation • Mileage reimbursement • Ability to lift and carry up to 50 lbs • Installation of NIC cards • Experience with POS equipment. (preferred)

2. Which of the jobs you found in your research would you like to have? Explain why you are interested in this job. An example has been provided for you.

Gentronics Flexible Solutions Field Service Representative – I am not able to travel far away from my family and this job allows me to travel locally. Also, this job offers educational opportunities so that I can advance further in the IT field.

_____

_____

_____

_____

_____

_____

_____

_____

11.2.2 Lab: Using a Multimeter and a Power Supply Tester

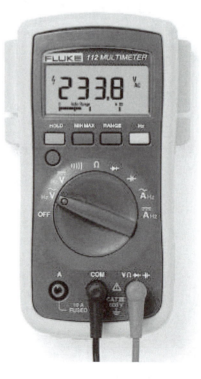

Introduction

In this lab, you will learn how to use and handle a multimeter and a power supply tester.

Recommended Equipment

- A digital multimeter - a Fluke 110 series or similar
- The multimeter manual
- A battery
- A power supply tester
- A manual for the tester
- A power supply

NOTE: The multimeter is a sensitive piece of electronic test equipment. Do not drop it or handle it carelessly. Be careful not to accidentally nick or cut the red or black wire leads, called probes. Because it is possible to check high voltages, extra care should be taken to avoid electrical shock.

Part 1: Multimeter

Step 1: Set Up the Multimeter

a. Insert the red and black leads into the proper jacks on the meter. The black probe should go in the COM jack and the red probe should go in the + (plus) jack.

b. Turn on the multimeter.(Consult the manual if there is no ON/OFF switch.)

What is the model of the multimeter?

What action must be taken to turn the meter on?

Step 2: Explore the Different Multimeter Measurements

a. Switch or turn to different measurements. For example, switch the multimeter to ohms.

How many different switch positions does the multimeter have?

What are they?

b. Switch or turn the multimeter to the voltage measurement.

What is the symbol shown for this?

Step 3: Measure the Voltage of a Battery

Place the battery on the table. Touch the tip of the red (positive) probe on the positive side of a battery. Touch the tip of the black, (negative) probe on the other end of the battery.

What is shown on the display?

If the multimeter does not display a number close to the battery voltage, check the multimeter setting to ensure it is set to measure voltage, or replace the battery with a known good battery. If the number is a negative number, reverse the probes.

Name one thing that you should not do when using multimeter.

Name one important function of a multimeter.

Disconnect the multimeter from the battery. Switch the multimeter to OFF. Part 1 of the lab is complete. Have your instructor verify your work.

Part 2: Power Supply Tester

Complete only the steps for the connectors supported by the power supply tester that you are using.

Step 1: Check the testing ports for the Power Supply Tester

Many power supply testers have connector ports to test the following power supply connectors:

- 20-pin/24-pin motherboard connector
- 4-pin Molex connector
- 6-pin PCI-E connector
- P4 +12V connector
- P8 +12V EPS connector
- 4-pin Berg connector
- 5-pin SATA connector

Which connectors does the power supply tester you are using have?

Complete the following steps for the connectors supported by the power supply tester that you are using.

Step 2: Test the Power Supply Motherboard Connector

a. Set the power supply switch (if available) to the OFF (or 0) position.

b. Plug the 20-pin or 24-pin motherboard connector into the tester.

c. Plug the power supply into an AC outlet.

d. Set the power supply switch (if available) to the ON (or 1) position.

If the power supply is working, LEDs will illuminate and you might hear a beep. If the LED lights do not illuminate, it is possible the power supply might be damaged or the motherboard connector has failed. In this instance, you must check all connections, ensure the power supply switch (if available) is set to ON (or 1) and try again. If the LEDs still do not illuminate, consult your instructor.

Possible LED lights include +5 V, -5 V, +12 V, +5 VSB, PG, -12 V, +3.3 V.

Which LED lights are illuminated?

Step 3: Test the Power Supply Molex Connector

Plug the 4-pin Molex connector into the tester. The LED illuminates on +12 V and +5 V. (If the power output fails, the LEDs will not illuminate.)

Which LED lights are illuminated?

Step 4: Test the 6-pin PCI-E Connector

Plug the 6-pin PCI-E connector into the tester. The LED will illuminate on +12 V. (If the power output fails, the LED will not illuminate.)

Does the LED light illuminate?

Step 5: Test the 5-pin SATA Connector

Plug the 5-pin SATA connector into the tester. The LED will illuminate on +12 V, +5 V, and +3.3 V. (If the power output fails, the LEDs will not illuminate.)

Which LED lights are illuminated?

Step 6: Test the 4-pin Berg connector

Plug the 4-pin Berg connector into the tester. The LED will illuminate on +12 V and +5 V. (If the power output fails, the LEDs will not illuminate.)

Which LED lights are illuminated?

Step 7: Test the P4/P8 connectors

a. Plug the P4 +12 V connector into the tester. The LED will illuminate on +12 V. (If the power output fails, the LEDs will not illuminate.)

b. Plug the P8 +12 V connector into the tester. The LED will illuminate on +12 V. (If the power output fails, the LEDs will not illuminate.)

Which LED lights are illuminated?

Switch the power supply to OFF (or 0) if available. Disconnect the power supply from the AC outlet. Disconnect the power supply from the power supply tester. The lab is complete. Have your instructor verify your work.

11.2.2 Lab: Testing UTP Cables Using a Loopback Plug and a Cable Meter

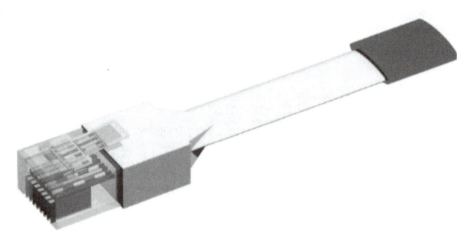

Loopback Plug

Coupler

Introduction

In this lab, you will use a loopback plug and a cable meter to test an Ethernet cable.

Recommended Equipment

- A LAN hub or switch
- Loopback plug and coupler
- A known good Ethernet cable
- A Fluke series 620 LAN CableMeter
- A manual for the cable meter
- Good Category 5 straight-through cables of different colors
- Good Category 5 crossover cables (T568A on one end and T568B on the other end)
- Category 5 straight-through cables of different colors and different lengths with open connections in the middle, or one or more conductors shorted at one end
- Category 5 straight-through cable with a split pair or a mis-wire

Wire maps can be very helpful in troubleshooting cabling problems with UTP cable. A wire map shows which wire pairs connect to what pin on the plug or socket.

Cables should be numbered to simplify the testing process and to maintain consistency. A cable meter should be available that can test continuity, cable length, and check the wire map. This lab can be performed individually, in pairs, or in groups.

Part 1: Loopback Plug

Step 1: Test an Ethernet cable using a loopback plug

    a.   Plug the loopback plug into one end of the coupler.

    b.   Plug one end of the Ethernet cable into the other end of the coupler.

    c.   Power on the hub or switch.

    d.   Plug the other end of the Ethernet cable into a port on the hub or switch.

After plugging the cable into the port, does a link light appear on the port?

If a link light does not appear, the problem is with the hub or switch. If the port displays a link light, then the cable has passed the continuity test.

Part 1 of the lab is complete. Ask your instructor to verify your work.

Part 2: Cable meter

Testing UTP Cables

Step 1: Set Up the Cable Meter

    a.   On the cable meter, select the WIRE MAP function.

    b.   Ensure that the following settings (if available) are set properly.

Tester Option	Desired Setting - UTP
CABLE:	UTP
WIRING:	10BASE-T OR EIA/TIA 4PR
CATEGORY:	CATEGORY 5
WIRE SIZE:	AWG 24
CALIBRATE TO CABLE?	NO
BEEPING:	ON or OFF

    c.   Once the meter is set up, exit the setup mode.

Step 2: Test Cabling Procedure

When testing with a Fluke LAN CableMeter use the following procedure.

    a.   Place one end of the cable into the RJ-45 jack labeled UTP/FTP on the tester.

    b.   Place the other end of the cable into the RJ-45 female coupler (labeled LAN Use).

    c.   Insert the cable identifier (labeled Net Tool) into the other side of the coupler. The coupler and the cable identifier are accessories that come with many cable meters.

Coupler and Cable Identifier

Step 3: Use the Wire Map Function

The wire map function and a cable identifier can be used to determine the wiring of both the near and far end of the cable. One set of numbers displayed on the LCD screen is the near end, and the other set is the far end.

    a.   Perform a wire map test on each of the cables provided.

Fill in the following table based on the testing results for each Category 5 cable. For each cable, write down the identifying number of the cable and the cable color. Also write down whether the cable is straight-through or crossover, the tester screen test results, and a description of the problem.

Cable No.	Cable Color	Straight-through or Crossover	Displayed Test Results (Note: Refer to the meter manual for detailed description of test results for the wire map test.)	Problem/Description
			Top: Bot:	

			Top: Bot:	
			Top: Bot:	
			Top: Bot:	
			Top: Bot:	

Step 4: Use the Length Function

Using the tester LENGTH function, perform a basic cable test on the same cables used previously. Fill in the additional information for each cable.

Cable No.	Cable Length	Tester Test Results (Pass/Fail)

11.3.7 Worksheet: Research Computer Components

Print and complete this activity.

In this activity, you will use the Internet, a newspaper, or a local store to gather information about the components you will need to upgrade your customer's computer. Be prepared to discuss your selections.

1. Your customer already owns the case described in the table below. You will not need to research a new case.

Brand and Model Number	Features	Cost
Cooler Master CAC-T05-UW	ATX Mid Tower ATX, Micro ATX Compatible form factor 5 X External 5.25" drive bays 1 X External 3.5" drive bay 4 X Internal 5.25" drive bays 7 expansion slots USB, Firewire, Audio front ports	

2. Research a **power supply** that is compatible with the components that your customer owns. The new component must have improved performance or additional capabilities. Enter the specifications in the table below.

Brand and Model Number	Features	Cost
Antec SP-450	450 Watt Dual +12V rails > 70% Efficiency ATX12V form factor	$60.99

3. Research a **motherboard** that is compatible with the components that your customer owns. The new component must have improved performance or additional capabilities. Enter the specifications in the table below.

Brand and Model Number	Features	Cost
GIGABYTE GA-965P-DS3	LGA 775 DDR2 800 PCI Express x16 SATA 3.0Gb/s interface	

	1.8V-2.4V RAM voltage	
	1066/800/533MHz Front Side Bus	
	4 Memory Slots	
	Dual Channel Memory Supported	
	1XATA100 connector	
	RAID 0/1	
	4X USB 2.0	
	ATX Form Factor	

4. Research a **CPU** that is compatible with the components that your customer owns. The new component must have improved performance or additional capabilities. Enter the specifications in the table below.

Brand and Model Number	Features	Cost
Intel Core 2 Duo E6300 BX80557E6300	LGA 775 1.86GHz Operating Frequency 1066MHz Front Side Bus 2M shared L2 Cache 64 bit supported Conroe Core	$183.00

5. Research a **heat sink/fan assembly** that is compatible with the components that your customer owns. The new component must have improved performance or additional capabilities. Enter the specifications in the table below.

Brand and Model Number	Features	Cost
Intel Stock heat sink/fan	LGA 775 80mm fan 2 pin power Under recommended socket weight	Included with CPU

6. Research **RAM** that is compatible with the components that your customer owns. The new component must have improved performance or additional capabilities. Enter the specifications in the table below.

Brand and Model Number	Features	Cost
Patriot PDC22G6400LLK	240-Pin DDR2 SDRAM DDR2 800 (PC2 6400) Cas Latency 4 Timing 4-4-4-12 Voltage 2.2V	$194.99

7. Research a **hard disk drive** that is compatible with the components that your customer owns. The new component must have improved performance or additional capabilities. Enter the specifications in the table below.

Brand and Model Number	Features	Cost
Western Digital WD400BB	40 GB 7200 RPM 2 MB Cache	$37.99

8. Research a video adapter card that is compatible with the components that your customer owns. The new component must have improved performance or additional capabilities. Enter the specifications in the table below.

Brand and Model Number	Features	Cost
XFX PVT71PUDD3	PCI Express X16 600 MHz Core clock 256 MB GDDR3 1600 MHz Memory clock 256-bit memory interface	$189.99

1. List three components that must have the same or compatible form factor.

2. List three components that must conform to the same socket type.

3. List two components that must utilize the same front side bus speed.

4. List three considerations when you choose memory.

5. What component must be compatible with every other component of the computer?

6. What determines compatibility between a motherboard and a video card?

11.4.1 Lab: Install a NIC in Windows XP

Introduction

In this lab, you will install a NIC, verify NIC operation, and manually configure an IP address.

Recommended Equipment

- Computer running Windows XP Professional
- PCI NIC
- Driver files for PCI NIC on CD or floppy disk
- Anti-static wrist strap
- Tool kit

Step 1

Log on to the computer as an Administrator.

Click the **Start** button. Right-click **My Computer**, and then choose **Properties**.

The "System Properties" window appears.

Choose the **Hardware** tab, and then click the **Device Manager** button.

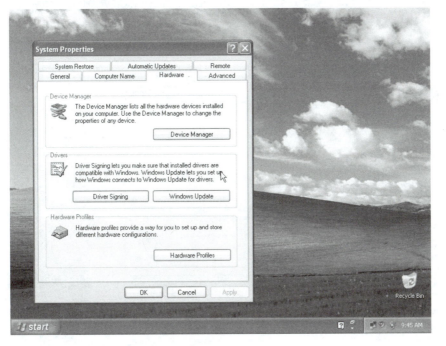

The "Device Manager" window appears.

Step 2

Expand **Network adapters**.

Right-click the NIC installed in your computer, and then choose **Disable**.

The "Disabling this device will cause it to stop functioning." confirmation window appears. Click **Yes**.

A red "X" appears over the icon of the NIC installed in your computer.

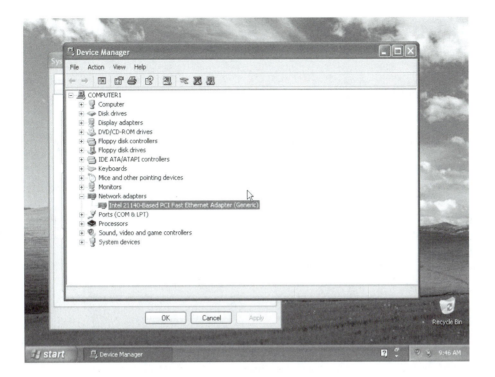

Close the Device Manager window.

Close the System Properties window.

Turn off your computer.

Step 3

Who is the manufacturer of the new NIC?

What is the model number of the new NIC?

What slot type is used to connect the new NIC to the motherboard?

Step 4

If a switch is present on the power supply, set the switch to "0" or "off".

Unplug the computer from the AC outlet.

Unplug the network cable from the computer.

Remove the side panels from the case.

Step 5

Choose an appropriate slot on the motherboard to install the new NIC.

You may need to remove the metal cover near the slot on the back of the case.

Make sure the NIC is properly lined up with the slot. Push down gently on the NIC.

Secure the NIC mounting bracket to the case with a screw.

Step 6

Replace the case panels.

Plug the network cable into the new NIC.

Plug the power cable into an AC outlet.

If a switch is present on the power supply, set the switch to "1" or "on".

Step 7

Boot your computer, and then log on as an administrator.

Choose **Start**. Right-click **My Computer,** and then choose **Properties**.

The "System Properties" window appears.

Choose the **Hardware** tab, and then click the **Device Manager** button.

Step 8

The "Device Manager" window appears.

Expand **Network adapters**.

How many Network adapters are present (enabled and disabled) in the list?

If the new card icon has a red X over it, right-click on that icon, and then click **Enable**.

Right-click the new NIC icon, and then choose **Properties**.

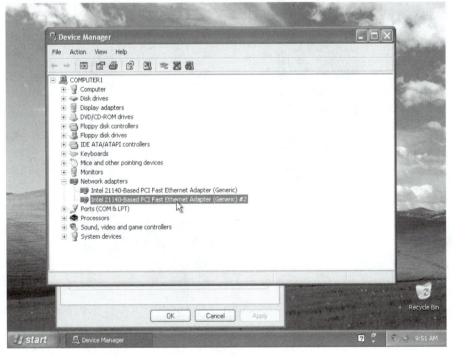

Choose the **Driver** tab. Click the **Update Driver...** button.

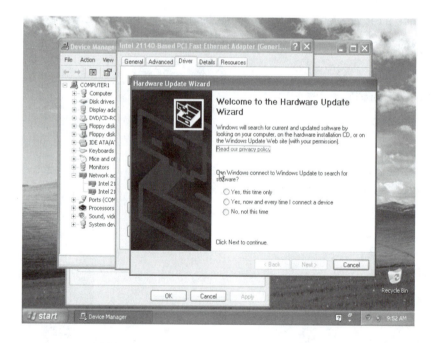

The "Hardware Update Wizard" appears.

If you are prompted to connect to Windows Update, click the **No, not this time** radio button, and then click **Next**.

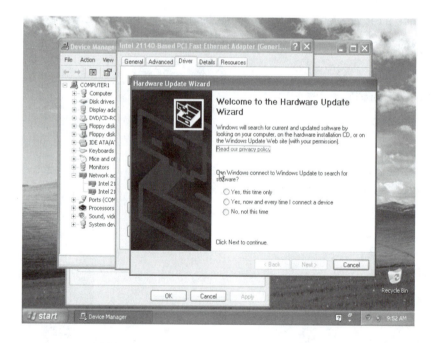

Choose the **Install from a list or specific location (Advanced)** radio button, and then click **Next**.

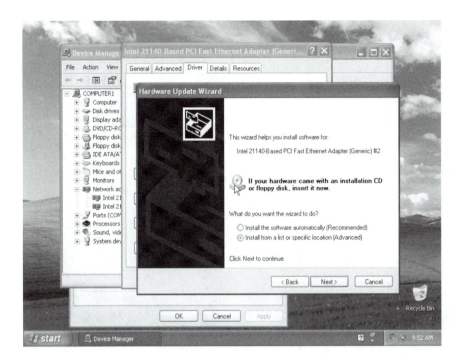

Insert the CD or floppy disk with the new NIC drivers, and then click **Next**.

The "Please wait while the wizard searches…" window appears.

Click **Finish** after Windows installs the new driver.

The Hardware Update Wizard window closes.

Click **Close**.

The "NIC Properties" window closes.

Close the Device Manager.

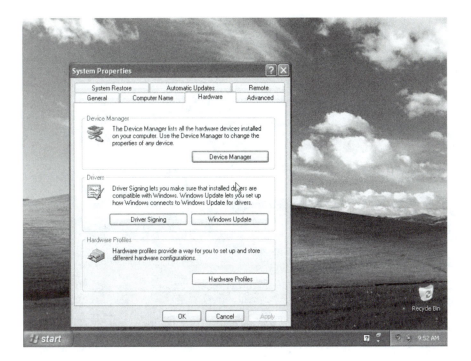

Step 9

Choose **Start > Run**.

Type **cmd** in the **Open:** field, and then click **OK**.

The "C:\WINDOWS\System32\cmd.exe" window appears.

Type **ipconfig** and press **Enter**.

The settings of the new NIC are displayed.

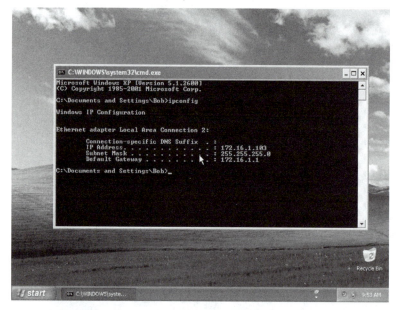

What is the IP address?

What is the subnet mask?

What is the default gateway?

Step 10

Choose **Start > Control Panel**.

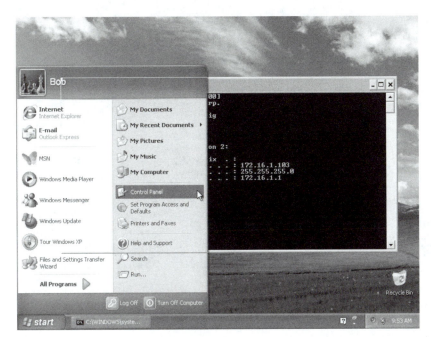

Click **Network and Internet Connections**.

The "Network and Internet Connections" window appears.

Click **Network Connections**.

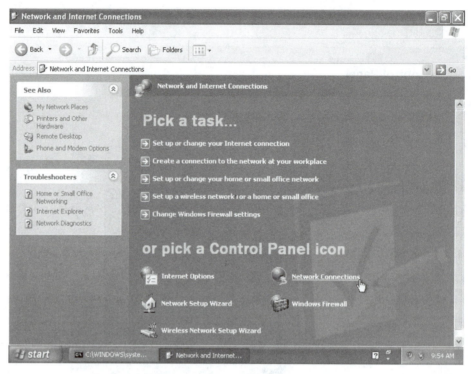

The "Network Connections" window appears.

Step 11

Right-click the connected "Local Area Connection" and choose **Properties**.

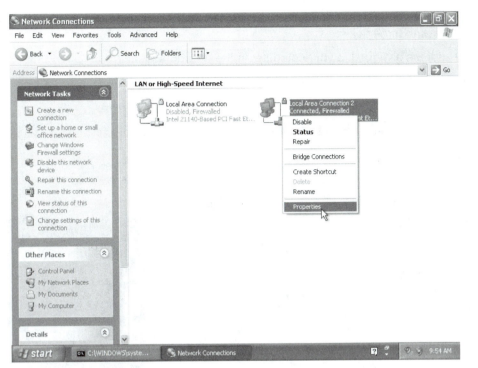

The "Local Area Connection Properties" window appears.

Choose Internet Protocol (TCP/IP) and click **Properties**.

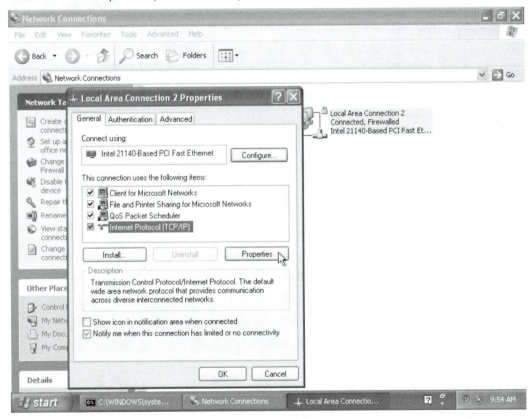

Click the **Use the Following IP address:** radio button.

NOTE: Use the IP address, subnet mask, and default gateway you wrote down earlier in the lab to fill in the following three fields:

Type the IP address assigned to your computer in the "IP address" field.

Type the subnet mask assigned to your network in the "Subnet mask:" field.

Type the default gateway assigned to your network in the "Default gateway:" field.

Click **OK**.

The "Internet Protocol (TCP/IP) Properties" window closes.

Click **Close**.

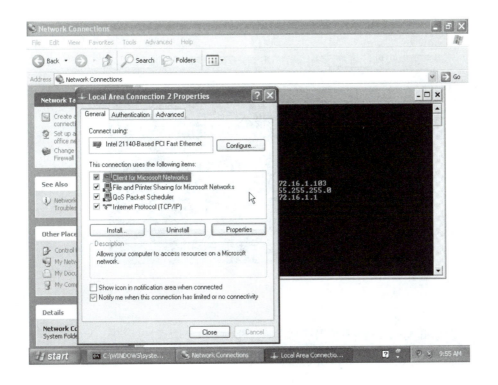

The "Local Area Connection Properties" window closes.

Step 12

The "C:\WINDOWS\System32\cmd.exe" window is revealed.

Type **ipconfig /all**, and then press **Enter**.

Does the NIC have DHCP Enabled?

Type **ping** and your IP address. For example, **ping 172.16.1.103**.

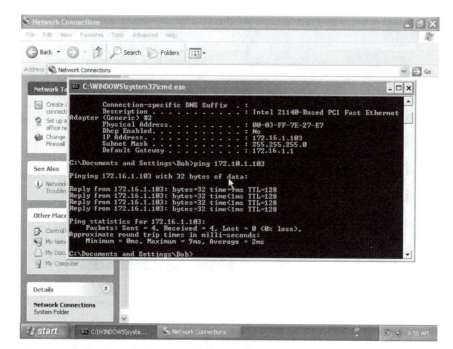

Write one of the replies of your ping command:

Type **exit,** and then press **Enter**.

Step 13
Choose **Start > Control Panel**.

Click **Network and Internet Connections**.

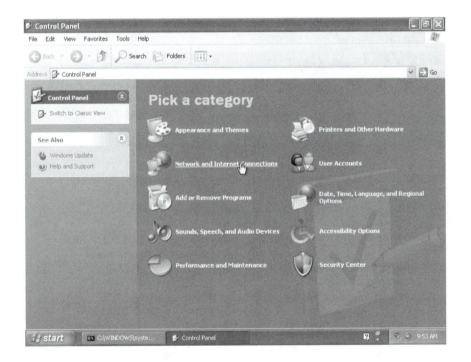

The "Network and Internet Connections" window appears.

Click **Network Connections**.

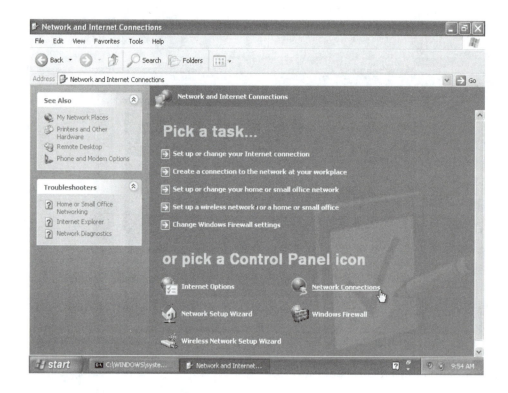

The "Network Connections" window appears.

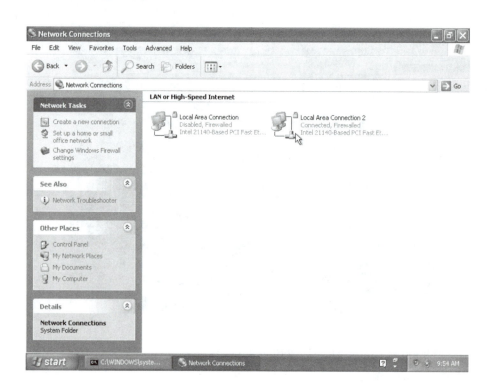

Step 14

Right-click the connected "Local Area Connection" and choose **Properties**.

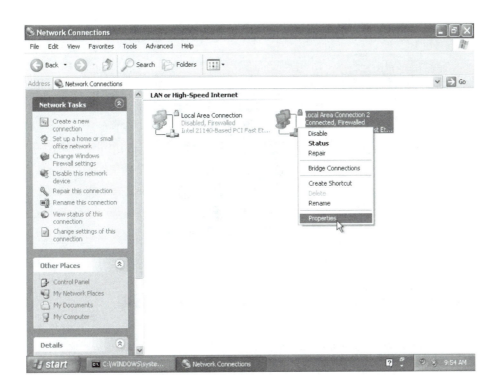

The "Local Area Connection Properties" window appears.

Choose Internet Protocol (TCP/IP) and click **Properties**.

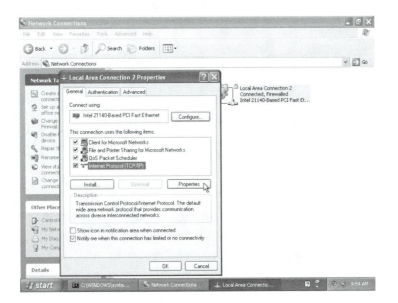

Click the **Obtain an IP address Automatically** radio button.

Click **OK**.

The "Internet Protocol (TCP/IP) Properties" window closes.

Click **Close**.

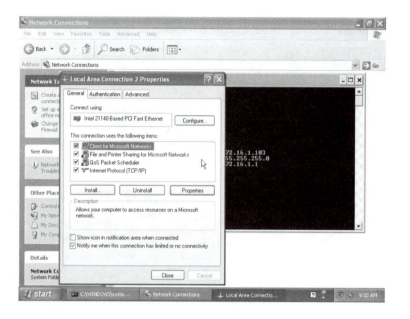

The "Local Area Connection Properties" window closes.

11.4.1 Optional Lab: Install a NIC in Windows Vista

Introduction

In this lab, you will install a NIC, verify NIC operation, and manually configure an IP address, and set the NIC to use DHCP in Windows Vista.

Recommended Equipment

- Computer running Windows Vista
- PCI NIC
- Driver files for PCI NIC on CD or floppy disk
- Antistatic wrist strap
- Tool kit

Step 1: Open the Device Manager

Log on to the computer as an Administrator.

Click the **Start** button. Right-click **Computer**, and then choose **Properties**.

The "System" window appears.

Choose the **Device Manager** link.

The Device Manager window appears.

Step 2: Disable the NIC

Expand **Network adapters**.

Right-click the NIC installed in your computer, and then choose **Disable**.

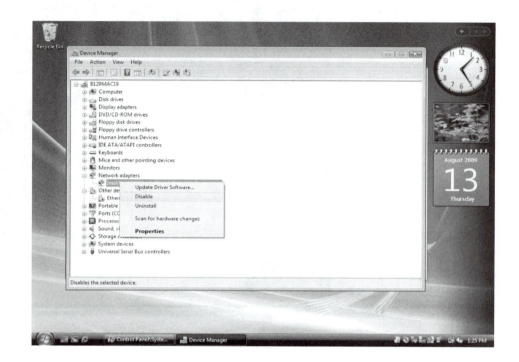

The "Disabling this device will cause it to stop functioning." confirmation window appears.

Click **Yes**.

A black arrow (↓) appears over the icon of the NIC installed in your computer.

Close the Device Manager window.

Close the System window.

Turn off your computer.

Who is the manufacturer of the new NIC?

What is the model number of the new NIC?

What slot type is used to connect the new NIC to the motherboard?

Step 3: Open the Case

If a switch is present on the power supply, set the switch to "0" or "OFF".

Unplug the computer from the AC outlet.

Unplug the network cable from the computer.

Remove the side panels from the case.

Step 4: Insert the NIC

Choose an appropriate slot on the motherboard to install the new NIC. You may need to remove the metal cover near the slot on the back of the case.

Make sure the NIC is properly lined up with the slot.

Push down gently on the NIC.

Secure the NIC mounting bracket to the case with a screw.

Step 5: Close Case and Restart the Computer

Replace the case panels.

Plug the network cable into the new NIC.

Plug the power cable into an AC outlet.

If a switch is present on the power supply, set the switch to "1" or "ON".

Boot your computer, and then log on as an administrator.

Choose **Start**. Right-click **Computer,** and then choose **Properties**.

Click the **Device Manager** link.

Step 6: Install a New Driver

The "Device Manager" window appears.

Expand **Network adapters**.

How many Network adapters are present (enabled and disabled) in the list?

Right-click the new NIC icon or Ethernet controller, and then choose **Properties**.

Choose the **Driver** tab. Click the **Update Driver** button.

The "Hardware Update Wizard" appears.

If you are prompted to connect to Windows Update, click the **No, not this time** radio button, and then click **Next**.

Choose the **Install from a list or specific location (Advanced)** radio button, and then click **Next**.

Insert the CD or floppy disk with the new NIC drivers, and then click **Next**.

The "Please wait while the wizard searches…" window appears.

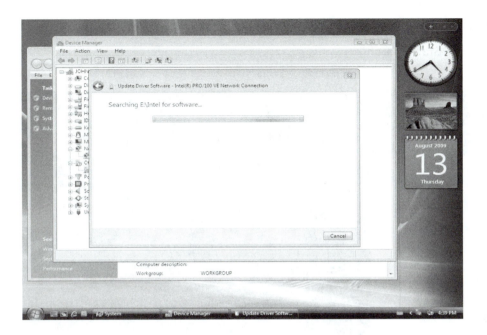

Click Finish after Windows installs the new driver.

The Hardware Update Wizard window closes.

Click **Close**.

The "NIC Properties" window closes.

Close the Device Manager.

Step 7: View the NIC Settings

Choose **Start > Start Search**.

Type **cmd** and press **Enter**.

The "C:\WINDOWS\System32\cmd.exe" window appears.

Type **ipconfig** and press **Enter**.

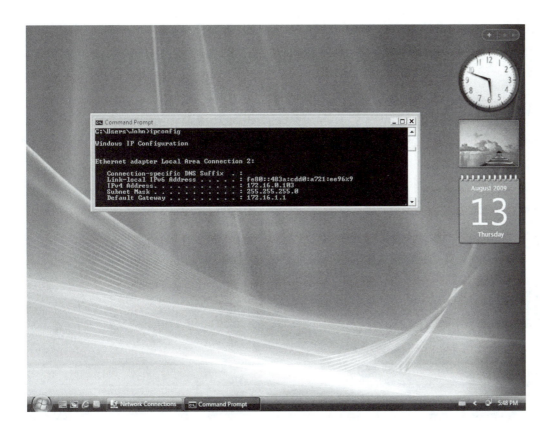

The settings of the new NIC are displayed.

What is the IP address?

What is the subnet mask?

What is the default gateway?

Step 8: Open the Network Connections Window

Choose **Start > Network**.

Click **Network and Sharing Center**.

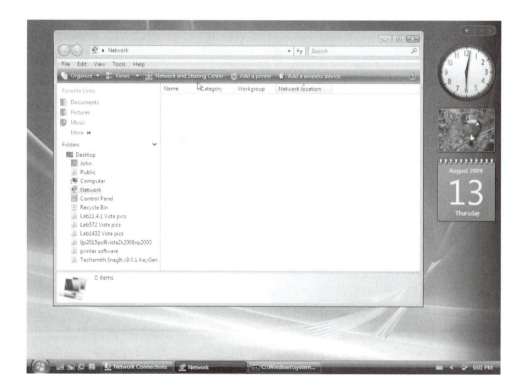

The "Network and Sharing Center" window appears.

Click **Manage network connections**.

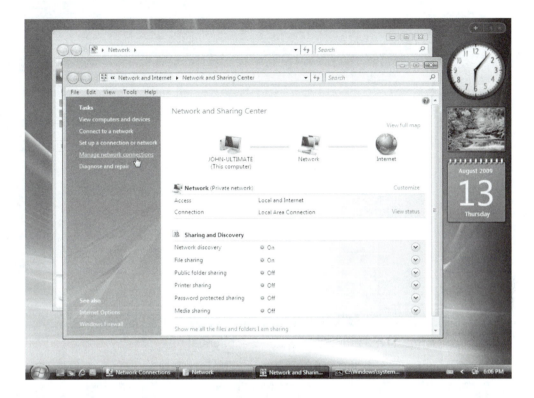

The "Network Connections" window appears.

Step 9: Set a Static IP Address

Right-click the connected "Local Area Connection 2" and choose **Properties**.

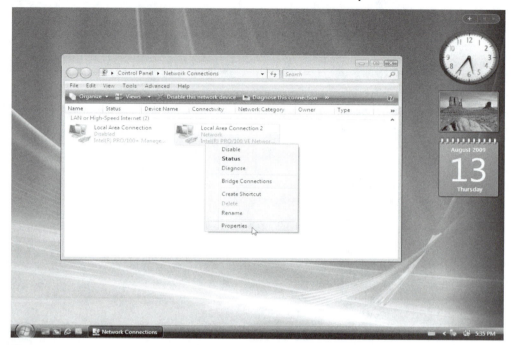

The "Local Area Connection 2 Properties" window appears.

Choose Internet Protocol Version 4 (TCP/IPv4) and click **Properties**.

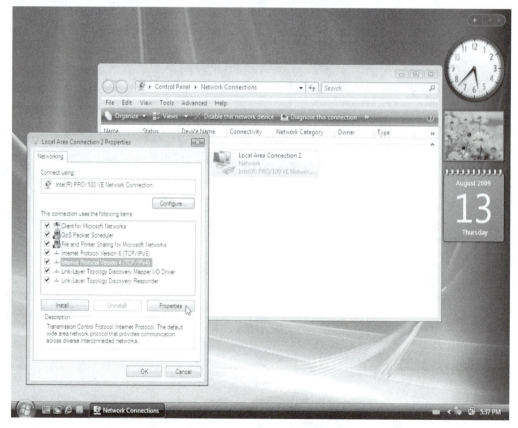

Click the **Use the Following IP address:** radio button.

NOTE: Use the IP address, subnet mask, and default gateway you wrote down earlier in the lab to fill in the following three fields:

Type the IP address assigned to your computer in the "IP address" field.

Type the subnet mask assigned to your network in the "Subnet mask:" field.

Type the default gateway assigned to your network in the "Default gateway:" field.

Click **OK**.

The "Internet Protocol (TCP/IP) Properties" window closes.

Click **OK**.

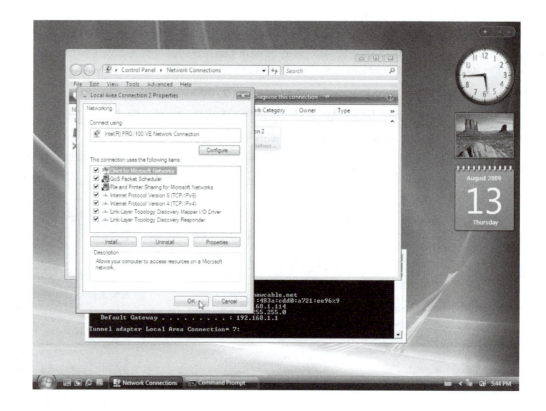

The "Local Area Connection Properties" window closes.

Step 10: Ping Your Computer

The "C:\WINDOWS\System32\cmd.exe" window is revealed.

Type **ipconfig /all**, and then press **Enter**.

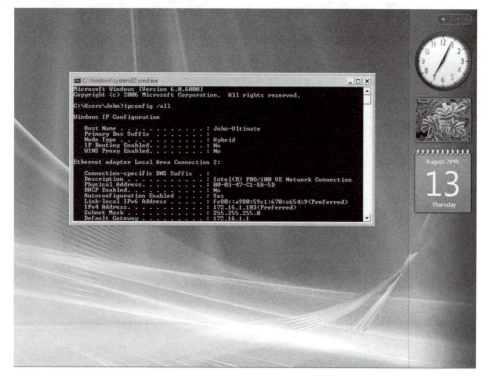

Does the NIC have DHCP enabled?

Type **ping** and your IP address. For example, **ping 172.16.1.103**.

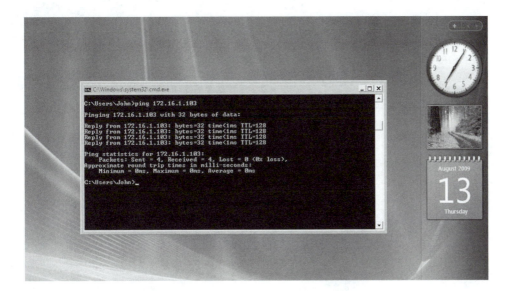

Write one of the replies of your ping command.

Type **exit,** and then press **Enter**.

Step 11: Set the NIC to Use DHCP

Choose **Start > Network**.

Click **Network and Sharing Center**.

The "Network and Sharing Center" window appears.

Click **Manage network connections** link.

The "Network Connections" window appears.

Right-click the connected "Local Area Connection 2" and choose **Properties**.

The "Local Area Connection 2 Properties" window appears.

Choose Internet Protocol Version 4 (TCP/IPv4) and click **Properties**.

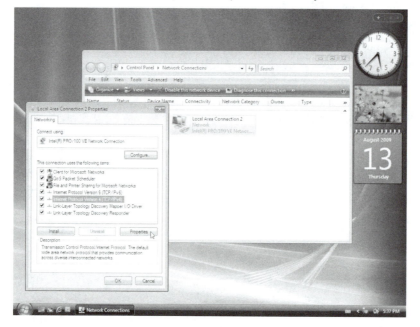

Click the **Obtain an IP address Automatically** radio button.

Click **OK**.

The "Internet Protocol (TCP/IP) Properties" window closes.

Click **OK**.

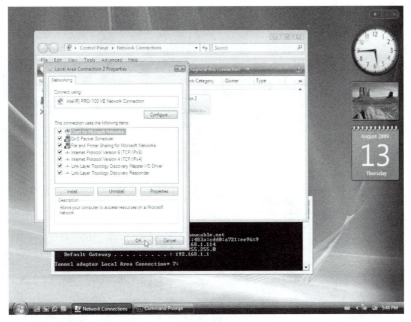

The "Local Area Connection Properties" window closes.

11.4.3 Lab: Install Additional RAM in Windows XP

Introduction

In this lab, you will install additional RAM.

Recommended Equipment

- Computer running Windows XP
- Available RAM slot on motherboard
- Additional RAM module(s)
- Tool kit
- Antistatic wrist strap
- Antistatic mat

Step 1

Log on to the computer as an administrator.

Click the **Start** button. Right-click **My Computer**, and then choose **Properties**.

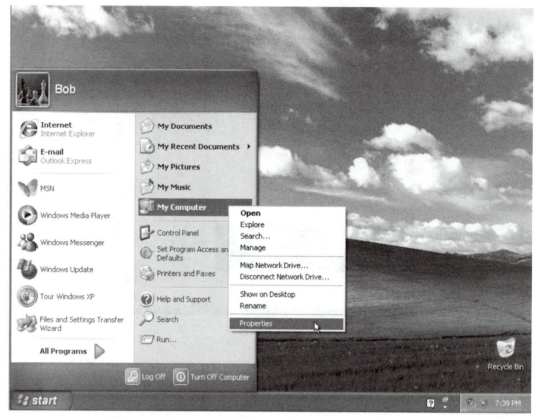

The "System Properties" window appears.

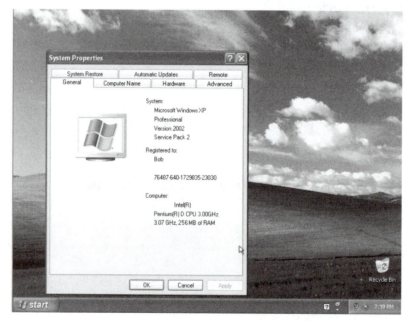

How much RAM is installed in your computer?

Close the "System Properties" window.

Step 2

Shut down your computer.

If a switch is present on the power supply, set the switch to "0" or "off".

Unplug the computer from the AC outlet.

Remove the side panels from the case.

Put on the antistatic wrist strap, and then clip it to the case.

Step 3

Press down on the retainer tabs at each end of a slot. The memory module will be lifted out of the memory slot. Remove the memory module.

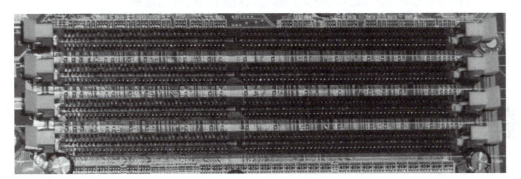

What type of memory is the module that you removed?

What is the speed of the memory in MHz?

Step 4

CAUTION: If, during re-installation of the RAM module, the module does not fit correctly or does not install easily, carefully remove the module and start the installation again.

Align the notch(es) at the bottom of the RAM module with the key(s) in the ram slot. Place the RAM module in the slot, and then push down firmly on the RAM module until the module is fully seated in the slot and the retainer tabs hold the module in place.

Press each retainer tab in toward the memory module to make sure that the RAM is held in place by the retainer tabs.

Install the RAM modules provided by your instructor.

Step 5

Remove the antistatic wrist strap from the case and from your wrist, and then replace the case panels.

Plug the power cable into an AC outlet.

If a switch is present on the power supply, set the switch to "1" or "on".

Boot your computer, and then log on as an administrator.

Open the "System Properties" window.

How much RAM is installed in your computer?

11.4.3 Optional Lab: Install Additional RAM in Windows Vista

Introduction

In this lab, you will install additional RAM.

Recommended Equipment

- Computer running Windows Vista
- Available RAM slot on motherboard
- Additional RAM module(s)
- Tool kit
- Antistatic wrist strap
- Antistatic mat

Step 1

Log on to the computer as an administrator.

Click the **Start** button. Right-click **Computer**, and then choose **Properties**.

The System window appears.

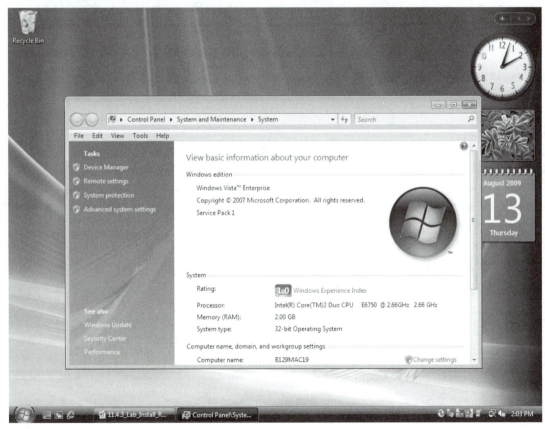

How much RAM is installed in your computer?

Close the System window.

Step 2

Shut down your computer.

If a switch is present on the power supply, set the switch to "0" or "off".

Unplug the computer from the AC outlet.

Remove the side panels from the case.

Put on the antistatic wrist strap, and then clip it to the case.

Step 3

Press down on the retainer tabs at each end of a slot. The memory module will be lifted out of the memory slot. Remove the memory module.

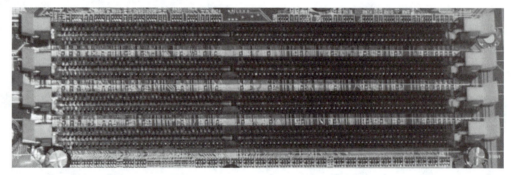

What type of memory is the module that you removed?

What is the speed of the memory in MHz?

Step 4

CAUTION: If, during re-installation of the RAM module, the module does not fit correctly or does not install easily, carefully remove the module and start the installation again.

Align the notches at the bottom of the RAM module with the key(s) in the ram slot. Place the RAM module in the slot, and then push down firmly on the RAM module until the module is fully seated in the slot and the retainer tabs hold the module in place.

Press each retainer tab in toward the memory module to make sure that the RAM is held in place by the retainer tabs.

Install the RAM modules provided by your instructor.

Step 5

Remove the antistatic wrist strap from the case and from your wrist, and then replace the case panels.

Plug the power cable into an AC outlet.

If a switch is present on the power supply, set the switch to "1" or "on".

Boot your computer, and then log on as an administrator.

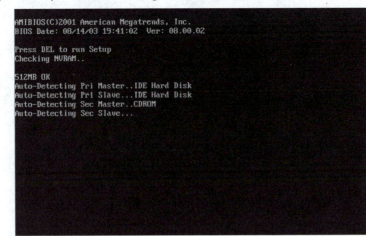

Open the "System Properties" window.

How much RAM is installed in your computer?

11.4.4 Lab: BIOS File Search

Introduction

In this lab, you will identify the current BIOS version, and then search for BIOS update files.

Recommended Equipment

- Computer running Windows XP Professional
- Internet access

Step 1

Boot your computer.

During POST, BIOS information is displayed on the screen for a short period of time.

```
AMIBIOS(C)2001 American Megatrends, Inc.
BIOS Date: 08/14/03 19:41:02  Ver: 08.00.02

Press DEL to run Setup
Checking NVRAM..

1024MB OK
Auto-Detecting Pri Master..IDE Hard Disk
Auto-Detecting Pri Slave...Not Detected
Auto-Detecting Sec Master..CDROM
Auto-Detecting Sec Slave...Not Detected
```

Do not log on to Windows.

What key or combination of keys is used to run Setup on your computer?

Restart your computer and enter Setup.

Step 2

The "BIOS Setup Utility" screen appears.

```
                        BIOS SETUP UTILITY
    Main    Advanced    Power    Boot    Security    Exit

    AMIBIOS Version :          08.00.02
    BIOS Build Date :          08/14/03


    System Memory   :          1024MB

    System Time                [12:39:37]
    System Date                [Sat 02/10/2007]



                                                →    Select Screen
                                                ↑↓   Select Item
                                                +-   Change Field
                                                Tab  Select Field
                                                F1   General Help
                                                F10  Save and Exit
                                                ESC  Exit


        v02.10 (C)Copyright 1985-2001, American Megatrends, Inc.
```

Who is the manufacturer of the BIOS?

Which BIOS version is installed in your computer?

GA-965P-DS3 (rev. 1.3)
Intel P965+ ICH8 chipset

◇ Enlarge View

◇ Related link

- Overview
- Specification
- Accessories
- BIOS
- Driver
- Manual
- FAQ
- Utility
- CPU Support List
- Memory Support List
- Comparison Sheet
- Awards
- Where To Buy

1. Supports Intel® Core™2 Extreme Quad-Core / Core™2 Duo processor
2. Supports Dual channel DDR2 800 memory
3. Features PCI-E graphics interface
4. Features SATA 3Gb/s interface with RAID function (2 ports with RAID function supported by GIGABYTE SATA2)
5. Intel High Definition 8 Channels Audio
6. Optimized Gigabit LAN connection
7. Industry's leading all solid capacitor motherboard design

◇ BIOS

Download	Version	Date	Description
Download from ...	F10	2007/01/12	1. Enhance FSB frequency flexibility
Download from ...	F9	2006/12/27	1. Update CPU ID 2. FSB 1333 MHz support for rev 3.3 only
Download from ...	F8	2006/12/19	1. Update CPU ID

CAUTION: Do not update your BIOS.

What is the current BIOS version available for the motherboard?

What features, if any, have been added to the new BIOS version?

What changes, if any, have been made to the new BIOS version to fix problems?

What are the instructions to update the new BIOS version?

11.4.5 Lab: Install, Configure, and Partition a Second Hard Drive in Windows XP

Introduction

In this lab, you will change the boot order, install a second hard drive, create partitions, and map drive letters to partitions.

Recommended Equipment

- Computer running Windows XP Professional
- Unpartitioned IDE hard disk drive
- IDE cable with a free connection

- Antistatic wrist strap
- Tool kit

Step 1

Boot your computer, and then enter the BIOS setup.

```
                          BIOS SETUP UTILITY
   Main    Advanced    Power    Boot    Security    Exit

   AMIBIOS Version :           08.00.02
   BIOS Build Date :           08/14/03


   System Memory   :           1024MB

   System Time                 [12:39:37]
   System Date                 [Sat 02/10/2007]



                                                 ←→    Select Screen
                                                 ↑↓    Select Item
                                                 +-    Change Field
                                                 Tab   Select Field
                                                 F1    General Help
                                                 F10   Save and Exit
                                                 ESC   Exit


            v02.10 (C)Copyright 1985-2001, American Megatrends, Inc.
```

Use the **left** and **right arrow** keys to move between tabs in the BIOS. Use the **up** and **down arrow** keys to move between items in each tab.

Navigate the BIOS setup program screens to the boot order configuration settings screen.

```
                          BIOS SETUP UTILITY
   Main    Advanced    Power    Boot    Security    Exit

   ▶ Boot Device Priority
   ▶ Hard Disk Drives
   ▶ Floppy Drives
   ▶ CDROM Drives



                                                 ←→    Select Screen
                                                 ↑↓    Select Item
                                                 Enter Go to Sub Screen
                                                 F1    General Help
                                                 F10   Save and Exit
                                                 ESC   Exit

            v02.10 (C)Copyright 1985-2001, American Megatrends, Inc.
```

Select the "Boot Device Priority". The "Boot Device Priority" may also be called the "Boot Options" or the "Boot Order".

Press the **Enter** key.

Change the order of the boot devices to:

1. CD-ROM
2. Hard Drive
3. Floppy Drive
4. Any other boot option available

```
                          BIOS SETUP UTILITY
                               Boot

                                                  Specifies the boot
   1st Boot Device          [Floppy Drive]        sequence from the
   2nd Boot Device          [CDROM]               available devices.
   3rd Boot Device          [Hard Drive]




                                                  ↔    Select Screen
                                                  ↑↓   Select Item
                                                  +-   Change Option
                                                  F1   General Help
                                                  F10  Save and Exit
                                                  ESC  Exit


        v02.10 (C)Copyright 1985-2001, American Megatrends, Inc.
```

On which screen was the boot device order found?

Save the changes to the BIOS and exit the BIOS utility by pressing the **F10** key.

Step 2

Confirm the change to the BIOS settings if you are prompted. The computer will restart.

Do not log on to Windows.

Shut down your computer.

If a switch is present on the power supply, set the switch to "0" or "off".

Unplug the computer from the AC outlet.

Remove the side panels from the case.

Put on the antistatic wrist strap, and then clip it to the case.

Step 3

Many hard drives will have the jumper settings indicated in a diagram on the drive. Follow the diagram to determine where the jumper will be installed.

Move the Master/Slave jumper on the installed hard disk drive to the Master position if it is in any other position.

Move the Master/Slave jumper on the second hard disk drive to the Slave position if it is in any other position.

Insert the second hard disk drive into the computer and attach it with the proper screws.

Plug the middle connector of the IDE cable into the second hard disk drive.

Plug a four-pin Molex power connector into the second hard disk drive.

Check the jumper settings and cable connections on both hard disk drives to make sure the settings are correct and the cables are secured.

Remove the antistatic wrist strap from the case and from your wrist, and then replace the case panels.

Plug the power cable into an AC outlet.

If a switch is present on the power supply, set the switch to "1" or "on".

Boot your computer.

Step 4

The new hard disk drive will be detected by the computer during the POST routine.

```
AMIBIOS(C)2001 American Megatrends, Inc.
BIOS Date: 08/14/03 19:41:02  Ver: 08.00.02

Press DEL to run Setup
Checking NVRAM..

1024MB OK
Auto-Detecting Pri Master..IDE Hard Disk
Auto-Detecting Pri Slave...IDE Hard Disk
Auto-Detecting Sec Master..CDROM
Auto-Detecting Sec Slave...Not Detected
Pri Master: 1. 1      Virtual HD
Pri Slave : 1. 1      Virtual HD
Sec Master:           Virtual CD
```

If you are prompted to accept changes to the computer, Press the **F1** key.

Log on to Windows as an administrator.

Step 5

Click the **Start** button, and then right-click **My Computer.**

Choose **Manage**.

The "Computer Management" window appears.

Click **Disk Management**.

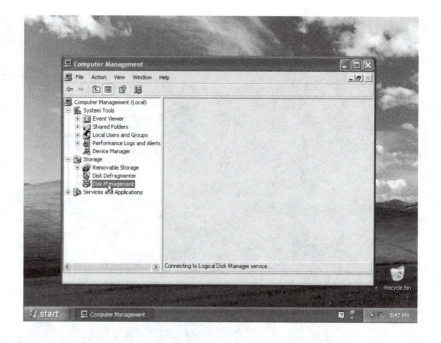

The "Initialize and Convert Disk Wizard" window appears. Click **Next**.

The "Select Disks to Initialize" window appears.

Check the "Disk 1" checkbox, and then click **Next**.

The "Select Disks to Convert" window appears.

Uncheck the "Disk 1" checkbox if it is already checked, and then click **Next**.

The "Completing the Initialize and Convert Disk Wizard" window appears.

Verify that you will "Initialize: Disk 1" and "Convert: None", and then click **Finish**.

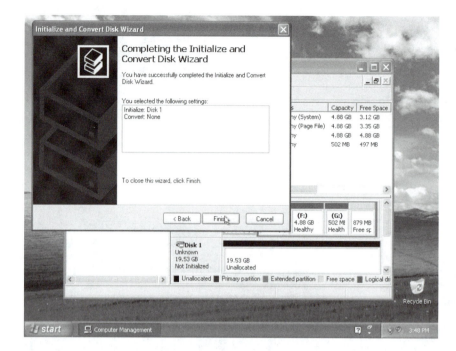

Step 6

The "Disk Management" area of "Computer Management" appears.

NOTE: If the hard disk drive is shown as offline or missing, the hard disk drive may be corrupted.

Right-click on the **Unallocated** space of "Disk 1" and choose **New Partition....**

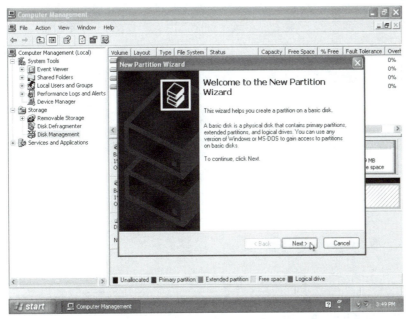

The "New Partition Wizard" window appears.

Click **Next**.

The "Specify Partition Size" window appears.

Type "5000" in the "Partition size in MB:" field, and then click **Next**.

The "Assign Drive Letter or Path" window appears.

Click the "Assign the following drive letter" radio button.

Choose "M" from the "Assign the following drive letter" drop-down box, and click **Next**.

The "Format Partition" window appears.

Click **Next**.

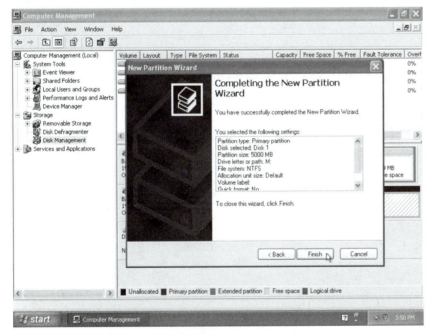

The "Completing the New Partition Wizard" window appears.

Verify that the settings you have chosen match the settings shown in the "Completing the New Partition Wizard" window, and then click **Finish**.

Windows formats the new partition and the status of the Volume changes to "Healthy".

The New Volume Setup Wizard partitioned the second hard drive. What type of partitions did the Setup Wizard create?

What other partitions could be created?

Step 7

Create a second partition in the Unallocated space of "Disk 1" with the drive label "N:".

Step 8

Choose **Start > My Computer**.

The "Hard Disk Drives" section of "My Computer" now shows the two "New Volumes", "M:" and "N:".

How many primary partitions can be created on the newly added second hard disk drive?

11.4.5 Optional Lab: Install, Configure, and Partition a Second Hard Drive in Windows Vista

Introduction

In this lab, you will change the boot order, install a second hard drive, create partitions, and map drive letters to partitions.

Recommended Equipment

- Computer running Windows Vista
- Unpartitioned IDE hard disk drive
- IDE cable with a free connection
- Antistatic wrist strap
- Tool kit

Step 1

Boot your computer, and then enter the BIOS setup.

```
                      BIOS SETUP UTILITY
   Main    Advanced   Power    Boot    Security    Exit

   AMIBIOS Version :         08.00.02
   BIOS Build Date :         08/14/03


   System Memory    :        1024MB

   System Time               [12:39:37]
   System Date               [Sat 02/10/2007]



                                              ↔     Select Screen
                                              ↑↓    Select Item
                                              +-    Change Field
                                              Tab   Select Field
                                              F1    General Help
                                              F10   Save and Exit
                                              ESC   Exit


        v02.10 (C)Copyright 1985-2001, American Megatrends, Inc.
```

Use the **left** and **right arrow** keys to move between tabs in the BIOS. Use the **up** and **down arrow** keys to move between items in each tab.

Click the Boot tab.

```
                      BIOS SETUP UTILITY
   Main    Advanced   Power    Boot    Security    Exit

   ▶ Boot Device Priority
   ▶ Hard Disk Drives
   ▶ Floppy Drives
   ▶ CDROM Drives




                                              ↔     Select Screen
                                              ↑↓    Select Item
                                              Enter Go to Sub Screen
                                              F1    General Help
                                              F10   Save and Exit
                                              ESC   Exit


        v02.10 (C)Copyright 1985-2001, American Megatrends, Inc.
```

Select the "Boot Device Priority". The "Boot Device Priority" may also be called the "Boot Options" or the "Boot Order".

Press the **Enter** key.

Change the order of the boot devices to:

1. CD-ROM
2. Hard Drive
3. Floppy Drive
4. Any other boot option available

```
                        BIOS SETUP UTILITY
                        Boot

    1st Boot Device          [Floppy Drive]      Specifies the boot
    2nd Boot Device          [CDROM]             sequence from the
    3rd Boot Device          [Hard Drive]        available devices.




                                                 ↔     Select Screen
                                                 ↑↓    Select Item
                                                 +-    Change Option
                                                 F1    General Help
                                                 F10   Save and Exit
                                                 ESC   Exit

          v02.10 (C)Copyright 1985-2001, American Megatrends, Inc.
```

On which screen was the boot device order found?

Save the changes to the BIOS and exit the BIOS utility by pressing the **F10** key.

Step 2

Confirm the change to the BIOS settings if you are prompted. The computer will restart.

Do not log on to Windows.

Shut down your computer.

If a switch is present on the power supply, set the switch to "0" or "off".

Unplug the computer from the AC outlet.

Remove the side panels from the case.

Put on the antistatic wrist strap, and then clip it to the case.

Step 3

Many hard drives will have the jumper settings indicated in a diagram on the drive. Follow the diagram to determine where the jumper will be installed.

Move the Master/Slave jumper on the installed hard disk drive to the Master position if it is in any other position.

Move the Master/Slave jumper on the second hard disk drive to the Slave position if it is in any other position.

Insert the second hard disk drive into the computer and attach it with the proper screws.

Plug the middle connector of the IDE cable into the second hard disk drive.

Plug a four-pin Molex power connector into the second hard disk drive.

Check the jumper settings and cable connections on both hard disk drives to make sure the settings are correct and the cables are secured.

Remove the antistatic wrist strap from the case and from your wrist, and then replace the case panels.

Plug the power cable into an AC outlet.

If a switch is present on the power supply, set the switch to "1" or "on".

Boot your computer.

Step 4

The new hard disk drive will be detected by the computer during the POST routine.

```
AMIBIOS(C)2001 American Megatrends, Inc.
BIOS Date: 08/14/03 19:41:02  Ver: 08.00.02

Press DEL to run Setup
Checking NVRAM..

1024MB OK
Auto-Detecting Pri Master..IDE Hard Disk
Auto-Detecting Pri Slave...IDE Hard Disk
Auto-Detecting Sec Master..CDROM
Auto-Detecting Sec Slave...Not Detected
Pri Master: 1. 1      Virtual HD
Pri Slave : 1. 1      Virtual HD
Sec Master:           Virtual CD
```

If you are prompted to accept changes to the computer, Press the **F1** key.

Log on to Windows as an administrator.

Step 5

Click the **Start** button, and then right-click **Computer.**

Choose **Manage**.

The "Computer Management" window appears.

Click **Disk Management**.

Right click Disk 1: Unallocated space and choose New Simple Volume from the dropdown menu.

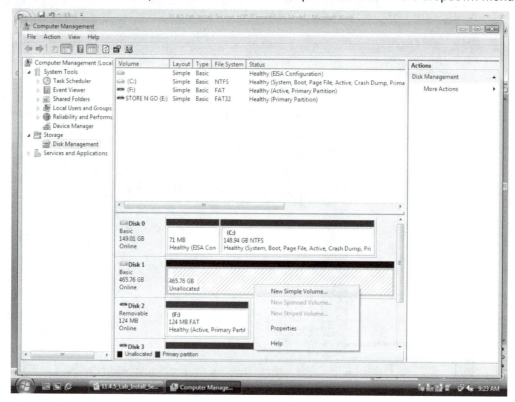

The "Welcome to the New Simple Volume Wizard" window appears. Click **Next**.

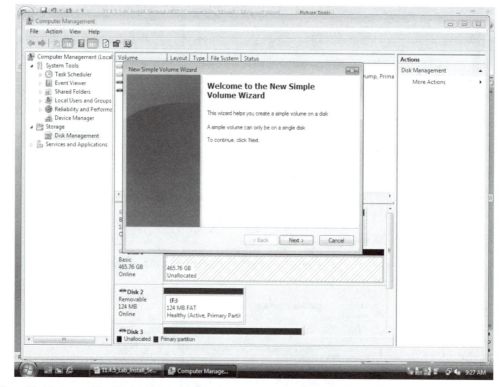

The "Specify Volume Size" window appears.

Type "5000" in the "Partition size in MB:" field, and then click **Next**.

The "Assign Drive Letter or Path" window appears.

Click the "Assign the following drive letter" radio button.

Choose "M" from the "Assign the following drive letter" drop-down box, and click **Next**.

The "Format Partition" window appears.

Click **Next**.

The "Completing the New Simple Volume Wizard" window appears.

Verify that the settings you have chosen match the settings shown in the "Completing the New Partition Wizard" window, and then click **Finish**.

Windows formats the new partition and the status of the Volume changes to "Healthy".

The New Volume Setup Wizard partitioned the second hard drive. What type of partitions did the Setup Wizard create?

What other partitions could be created?

Step 6

Create a second partition in the Unallocated space of "Disk 1" with the drive label "N".

Step 7

Choose **Start > Computer**.

The "Hard Disk Drives" section of "Computer" now shows the two "New Volumes", "M:" and "N:".

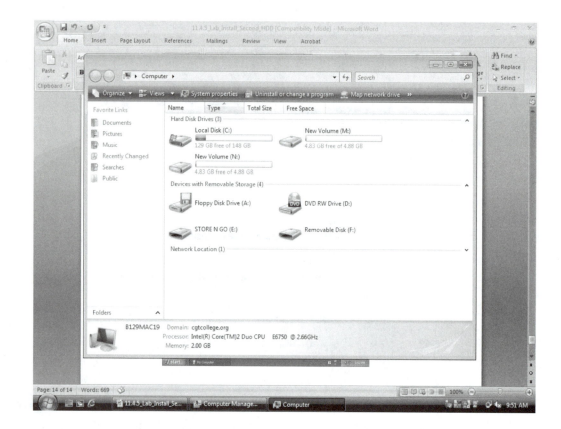

How many primary partitions can be created on the newly added second hard disk drive?

11.6.3 Lab: Repair Boot Problem

Introduction

In this lab, you will troubleshoot and repair a computer that does not boot.

Recommended Equipment

- A computer running Windows XP Professional
- Antistatic wrist strap
- Tool kit

Scenario

The computer will not start up. The computer beeps constantly.

Step 1

Unplug the power cable from the computer. Check the other external cables. Make sure all other external cables are in the correct position and the connections are secure. Make sure any power switches are set to "off" or "0".

Step 2

Open the case and check all internal data and power cable connections. Check the adapter cards and RAM modules to make sure they are seated completely.

Step 3

Remove your antistatic wrist strap. If there is a power switch on the power supply, turn it to "on" or "1". Turn on the computer.

What steps did you perform to fix the computer?

11.6.3 Lab: Remote Technician: Repair Boot Problem

(Student Technician Sheet)

In this lab, you will gather data from the customer, and then instruct the customer on how to fix a computer that does not boot. Document the customer's problem in the work order below.

Company Name: <u>JH Travel, Inc.</u>

Contact: <u>Dan Handy</u>

Company Address: <u>204 N. Main Street</u>

Company Phone: <u>1-866-555-0998</u>

Work Order

Generating a New Ticket

Category <u>Hardware</u>   Closure Code ____   Status <u>Open</u>

Type: _____   Escalated <u>Yes</u>   Pending _____

Item _____   Pending Until Date _____

Business Impacting? X Yes   O No

Summary <u>The computer will not start up. The computer beeps constantly.</u>

_____

Case ID#_____   Connection Type _____

Priority _____2_____   Environment _____

User Platform <u>Windows XP Pro</u>

Problem Description: <u>Computer will not boot. Customer does not know the</u>
<u>manufacturer of the BIOS. Cannot identify error from beep sequence. Customer</u>
<u>did not hear any strange sounds from the computer. Customer does not smell</u>
<u>smoke or burning electronics.</u>

_____

_____

Problem Solution: _____

(Student Customer Sheet)

Use the contact information and problem description below to report the following information to a level-two technician:

Contact Information

Company Name: JH Travel, Inc.

Contact: Dan Handy

Company Address: 204 N. Main Street

Company Phone: 1-866-555-0998

Problem Description

Ok, so I work with cars all the time and I know how they work, but I do not know how my computer works. This morning was pretty slow because I guess more and more people are using those Internet travel sites. So, after my morning coffee, I decided to figure out what makes my computer work. I opened up the case and just started looking at the different things inside. When I put everything back together, everything seemed to fit and I didn't see any leftover parts. Now it does not work at all. It beeps at me all the time.

(NOTE: Once you have given the level-two tech the problem description, use the Additional Information to answer any follow up questions the technician may ask.)

Additional Information

- Windows XP Pro
- Computer has no new hardware
- Computer has not been moved recently
- Except for the beeping, I did not hear any other strange sounds from the computer
- I do not smell any electronics burning or smoke
- Computer looks the same as it did yesterday

11.6.3 Lab: Troubleshooting Hardware Problems in Windows XP

Introduction

In this lab, the instructor will introduce various hardware problems. The student will diagnose the causes and solve the problems.

Recommended Equipment

The following equipment is required for this exercise:

- A computer running Windows XP

Scenario

You must solve hardware problems for a customer. You may need to troubleshoot both software and hardware used by the computer. Make sure you document and solve the problems, and then document the solutions.

There are several possible errors. Solve one problem at a time until you can successfully start the computer and all devices are fully functional.

Step 1

Start the computer.

Did the computer boot successfully?

If the computer started Windows XP, log on with the Administrator account.

Test all internal and external hardware devices.

Did all devices operate properly?

If the computer successfully started and all devices are fully functional, you have successfully solved all hardware problems. Hand the lab into your instructor.

If you could not successfully start the computer and all devices are not fully functional, continue troubleshooting the problem.

Students start by troubleshooting the computer for problems. Answer the following questions after each problem is solved.

What problem did you find?

What steps did you take to determine the problem?

What is causing the problem?

List the steps taken to fix the problem.

11.6.3 Optional Lab: Troubleshooting Hardware Problems in Windows Vista

Introduction

In this lab, the instructor will introduce various hardware problems, and you will diagnose the cause of these problems then fix them.

Recommended Equipment

The following equipment is required for this exercise:

- A computer running Windows Vista

Scenario

You must solve hardware problems for a customer. You may need to troubleshoot both software and hardware used by the computer. Make sure you document and solve the problems, and then document the solutions.

There are several possible errors. Solve one problem at a time until you can successfully start the computers and all devices are fully functional. You may need to ask the instructor for hardware when needed.

Step 1

Start the computer.

Did the computer boot successfully?

If the computer started Windows Vista, log on with the Administrator account.

Test all internal and external hardware devices.

Did all devices operate properly?

If the computer successfully started and all devices are fully functional, you have successfully solved all hardware problems. Hand the lab into your instructor.

If you could not successfully start the computer and all devices are not fully functional, continue troubleshooting the problem.

Students start by troubleshooting the computer for problems. Answer the following questions after each problem is solved.

What problem did you find?

What steps did you take to determine the problem?

What is causing the problem?

List the steps taken to fix the problem.

Chapter 12: Advanced Operating Systems

12.2.2 Lab: Advanced Installation of Windows XP

Introduction

In this lab, you will install a Windows XP operating system by using an answer file for automation. You will customize partition settings and create an administrative user and limited users.

Recommended Equipment

The following equipment is required for this exercise:

- A computer with a new installation of Windows XP
- Windows XP installation media
- A blank, formatted floppy disk

Step 1

Log on to the computer.

Insert the Windows XP Professional CD in the CD-ROM drive.

Click **Perform additional tasks**.

Step 2

Click **Browse this CD**.

Double-click the **Support** folder.

Double-click the **Tools** folder.

Double-click **Deploy.CAB**.

Highlight all of the files by clicking **Edit > Select All**.

Right-click **setupmgr.exe** and then click **Extract**.

Click **Make New Folder** to create a folder on the C: drive.

Name the folder "Deploy".

Click **Extract** to extract the files from the CD to C:\Deploy.

Browse to C:\Deploy.

Step 3

Double-click **setupmgr.exe**.

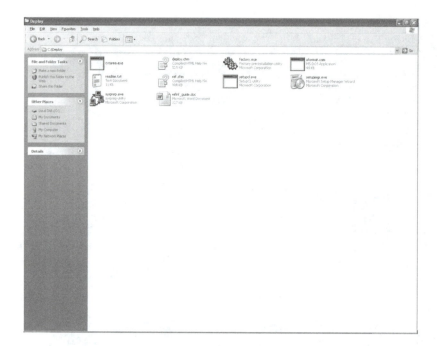

Step 4

The "Setup Manager" window appears.

Click **Next**.

The **Create new** button should be checked by default.

Click **Next**.

Click the **Unattended setup** radio button.

Note that a CD-based answer file name must be Winnt.sif.

Click the **Windows XP Professional** radio button, and then click **Next**.

Click the **Fully automated** radio button, and then click **Next**.

Click the **Set up from a CD** radio button, and then click **Next**.

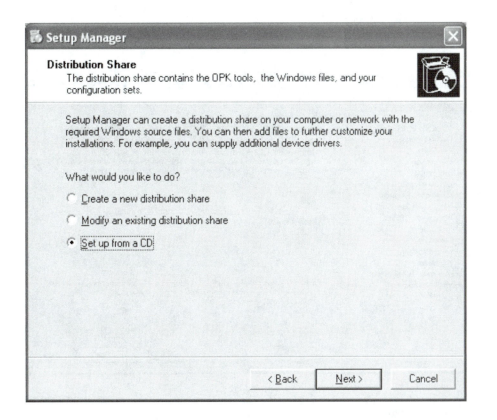

Click the **I accept the terms of the License Agreement** checkbox, and then click **Next**.

![Setup Manager - License Agreement dialog]

Setup Manager

License Agreement
    Do you accept the terms of the License Agreement for Windows?

You chose to fully automate the installation of Windows. To use this option, you must accept the terms of the End User License Agreement (EULA) and any Microsoft license agreements you have for the version of Windows you want to install.

For more information about the EULA, consult your documentation or your Microsoft license agreement.

To continue with Setup Manager, select the following check box, and then click Next.

☑ I accept the terms of the License Agreement

< Back   Next >   Cancel

Click **Name and Organization** in the list on the left.

Type the name and the organization name provided by your instructor.

Click **Next**.

Click **Time Zone** in the list on the left.

Click the time zone for your location from the "Time zone:" drop-down box, and then click **Next.**

Highlight **Product Key** in the list on the left.

Type the Windows XP Professional product key supplied by your instructor in the "Product Key:" fields.

Click **Next**.

Click **Computer Names** in the list on the left.

Type the computer name provided by your instructor in the "Computer name:" field, and then click **Add**.

The computer name will then display in the "Computers to be installed:" field.

Click **Next**.

Click **Administrative Password** in the list on the left.

Type your first initial of your first name and your complete last name in the "Password:" and "Confirm password:" fields. (For example, jsmith)

Click **Next**.

Click **Workgroup or Domain** in the list on the left.

Click the **Workgroup** radio button.

Type the Workgroup name **LabGroup1** in the "Workgroup:" field, and then click **Next**.

Click **Additional Commands** in the list on the left, and then click **Finish**.

Type "C:\Deploy\unattend.txt" in the "Path and file name:" field if it is not already displayed.

Click **OK**.

Click **File > Exit**.

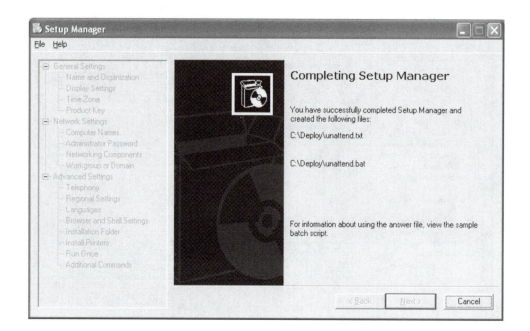

Step 5

Browse to "C:\Deploy".

Right-click **unattend.txt**, and then click **copy**.

Browse to "A:\".

Click **File > Paste**.

Right-click **unattend.txt**, and then click **rename**.

Type **Winnt.sif** as the new file name, and press **Enter**.

Copy **unattend.bat** to the floppy disk.

Remove the floppy disk from the floppy drive.

Click **Start > Turn Off Computer**.

Click **Restart**.

Step 6

When the "Press Any Key to Boot from CD" message appears, press any key on the keyboard. Insert the floppy disk. The system will inspect the hardware configuration.

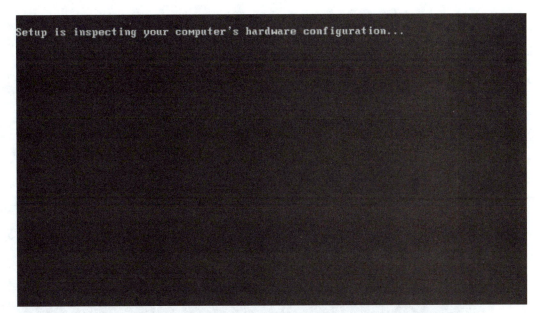

The Windows XP Setup screen appears while the program loads the necessary files.

Step 7

The Welcome to Setup screen appears. Press **Enter**.

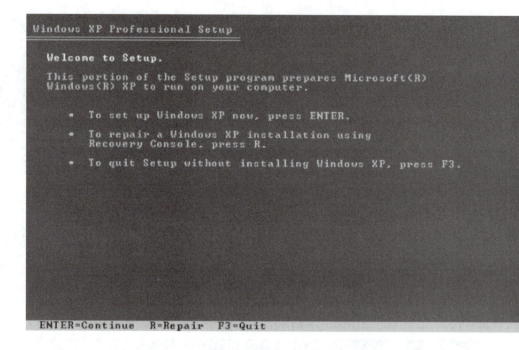

The "Windows XP Licensing Agreement" screen appears.

Press **F8**.

Windows XP Professional Setup will search to determine if another operating system already exists on the hard drive.

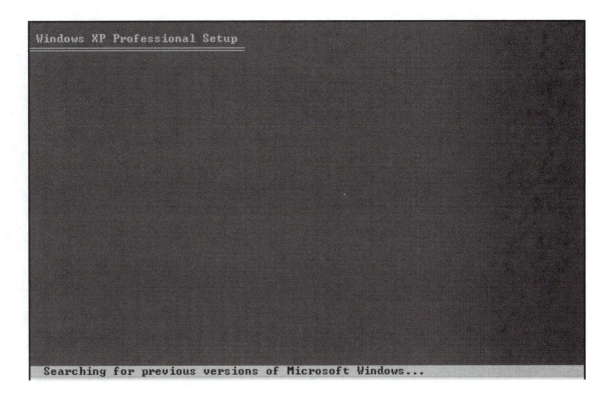

Press **ESC**.

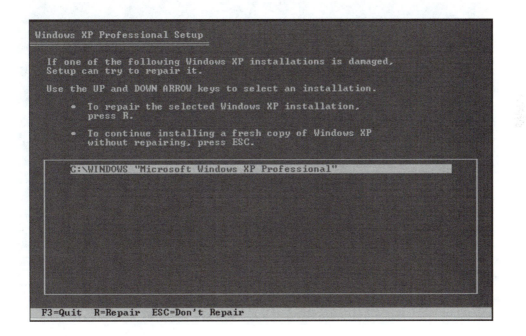

Press the **D** key.

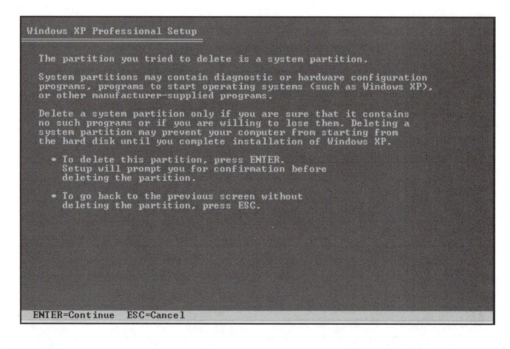

Press **Enter**.

Press the **L** key.

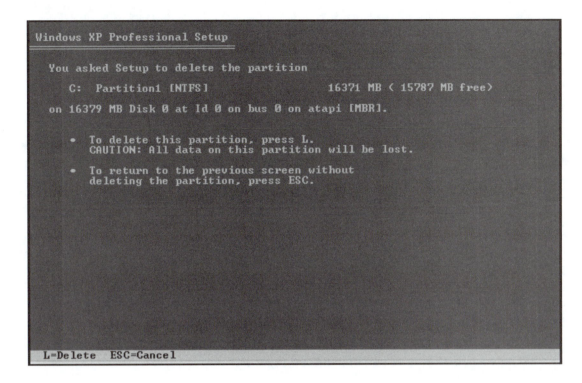

Press the **C** key.

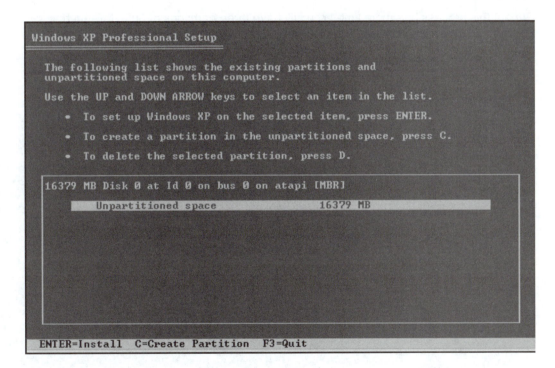

Type **5000** in the "Create partition of size (in MB):" field.

Press the **Enter** key.

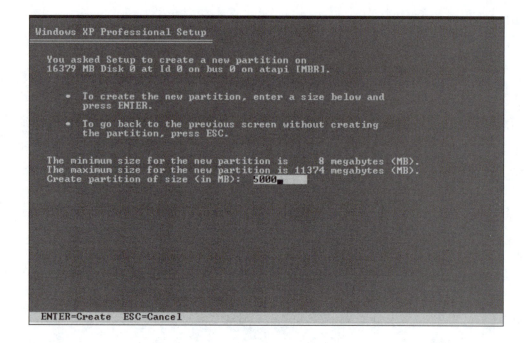

Press the **down arrow** key to select "Unpartitioned space".

Press the **C** key.

Create another partition of 5000 MB.

Repeat this process one more time. You will have three partitions of 5000 MB each.

Select **C: Partition1** and press the **Enter** key.

```
Windows XP Professional Setup

    The following list shows the existing partitions and
    unpartitioned space on this computer.

    Use the UP and DOWN ARROW keys to select an item in the list.

        •  To set up Windows XP on the selected item, press ENTER.

        •  To create a partition in the unpartitioned space, press C.

        •  To delete the selected partition, press D.

    16379 MB Disk 0 at Id 0 on bus 0 on atapi [MBR]

        C:  Partition1 [New (Raw)]              4997 MB (  4996 MB free)
        E:  Partition2 [New (Raw)]              4997 MB (  4996 MB free)
        F:  Partition3 [New (Raw)]              4997 MB (  4996 MB free)
            Unpartitioned space                 1381 MB
            Unpartitioned space                    8 MB

    ENTER=Install   D=Delete Partition   F3=Quit
```

Select "Format the partition using the NTFS file system".

Do not select ""Format the partition using the NTFS file system <Quick>".

Press the **Enter** key.

```
Windows XP Professional Setup

    A new partition for Windows XP has been created on

    16379 MB Disk 0 at Id 0 on bus 0 on atapi [MBR].

    This partition must now be formatted.

    From the list below, select a file system for the new partition.
    Use the UP and DOWN ARROW keys to select the file system you want,
    and then press ENTER.

    If you want to select a different partition for Windows XP,
    press ESC.

        Format the partition using the NTFS file system (Quick)
        Format the partition using the FAT file system (Quick)
        Format the partition using the NTFS file system
        Format the partition using the FAT file system

    ENTER=Continue   ESC=Cancel
```

The "Please wait while Setup formats the partition" screen appears.

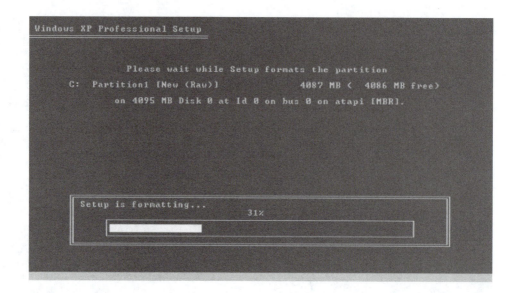

The system will restart automatically.

After the system restarts, the message "Press Any Key to Boot from CD" appears.

Do not press any keys.

The installation should continue without prompting you for any settings.

The system will restart automatically.

After the system restarts, the message "Press Any Key to Boot from CD" appears.

Do not press any keys.

Step 8

The "Welcome to Microsoft Windows" screen appears.

Click **Next**.

Click the **Help protect my PC by turning on Automatic Updates now** radio button.

Click **Next**.

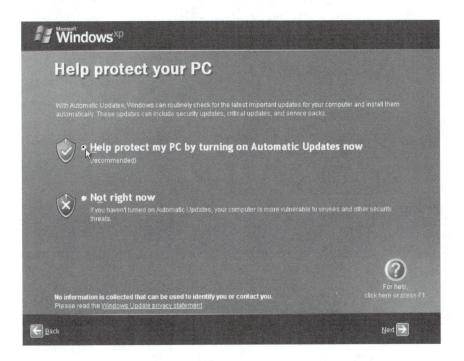

Click the **Yes, this computer will connect through the local area network or home network** radio button.

Click **Next**.

Click the **No, not at this time** radio button, and then click **Next**.

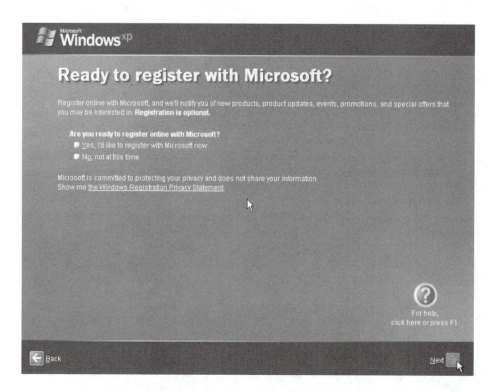

Type the name provided by your instructor in the "Your name:" field.

Click **Next**.

The "Thank you!" screen appears.

Click **Finish**.

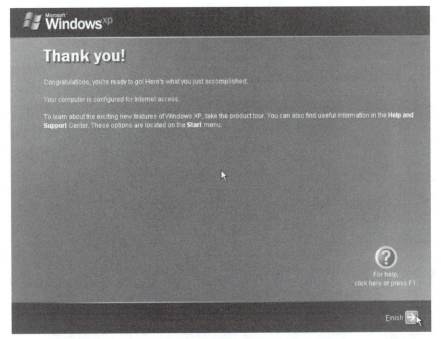

Step 9

The "Windows XP Professional" desktop appears.

Click **Start > Control Panel**.

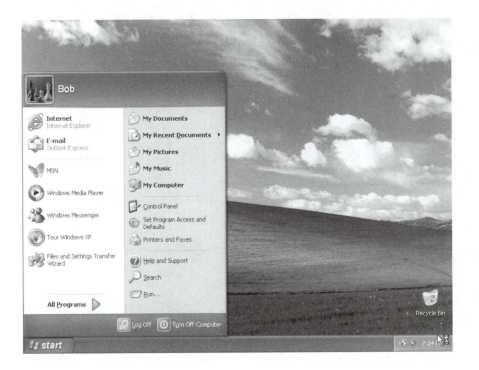

Step 10

Click **User Accounts**.

Click **Create a new account** from the "Pick a task…" list.

Type the name provided by your instructor in the "Type a name for the new account:" field.

Click **Next**.

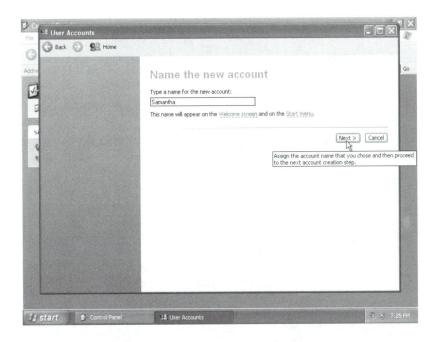

Click the **Limited** radio button.

Click **Create Account**.

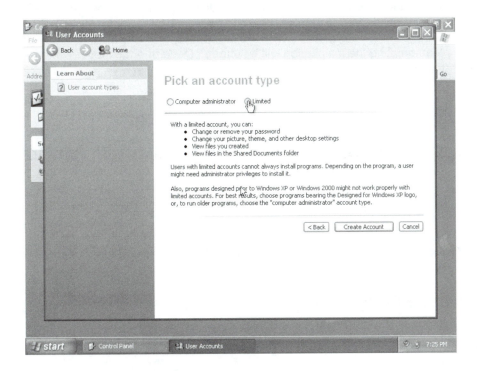

The "User Accounts" window appears.

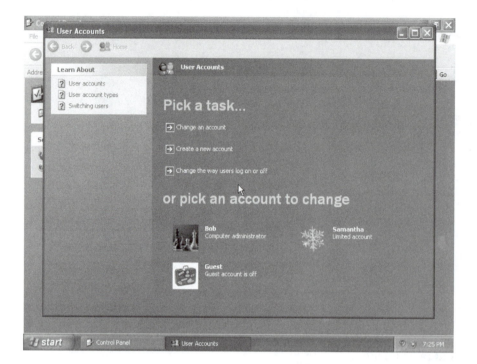

Create a second limited user. Your instructor will provide the name of the user.

What was the name of the file used to automate the installation located on the floppy disk?

How do you think automating the installation will help the IT Department if they have to repeat the procedure on 100 computers?

12.2.2 Optional Lab: Advanced Installation of Windows Vista

Introduction

In this lab, you will install a Windows Vista operating system by using an answer file for automation. You will customize partition settings and create an Administrator account and User accounts.

Recommended Equipment

The following equipment is required for this exercise:

- A computer with a new installation of Windows Vista
- Windows Automated Installation Kit (AIK) installation media
- Windows Vista installation media
- A blank, formatted floppy disk or a USB flash drive

Step 1

Ask the instructor for the following required information for the answer file:

Regional and language settings _____

Windows Vista product key _____

Partition sizes: Primary _____ Logical 1 _____ Logical 2 _____

Administrator account: Username _____

Password _____

User account: Username _____

Password _____

Computer name _____

Registered organization _____

Registered owner _____

Time zone _____

Step 2

Log on to the computer as Administrator.

Insert the Windows Automated Installation Kit (AIK) DVD in the DVD-ROM drive.

When the **AutoPlay** window appears, click **Run StartCD.exe**.

The **Welcome to Windows Automated Installation Kit** window appears, click **Windows AIK Setup**.

When the setup wizard appears click **Next**.

Select **I Agree** to license terms and then click **Next**.

For the **Select Installation Folder** window, keep the default settings and click **Next**.

Click **Next** to confirm and start the installation.

When the **Installation Complete** window appears, click **Close**.

Click **Exit**.

Step 3

Create a folder called **Vista_Installation** at the root of C:. Example: **C:\Vista_Installation**.

Insert the Windows Vista media in the appropriate drive.

Close the **Install Windows** window if it opens.

Navigate and copy **install.wim** from the Windows Vista installation media to C:\Vista_Installation.

NOTE: The install.wim file is 2.6GB and may take several minute to copy.

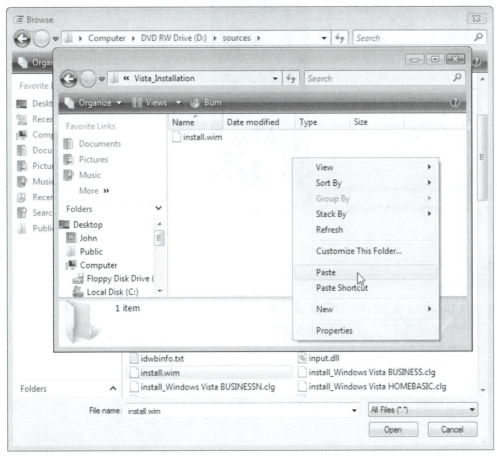

Step 4

Start > All Programs > Microsoft Windows AIK > Windows System Image Manager.

Step 5

The **Windows System Image Manager** window appears.

Right-click **Select a windows image or catalog file > Windows Image**.

Browse to **C:\Vista_Installation > install.wim > Open**.

Select **Windows Vista > OK**.

Click **Yes > Continue**. This may take several minutes.

A catalog file is generated in the **Windows Image** area.

Right-click **Create or open an answer file > New Answer File**.

A new answer file is created in the **Answer File** area.

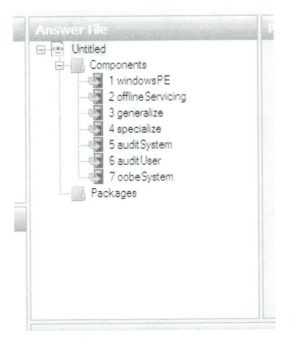

To name the file select the root node **Untitled**.

Click **File > Save Answer File >** name the file **autounattend**. Make sure the **Vista_Installation** folder is selected then click **Save**.

NOTE: It is important to name the file **autounattend** as Vista will only search for that file name when performing an unattended installation.

Step 6

In the **Windows Image** area, expand **Components**.

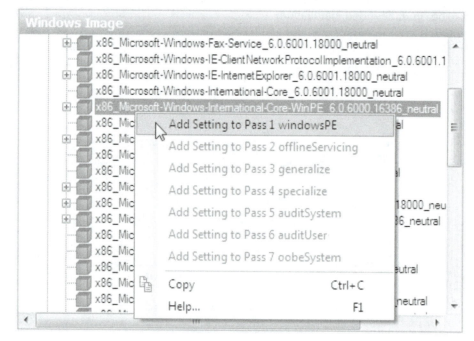

NOTE: The name of the components will have a prefix and suffix attached, for example: **x86_Microsoft-Windows-International-Core-WinPE_6.0.6000.16386_neutral**. The prefix is **x86** and the suffix is **6.0.6000.16386_neutral**. For simplicity, the prefix and suffix will be left out in the lab instructions.

Right-click **Microsoft-Windows-International-Core-WinPE > Add Settings to Pass 1 windowsPE**.

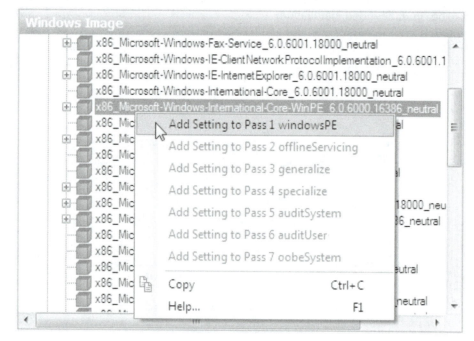

Notice that **Microsoft-Windows-International-Core-WinPE** has been added to the **Answer File** and **Properties** areas.

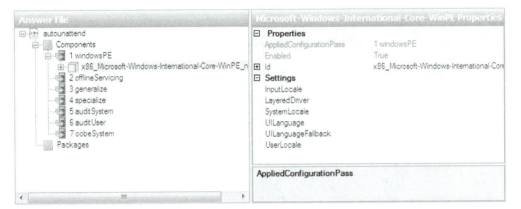

Select **Microsoft-Windows-International-Core-WinPE** in the **Answer File** area. In the **Microsoft-Windows-International-Core-WinPE Properties** area type the language settings provided by your instructor in the following locations: InputLocale, SystemLocale, UILanguage, UILanguageFallback, and UserLocale. For example: **en-us**.

NOTE: Place the curser next to a setting in the **Properties** area and press the F1 key to view the Windows Help file for the setting. Supported regional and language settings are located here: http://technet.microsoft.com/en-us/library/cc722435(WS.10).aspx.

In the **Answer File** area expand **Microsoft-Windows-International-Core-WinPE >** select **SetupUILanguage.** In the **SetupUILanguage Properties** area, type the language settings provided by your instructor in the UILanguage location. For example: **en-us**.

Confirm **OnError** is selected for **WillShowUI**.

Step 7

In the **Windows Image** area, locate and expand the component **Microsoft-Windows-Setup >** right-click **UserData > Add Setting to Pass 1 windowsPE**.

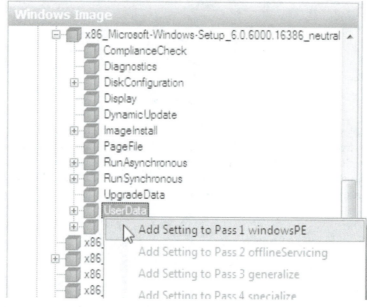

Select **UserData** in the **Answer File** area. In the **UserData Properties** area, click in the box to the right of **AcceptEula > true**.

In the **Answer File** area, expand **UserData > ProductKey.** In the **ProductKey Properties** area, click in the box to the right of **Key** and enter the Windows Vista product key provided by the instructor.

Click in the box to the right of the **WillShowUI > Never**.

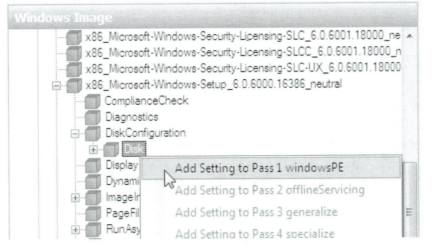

Step 8

In the **Windows Image** area, locate and expand component **Microsoft-Windows-Setup\DiskConfiguration** > right-click **Disk** > **Add Setting to Pass 1 windowsPE**.

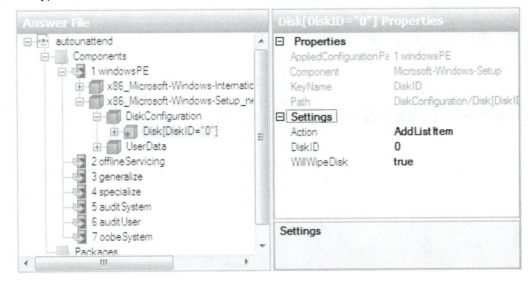

Select **Disk** in the **Answer File** area. In the **Disk Properties** area, click in the box to the right of **DiskID** and type the number **0**. Set **WillWipeDisk** to **true**.

In the **Answer File** area, expand **Disk[DiskID="0"]** > right-click **CreatePartitions** > **Insert New CreatePartition**.

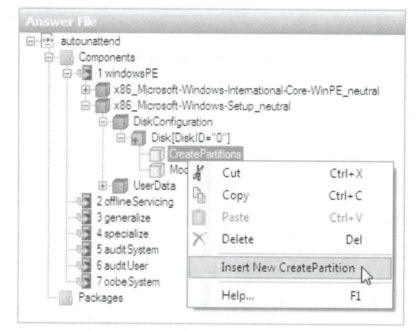

Add three more **CreatePartition** objects, for a total of four objects.

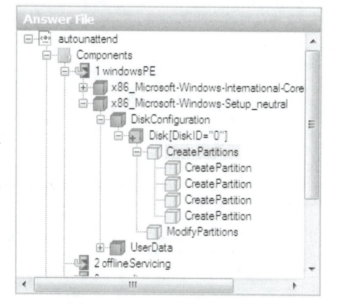

Select the top **CreatePartition** in the **Answer File** area. In the **CreatePartition Properties** area, set the following values: Extend = **false**, Order = **1** and Type = **Primary**. For Size, use the primary partition size provided by the instructor. For example: Size = **15000**.

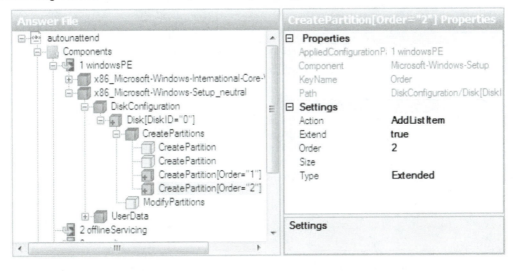

Notice that the newly configured partition moves to the bottom of the four **CreatePartition** objects.

Select the top **CreatePartition** in the **Answer File** area. In the **CreatePartition Properties** area, set the following values: Extend = **True**, Order = **2**, and Type = **Extended**.

Select the top **CreatePartition** in the **Answer File** area. In the **CreatePartition Properties** area, set the following values: Extend = **false**, Order = **3** and Type = **Logical**. For Size, use the logical 1 partition size provided by the instructor. For example: Size = **5000**.

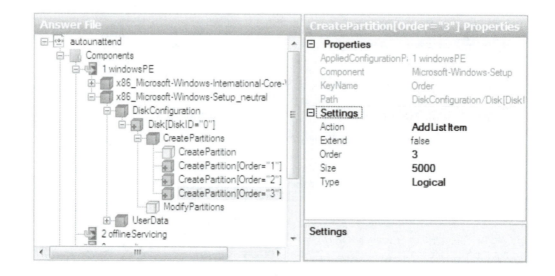

Select the top **CreatePartition** in the **Answer File** area. In the **CreatePartition Properties** area, set the following values: Extend = **false**, Order = **4** and Type = **Logical**. For Size, use the logical 2 partition size provided by the instructor. For example: Size = **5000**.

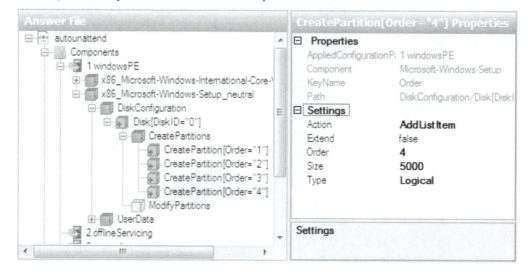

In the **Answer File** area, right-click **ModifyPartitions > Insert New ModifyPartition**.

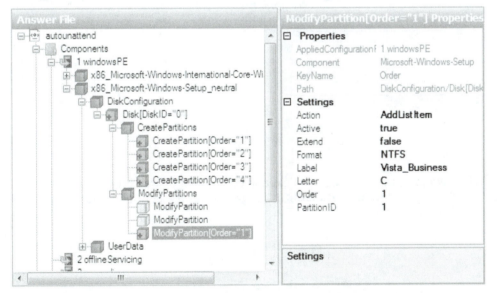

Add two more **ModifyPartition** objects, for a total of three objects.

Select the top **ModifyPartition** in the **Answer File** area. In the **ModifyPartition Properties** area, set the following values: Action = **AddListItem**, Active = **true**, Extend = **false**, Format = **NTFS**, Label = **Vista_Business**, Letter = **C**, Order = **1**, and PartitionID = **1**.

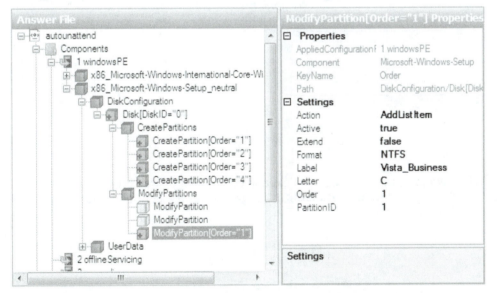

Select the top **ModifyPartition** in the **Answer File** area. In the **ModifyPartition Properties** area, set the following values: Action = **AddListItem**, Active = **false**, Extend = **false**, Letter = **E**, Order = **2**, and PartitionID = **2**.

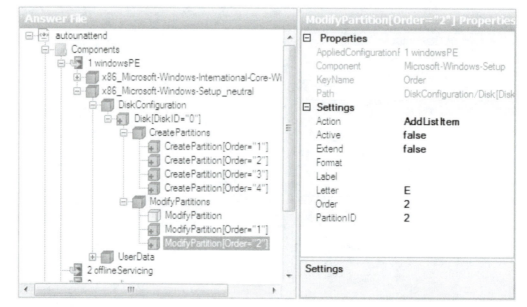

Select the top **ModifyPartition** in the **Answer File** area. In the **ModifyPartition Properties** area set the following values: Action = **AddListItem**, Active = **false**, Extend = **false**, Letter = **F**, Order = **3**, and PartitionID = **3**.

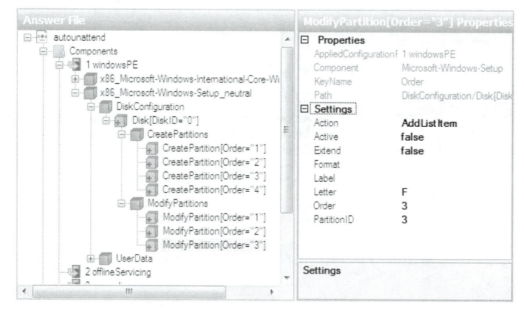

In the **Windows Image** area, locate and expand component **Microsoft-Windows-Setup\DiskConfiguration\ImageInstall\OSImage\InstallTo** > right-click **InstallTo** > **Add Setting to Pass 1 windowsPE**.

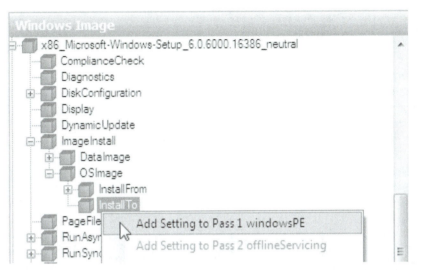

Select **InstallTo** in the **Answer File** area. In the **InstallTo Properties** area, set the following values: DiskID = **0**, and PartitionID = **1**.

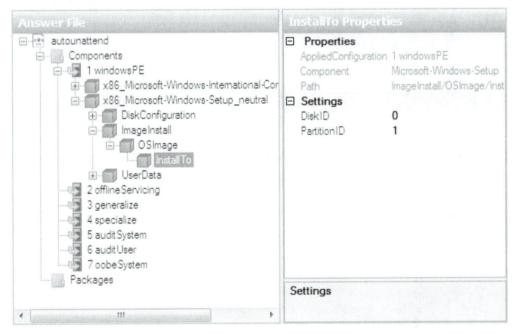

Step 9

In the **Windows Image** area, locate and expand component **Microsoft-Windows-Shell-Setup\UserAccounts\LocalAccounts >** right-click **LocalAccount > Add Setting to Pass 7 oobeSystem**.

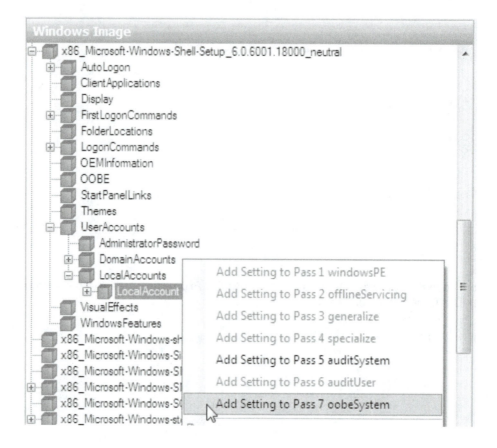

In the **Answer File** area, right-click **LocalAccounts** > select **Insert New LocalAccounts**.

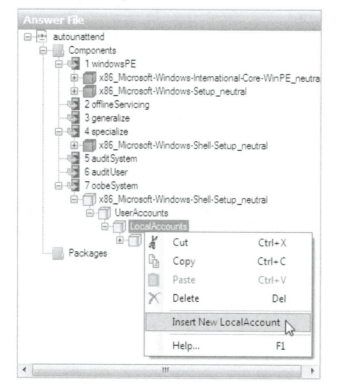

You should now have two **LocalAccounts** objects.

Setup an Administrators account.

Select the top **LocalAccount** in the **Answer File** area. In the **LocalAccount Properties** area, type the **DisplayName** and the **Name** provided by your instructor. Example: **John** and **John M**.

Type **Administrators** for the Group.

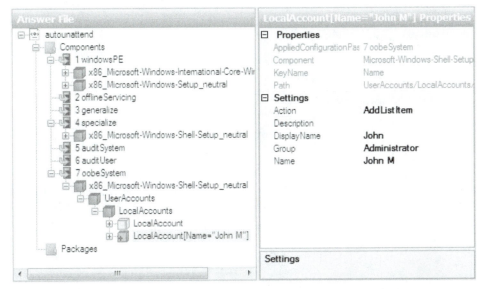

Expand **LocalAccount[Name="John M"] > Password**. In the **Password Properties** area, type the **password** provided by your instructor in the Value setting. Example: **Pa$$w0rd**.

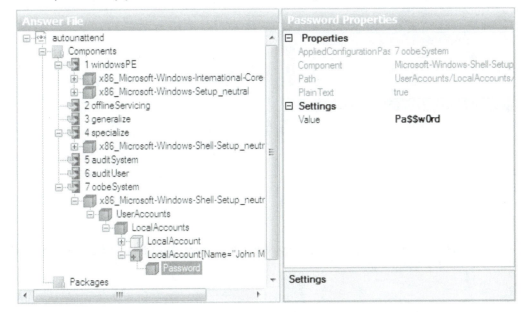

Set up a User account.

Select the top **LocalAccount** in the **Answer File** area. In the **LocalAccount Properties** area, type the **DisplayName** and the **Name** provided by your instructor. Example: **Nathan** and **Nathan W**.

Type **Users** for the Group.

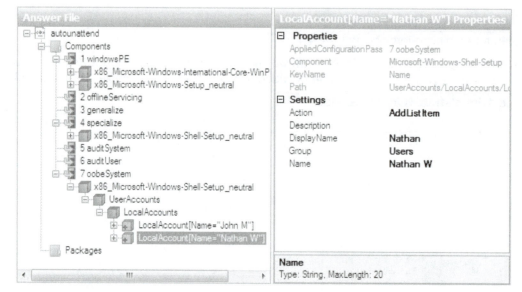

Expand **LocalAccount[Name="Nathan W"] > Password**. In the **Password Properties** area, type the **password** provided by your instructor in the Value setting. Example: **Pa$$w0rd**.

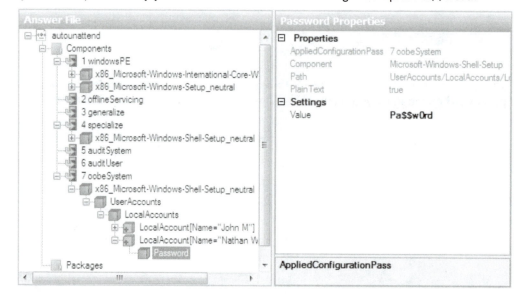

Step 10

In the **Windows Image** area, locate and right-click **Microsoft-Windows-Shell-Setup > Add Setting to Pass 4 specialize**.

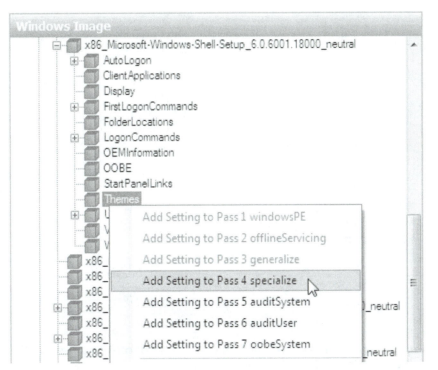

Select **Microsoft-Windows-Shell-Setup** in the **Answer File** area below **component 4 specialize**. In the **Microsoft-Windows-Shell-Setup Properties** area, type the ComputerName, RegisteredOrganization and RegisteredOwner provided by your instructor. Example: **Computer1, Cisco, and John**.

Expand **Microsoft-Windows-Shell-Setup** in **component 4 specialize** of the **Answer File** area. Locate and select **Themes**. In the **Themes Properties** area, set the following value: DefaultThemesOff = **false**.

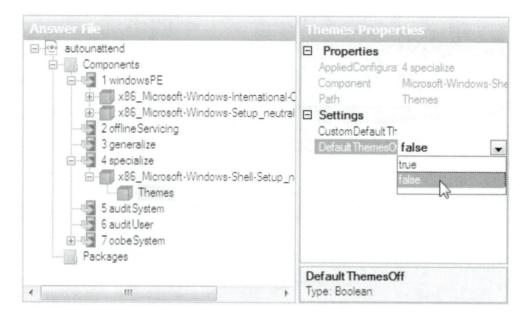

Step 11

In the **Windows Image** area, locate and expand component **Microsoft-Windows-Shell-Setup >** right-click **OOBE > Add Setting to Pass 7 oobeSystem**.

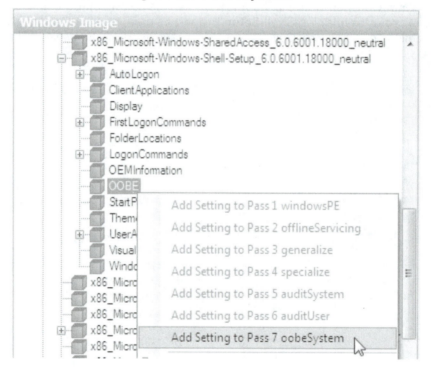

Select **Microsoft-Windows-Shell-Setup** in the **Answer File** area below **component 7 oobe System**. In the **Microsoft-Windows-Shell-Setup Properties** area, type the time zone in the **TimeZone** setting, provided by your instructor. Example: TimeZone = **Pacific Standard Time**.

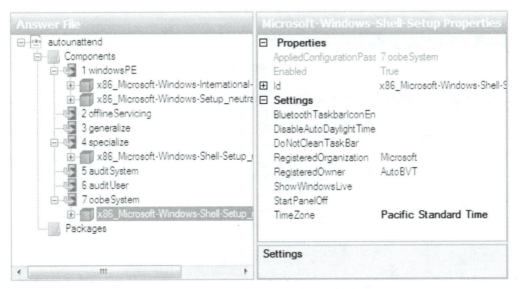

Select **OOBE** in the **Answer File** area. In the **OOBE Properties** area, set the following value: NetworkLocation = **Work** and ProtectYourPC = **3.** This will disable automatically installed updates.

NOTE: Normally you would set ProtectYourPC to 1, automatically install updates. But to reduce the installation time for this lab we will set the value to 3.

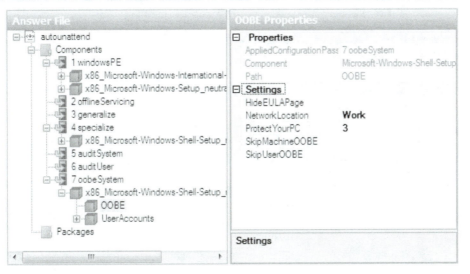

Step 12

Before validating the answer file, expand all components in the **autounattend** file to make sure everything is properly added.

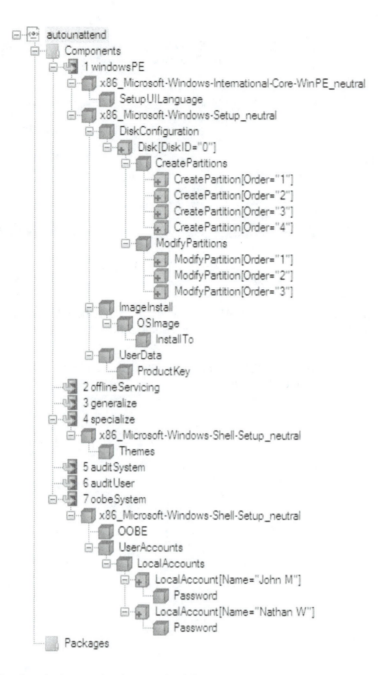

If anything is missing, go back over the lab and add the missing components or settings.

Click **Tools > Validate Answer File**.

Select the **Validation** tab in the **Messages** area.

If you see any error or warning messages, ask your instructor for assistance in correcting them before proceeding with the lab.

If there are no error or warning messages click **File > Save Answer File**.

Step 13

Copy the autounattend.xml file from **C:\Vista_Installation** to the root of the floppy disk or USB flash drive.

Insert the floppy disk in the floppy drive or connect the USB flash drive to a USB port.

Insert the Windows Vista media in the appropriate drive.

Restart the computer.

Step 14

When the **Press Any Key to Boot from CD or DVD** message appears, press any key on the keyboard.

The installation of Windows Vista will proceed in a completely unattended fashion, then Vista will run a performance check, and finally you will be presented with the logon screen.

NOTE: The system will flash on and off several times, restart several times, and other times only a black or blue screen will appear with nothing else shown during the installation.

Logon to the computer using the administrator name and password used in the **autounattend** file.

What was the name of the file used to automate the installation located on the floppy disk or USB flash drive?

How do you think automating the installation will help the IT Department if they have to repeat the procedure on 100 computers?

12.2.3 Lab: Create a Partition in Windows XP

Introduction

In this lab, you will create a FAT32 formatted partition on a disk. You will convert the partition to NTFS. You will identify the differences between the FAT32 format and the NTFS format.

Recommended Equipment

* Computer running Windows XP
* Unpartitioned space of at least 1 GB on the hard disk drive

Step 1

Log on to Windows as an administrator.

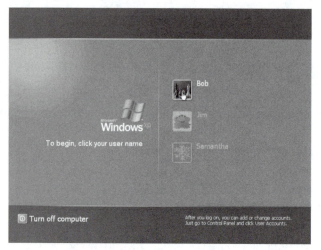

Step 2

Click **Start**.

Right-click **My Computer**, and then click **Manage**.

Step 3

The "Computer Management" window appears.

Click **Disk Management** on the left side of the screen.

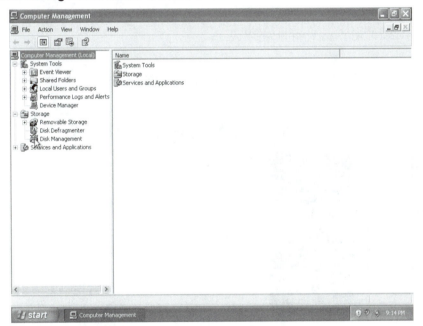

Right-click the green-outlined block of **Free Space**.

Click **New Logical Drive….**

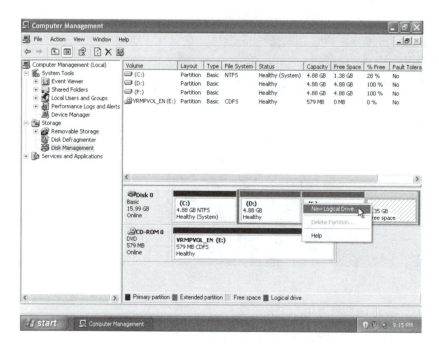

Step 4

The "New Partition Wizard" window appears.

Click **Next**.

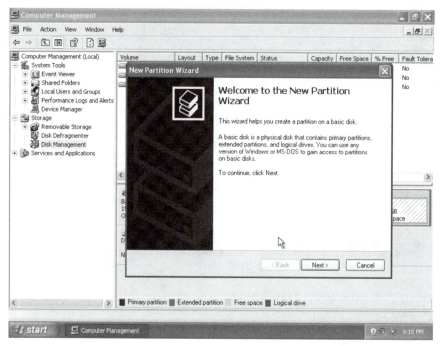

Click the **Logical drive** radio button, and then click **Next**.

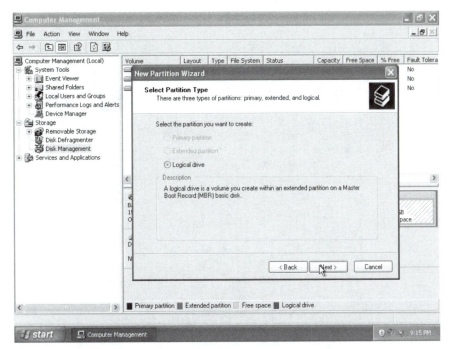

Type **500** in the "Partition size in MB:" field.

Click the **Assign the following drive letter:** radio button.

Select **G** from the drop-down menu.

Click **Next**.

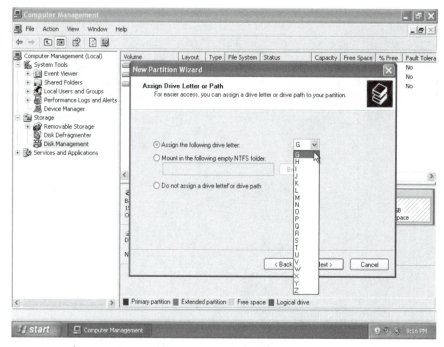

Click the **Format this partition with the following settings:** radio button.

Click **Next**.

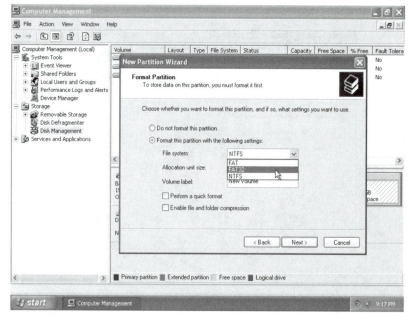

Click **Finish**.

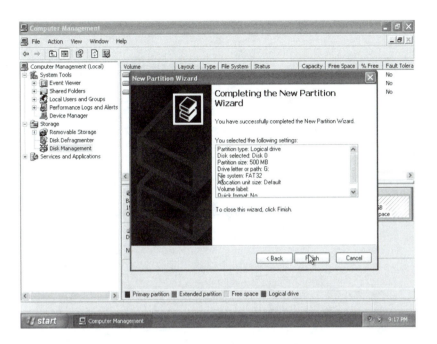

Step 5

The "Computer Management" window re-appears while the new volume is formatted.

The "Computer Management" window shows the new "Healthy" volume.

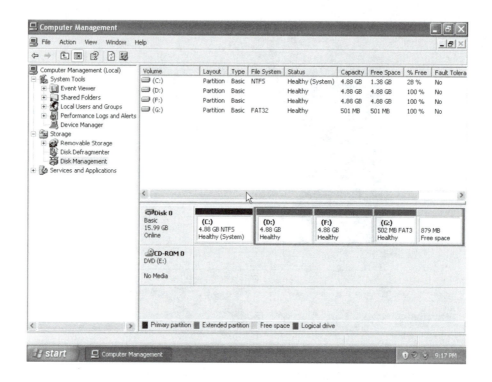

Step 6

Open **My Computer**.

Click the **Local Disk (G:)** drive.

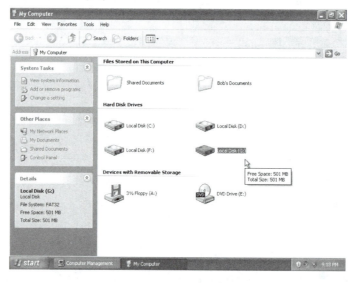

The "Details" area on the left of the "My Computer" window displays information about the G: drive.

What is the File System?

How much Free Space is shown?

Right-click the **Local Disk (G:)** drive.

Choose **Properties**.

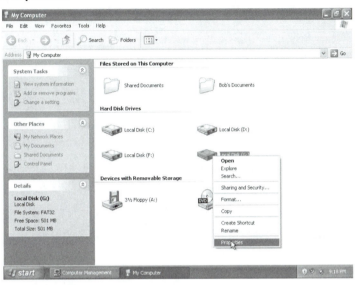

Step 7

The "Local Disk (G:) Properties" window appears.

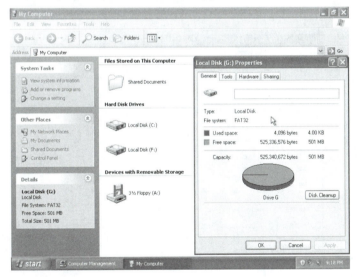

What is the File system of the G: drive?

List the tabs found in the "Local Disk (G:) Properties" window.

Click **OK**.

Double-click the **Local Disk (G:)** drive.

Step 8

Right-click anywhere in the white space of the window.

Choose **New > Text Document**.

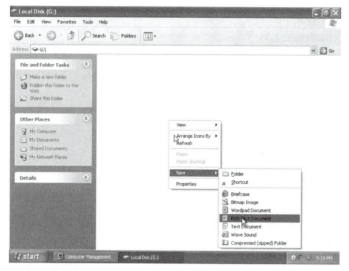

Type **Test** and press **Return**.

Step 9

Right-click the **Test** document in the window and choose **Properties**.

The "Test Properties" window appears.

Notice that there is a tab in the "Test Properties" window called "General".

Click **OK**.

Step 10

Choose **Start > Run**.

In the "Open:" field, type **cmd**, and then click **OK**.

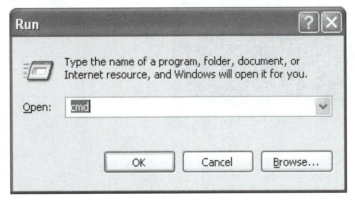

Step 11

The "C:\WINDOWS\system32\cmd.exe" window appears.

Type **convert G: /fs:NTFS**.

The **convert** command changes the file system of a volume without losing data.

Press the **Enter** key.

Type **exit**, and then press **Return**.

Step 12

The "C:\WINDOWS\System32\cmd.exe" window closes.

What is the File System of the **G:** drive?

Step 13

Open **My Computer**.

Right-click the **G:** drive, and then click **Properties**.

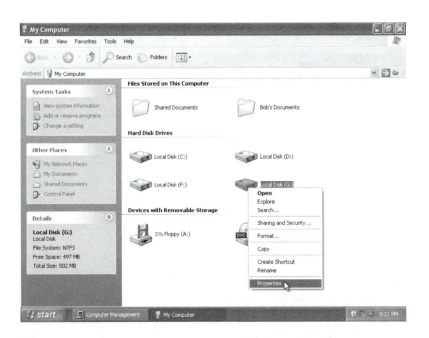

Step 14

The "Local Disk (G:) Properties" window appears.

What are the tabs in the "Local Disk (G:) Properties" window?

When the volume was FAT32, there were four tabs. What is the name of the new tab that was added after the volume was converted to NTFS?

Click **Cancel**, and then double-click the G: drive.

Step 15

Right-click the **Test** document, and then click **Properties**.

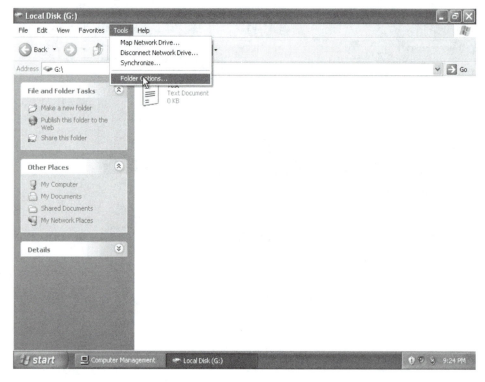

What are the tabs in the "Test Properties" window?

When the volume was FAT32, there was one tab. What is the name of the new tab that was added after the volume was converted to NTFS?

Click **OK**.

Step 16

Choose **Tools > Folder Options**.

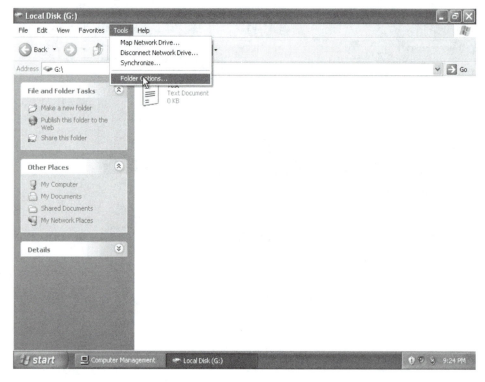

Step 17

The "Folder Options" window appears.

Click the **View** tab.

Scroll to the bottom of the "Advanced settings:" area, and then uncheck **Use simple file sharing (Recommended)**.

Click **OK**.

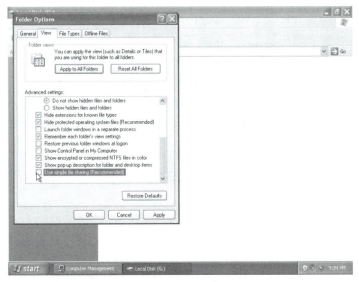

The "Folder Options" window closes.

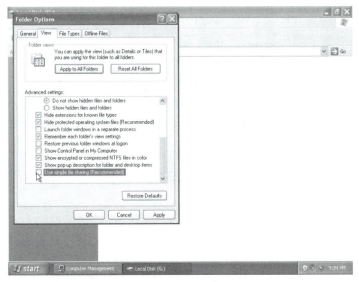

What are the tabs in the "Test Properties" window?

When "simple file sharing" was enabled, there were two tabs. What is the name of the new tab that was added after "simple file sharing" was turned off?

Step 18

Right-click the **G:** drive, and then choose **Properties**.

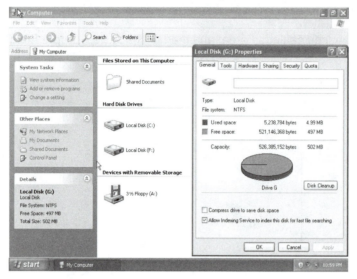

What are the tabs in the "Local Disk (G:) Properties" window?

When "simple file sharing" was enabled, there were five tabs. What is the name of the new tab that was added after "simple file sharing" was turned off?

12.2.3 Optional Lab: Create a Partition in Windows Vista

Introduction

In this lab, you will create a FAT32 formatted partition on a disk. You will convert the partition to NTFS. You will identify the differences between the FAT32 format and the NTFS format.

Recommended Equipment

- Computer running Windows Vista
- Unpartitioned space of at least 1 GB on the hard disk drive

Step 1

Log on to Windows as an Administrator.

Click **Start**.

Right-click **Computer > Manage**.

Step 2

The **Computer Management** window appears.

Click **Disk Management** on the left side of the screen.

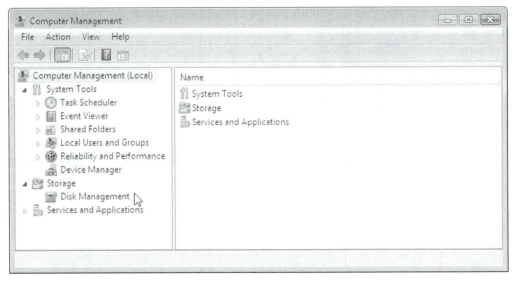

Right-click the green-outlined block of **Free Space**.

Click **New Simple Volume....**

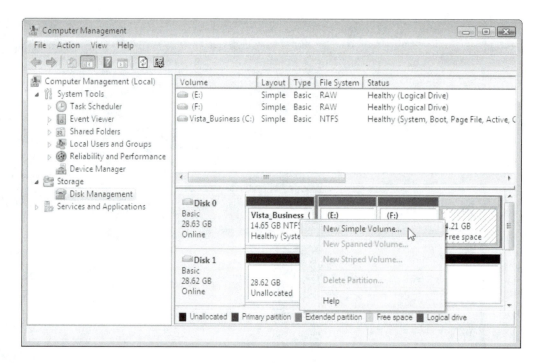

Step 3

The **New Simple Volume Wizard** window appears.

Click **Next**.

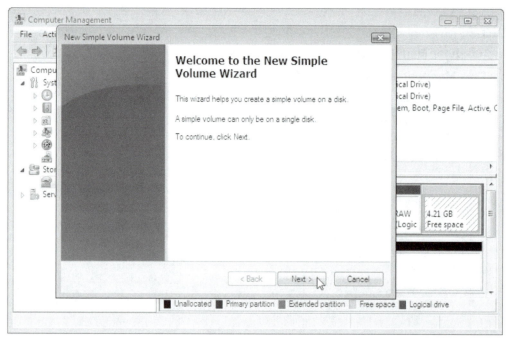

Type **500** in the **Simple volume size in MB**: field.

Click **Next**.

Click the **Assign the following drive letter:** radio button.

Select **G** from the drop-down menu.

Click **Next**.

Click the **Format this volume with the following settings:** radio button.

Select **FAT32** from the File system drop-down menu.

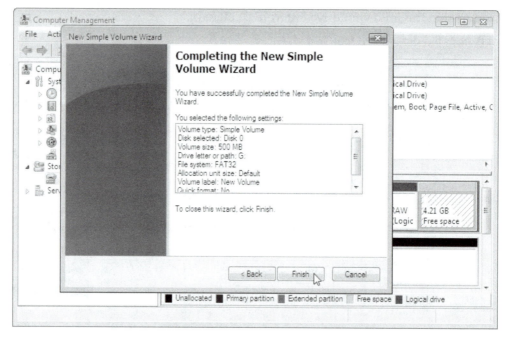

Click **Next.**

Click **Finish**.

Step 4

The **Computer Management** window re-appears while the new volume is formatted.

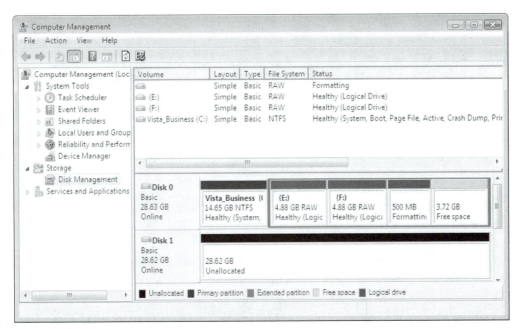

The **Computer Management** window shows the new **Healthy (Logical Drive)** volume.

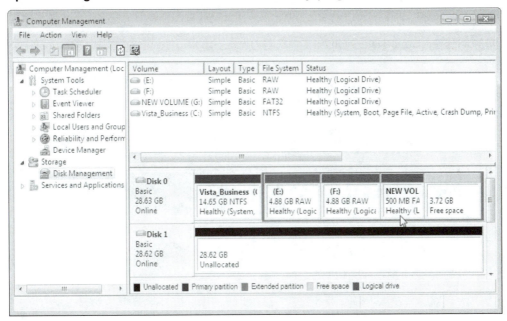

Step 5

Open **Computer**.

Click the **NEW VOLUME (G:)** drive.

The **Details** area on the bottom of the **Computer** window displays information about the G: drive. What is the File System?

How much Free Space is shown?

Right-click the **NEW VOLUME (G:)** drive.

Click **Properties**.

Step 6

The **NEW VOLUME (G:) Properties** window appears.

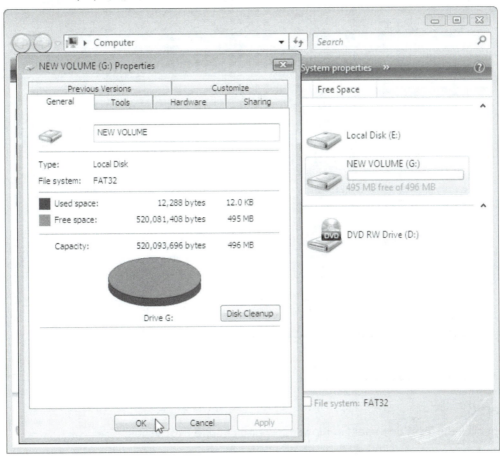

What is the File system of the G: drive?

List the tabs found in the **NEW VOLUME (G:) Properties** window.

Click **OK**.

Double-click the **NEW VOLUME (G:)** drive.

Step 7

Right-click anywhere in the white space of the window.

Click **New > Text Document**.

Type **Test** and press **Enter**.

Step 8

Right-click the **Test** document in the window and choose **Properties**.

The **Test Properties** window appears.

List the tabs found in the **Test Properties** window?

Click **OK**.

Close any windows open for the G: drive.

Step 9

Click **Start**.

In the **Start Search** field, type **cmd**. When the cmd program appears, right-click **cmd > Run as administrator**.

Step 10

The **Administrator: C:\Windows\System32\cmd.exe** window appears.

Type **convert G: /fs:NTFS >** press the **Enter** key.

The **convert** command changes the file system of a volume without losing data.

You will be prompted to enter the current volume label for drive G:. Type **NEW VOLUME** and the **Enter** key.

After the drive is converted, type **exit** in the **Administrator: C:\Windows\System32\cmd.exe** window, and then press **Enter**.

Step 11

The **C:\WINDOWS\System32\cmd.exe** window closes.

What is the File System of the **G:** drive?

Step 12

Open **Computer**.

Right-click **NEW VOLUME (G:) > Properties**.

Step 13

The **NEW VOLUME (G:) Properties** window appears.

What are the tabs in the **NEW VOLUME (G:) Properties** window?

When the volume was FAT32, there were four tabs. What are the names of the new tabs that were added after the volume was converted to NTFS?

Click **Cancel**. Double-click the **NEW VOLUME (G:)** drive.

Step 14

Open the **Cisco** folder.

Right-click the **Test** document **> Properties**.

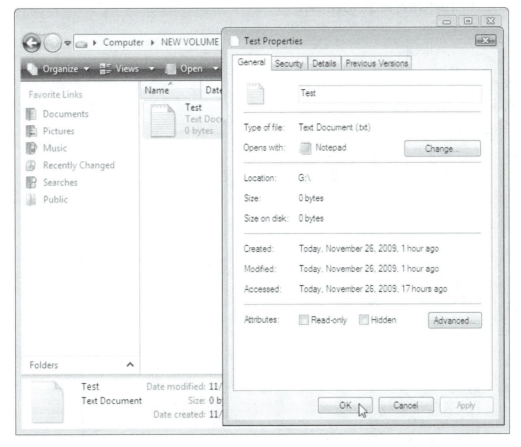

What are the tabs in the **Test Properties** window?

When the volume was FAT32, there were three tabs. What is the name of the new tab that was added after the volume was converted to NTFS?

Click **OK**.

12.2.4 Lab: Customize Settings in Windows XP

Introduction

This lab is comprised of five parts. This lab is designed to be completed in multiple lab sessions.

Part 1: Managing Virtual Memory, Startup Options, and Windows Update in Windows XP

In this part of the lab, you will customize Virtual Memory settings. You will customize the Startup Folder and RunOnce Key in the Registry. You will change the default Windows Update option.

Recommended Equipment

- A computer running Windows XP Professional
- Internet access

Step 1

Log on to Windows as an administrator.

Choose **Start**. Double-click **My Computer**.

The **My Computer** window appears.

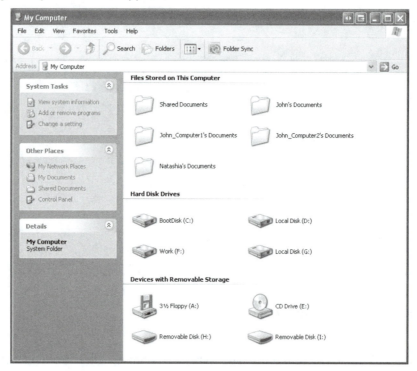

Step 2

Double click the **D**: drive.

The **Disk is not formatted** window appears.

Click **Yes**.

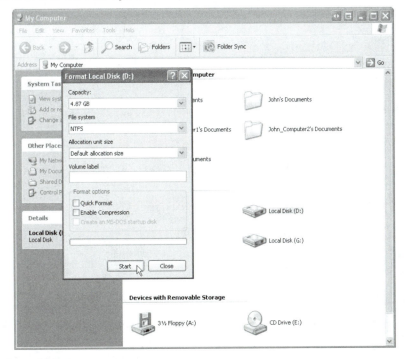

Step 3

The **Format Local Disk (D:)** window appears.

Choose **NTFS** in the **File system** drop-down menu, and then click **Start**.

A warning window appears.

Click **OK**.

Windows formats the drive.

When the **Format Complete** window appears, Click **OK**.

The **Format Local Disk (D:)** window re-appears.

Click **Close**.

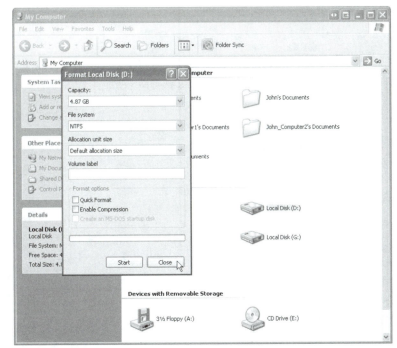

Close all open windows.

Step 4

Choose **Start**.

Right-click **My Computer**, and then click **Properties**.

The **System Properties** window appears.

Click the **Advanced** tab.

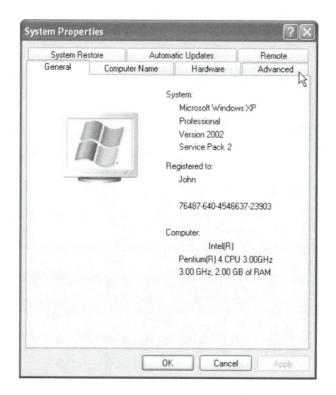

Click **Settings** in the **Performance** area.

Step 5

The **Performance Options** window appears.

Click the **Advanced** tab.

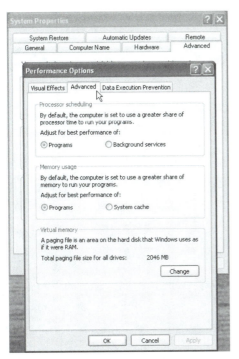

What is the current size of the Virtual Memory (paging file)?

Click **Change** in the Virtual Memory area.

The **Virtual Memory** window appears.

What **Drive [Volume Label]** contains the paging file?

Choose the **D:** drive.

Click the **Custom size** radio button.

Look at the recommended size in the **Total paging file size for all drives** section of the **Virtual Memory** window.

Type the recommended file size in **the Initial size (MB)** field.

Type the recommended file size again in the **Maximum size (MB)** field.

Click **Set**.

Choose the **C:** drive.

Click the **No paging file** radio button, and then click **Set**.

Click **OK**.

The **System Control Panel Applet** message window appears.

Click **OK**.

Click **OK**.

Click **OK**.

The **System Settings Change** window appears.

Click **Yes** to restart your computer now.

Step 6

Log on to Windows as an administrator.

Open the **Virtual Memory** window.

What **Drive [Volume Label]** contains the paging file?

Click **Cancel**.

Click **Cancel**.

The **Performance Options** window closes.

Click **Cancel**.

Step 7

Choose **Start > All Programs > Games >** right-click **FreeCell > Send To > Desktop (create shortcut)**.

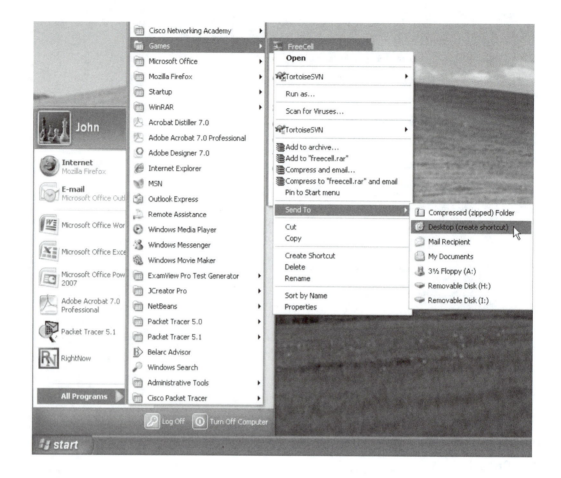

Step 8

Click and drag the **Freecell** to the **Start** button.

The **Start menu** appears.

Do not release the shortcut icon.

Drag the icon to **All Programs**.

The **All Programs** menu appears.

Drag the icon to **Startup**.

The **Startup** menu appears.

Drag the icon to the Startup menu.

Release the icon.

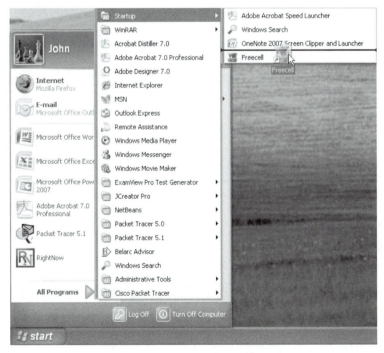

Step 9

Log off Windows.

Log on to Windows as an administrator.

What happens when you log in?

Close the Freecell application.

Step 10

Choose **Start > Run**.

Type **regedit** In the Open: field > **OK**.

CAUTION: Incorrect changes to the registry can cause system errors and/or system instability.

The **Registry Editor** window appears.

Expand the **HKEY_CURRENT_USER** Key.

Expand the **Software** Key.

Expand the **Microsoft** Key.

Expand the **Windows** Key.

Expand the **CurrentVersion** Key.

Select the **RunOnce** Key.

Right-click anywhere in the white space of the window.

Hover over **New**, and then select **String Value**.

Right-click **New Value #1**, and then choose **Rename**.

Type **Solitaire**, and then press **Enter**.

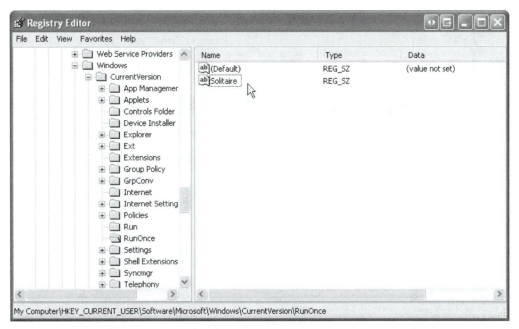

Right-click **Solitaire**, and then choose **Modify**.

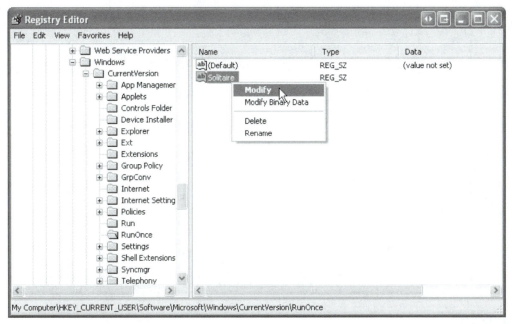

Type **C:\Windows\system32\sol.exe** in the Value data field.

Click **OK**.

Close the **Registry Editor** window.

Step 11

Log off Windows.

Log on to Windows as an administrator.

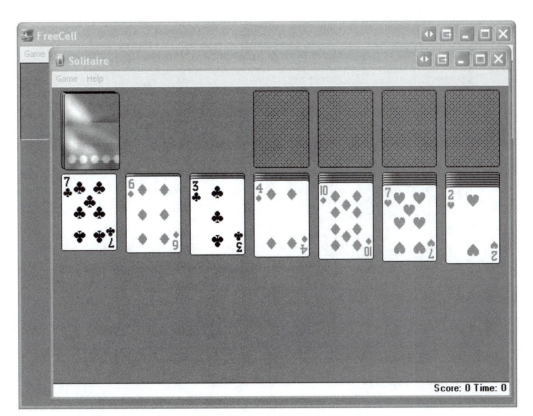

What happens when you log in?

Close all open Windows.

Step 12

Choose **Start > All Programs**.

Right-click **My Computer**, and then choose **Properties**.

Click the **Automatic Updates** tab.

Click the **Download updates for me, but let me choose when to install them** radio button.

Click **Apply**, and then click **OK**.

Step 13

Windows checks for updates.

The **Updates are ready for your computer** balloon appears.

Double-click the **shield** icon in the system tray.

Click **Custom Install (Advanced)**, and then click **Next**.

The **Choose updates to install** window appears.

Click **Install**.

The **Installing updates** balloon appears.

Reboot the computer.

Part 2: Windows XP Hard Drive Maintenance

In this part of the lab, you will examine the results after using Disk Check and Disk Defragmenter on a hard drive.

Recommended Equipment

- A computer running Windows XP Professional

Step 1

Log on to Windows as an administrator.

Start > My Computer > double-click **New Volume (G:)**.

Right-click anywhere in the white space of the folder area for drive **G: > Properties > Tools** tab > **Check Now**.

When the **Check Disk New Volume (G:)** window appears, click **Start**.

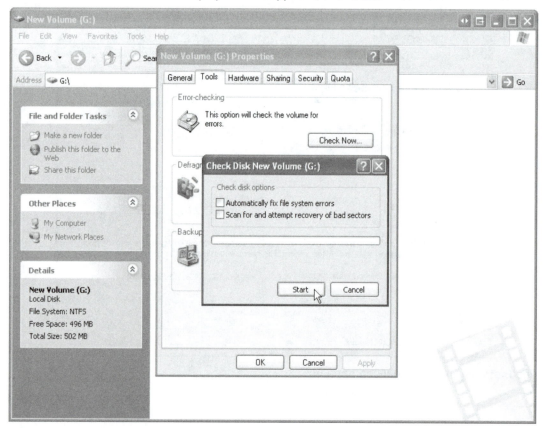

The **Disk Check Complete** window appears.

How many phases were checked?

Click **OK**.

Select the **Tools** tab, click **Check Now**.

Place a check mark in the check box next to **Scan for and attempt recovery of bad sectors >
Start**.

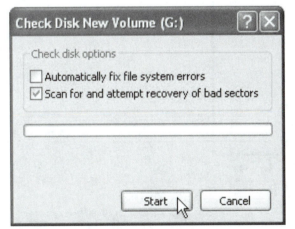

The **Disk Check Complete** Window appears.

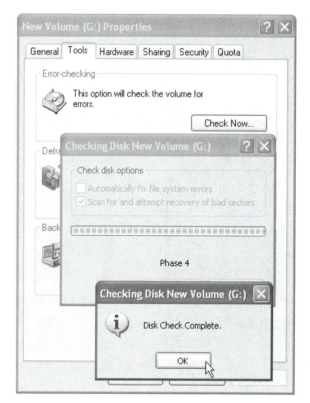

How many phases were checked?

Click **OK**.

Select the **Tools** tab, click **Check Now**.

Place a check mark in both check boxes and click **Start**.

An information window opens.

Why will CHKDSK not start?

NOTE: This message is displayed because a boot partition will be scanned, or a non-boot partition that is going to be scanned is open.

Click **Yes** and then **OK** to close the **New Volume (G:) Properties** window.

Make sure drive **G:** stays open.

NOTE: To force CHKDSK to create a log file, when it scans a non-boot partition with no bad sectors, the non-boot partition drive must be open.

Click **Start > Shutdown > Restart**.

Step 2

The **Checking file system on G:** window appears.

How many stages in the scan are there?

What is being verified in each of the stages?

Were any problems found with the volume?

If so what are they?

Step 3

Log on to Windows as an administrator.

Start > Control Panel > Administrative Tools > Event Viewer > in the left pane select **Application**.

Double-click the top event in the right pane. Click the black down arrow until the disk check event appears.

Checking file system on G:
The type of the file system is NTFS.
Volume label is New Volume.

A disk check has been scheduled.
Windows will now check the disk.
Cleaning up 2 unused index entries from index $SII of file 0x9.
Cleaning up 2 unused index entries from index $SDH of file 0x9.
Cleaning up 2 unused security descriptors.
CHKDSK is verifying file data (stage 4 of 5)...
File data verification completed.
CHKDSK is verifying free space (stage 5 of 5)...
Free space verification is complete.

```
  514048 KB total disk space.
      24 KB in 9 files.
      16 KB in 15 indexes.
       0 KB in bad sectors.
    5203 KB in use by the system.
    4624 KB occupied by the log file.
  508804 KB available on disk.

     512 bytes in each allocation unit.
 1028096 total allocation units on disk.
 1017609 allocation units available on disk.
```

Internal Info:
```
30 00 00 00 23 00 00 00 26 00 00 00 00 00 00 00  0...#...&......
01 00 00 00 00 00 00 00 0d 00 00 00 00 00 00 00  ...............
76 b0 10 00 00 00 00 00 92 fe 1e 00 00 00 00 00  v...............
38 9c 1c 00 00 00 00 00 c2 eb 0b 00 00 00 00 00  8...............
ba f0 a0 04 00 00 00 00 aa a0 68 0b 00 00 00 00  ..........h.....
40 01 bb b2 00 00 00 00 d0 3c 07 00 09 00 00 00  @.......<......
00 00 00 00 00 60 00 00 00 00 00 00 0f 00 00 00  .....`..........
```

For more information, see Help and Support Center at
http://go.microsoft.com/fwlink/events.asp.

Which stages are shown as completed?

Close all open windows.

Step 4

Start > My Computer > right-click drive **(C:) > Properties > Tools tab > Defragment Now**.

The **Disk Defragmenter** window appears. Notice drive (C:) is selected.

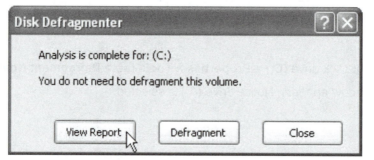

What are the file types and colors, grouped by Disk Defragmenter?

Click **Analyze**.

When the **Analysis is complete for: (C**:) window appears, click **View Report**.

The **Analysis Report** window opens. Does the volume need defragmenting?

Analysis Report [?][X]

Analysis is complete for: (C:)
You do not need to defragment this volume.

Volume information:

Volume (C:)		
Volume size	=	3.99 GB
Cluster size	=	4 KB
Used space	=	2.16 GB
Free space	=	1.83 GB
Percent free space	=	45 %
Volume fragmentation		

Most fragmented files:

Fragments	File Size	File Name
112	11 MB	\Documents and Settings\Administrator\Loca.
103	6 MB	\Documents and Settings\Administrator\Loca.
67	704 KB	\Documents and Settings\Default User\Local .
63	1 KB	\WINDOWS\system32\config\system.LOG
60	249 KB	\WINDOWS\setupapi.log
51	3 MB	\Documents and Settings\Administrator\Loca.
48	8 MB	\Program Files\TechSmith\Snagit 9\SnagitEdi...
46	39 MB	\Documents and Settings\Administrator\Desk.

[Print...] [Save As...] [Defragment] [Close]

Click on the scroll down bar to view volume information.

Volume (C:)		
Volume size	=	3.99 GB
Cluster size	=	4 KB
Used space	=	2.16 GB
Free space	=	1.83 GB
Percent free space	=	45 %
Volume fragmentation		
Total fragmentation	=	10 %
File fragmentation	=	20 %
Free space fragmentation	=	0 %
File fragmentation		
Total files	=	10,655
Average file size	=	246 KB
Total fragmented files	=	634
Total excess fragments	=	2,046
Average fragments per file	=	1.19
Pagefile fragmentation		
Pagefile size	=	768 MB
Total fragments	=	1
Folder fragmentation		
Total folders	=	748
Fragmented folders	=	17
Excess folder fragments	=	118
Master File Table (MFT) fragmentation		
Total MFT size	=	11 MB
MFT record count	=	11,420
Percent MFT in use	=	99
Total MFT fragments	=	2

Click the **Close** button.

Drive (C:) has what percentage of free space?

Click the **Defragment** button.

The defragmenting process begins.

When the **Defragmentation is complete for: (C:)** window appears click **View Report**.

Click on the scroll down bar to view volume information.

```
Volume  (C:)
   Volume size                              =   3.99 GB
   Cluster size                             =   4 KB
   Used space                               =   2.15 GB
   Free space                               =   1.84 GB
   Percent free space                       =   46 %
Volume fragmentation
   Total fragmentation                      =   0 %
   File fragmentation                       =   0 %
   Free space fragmentation                 =   0 %
File fragmentation
   Total files                              =   10,673
   Average file size                        =   245 KB
   Total fragmented files                   =   0
   Total excess fragments                   =   0
   Average fragments per file               =   1.00
Pagefile fragmentation
   Pagefile size                            =   768 MB
   Total fragments                          =   1
Folder fragmentation
   Total folders                            =   748
   Fragmented folders                       =   1
   Excess folder fragments                  =   0
Master File Table (MFT) fragmentation
   Total MFT size                           =   11 MB
   MFT record count                         =   11,438
   Percent MFT in use                       =   99
   Total MFT fragments                      =   2
```

Volume (C:) has what percentage of free space?

Close all open windows.

Part 3: Managing Processes, and Regional and Language Settings in Windows XP

In this part of the lab, you will examine regional and language settings, and explore how to manage processes in Task Manager.

Recommended Equipment

- A computer running Windows XP Professional

Step 1

Log on to Windows as an administrator.

Press **Ctrl-Alt-Delete**.

Click the **Processes** tab.

Double-click the border around the tabs.

Image Name	User Name	CPU	Mem Usage
Acrobat.exe	John	00	43,500 K
taskmgr.exe	John	02	5,920 K
iexplore.exe	John	00	85,504 K
WINWORD.EXE	John	00	49,564 K
SnagitEditor.exe	John	00	46,788 K
aolsoftware.exe	John	00	6,548 K
SnagPriv.exe	John	00	3,028 K
TscHelp.exe	John	00	3,432 K
WindowsSearch.exe	John	00	11,048 K
Snagit32.exe	John	00	25,536 K
UltraMonTaskbar.exe	John	00	3,452 K
aim6.exe	John	00	61,736 K
ctfmon.exe	John	00	4,736 K
jusched.exe	John	00	7,424 K
hpwuschd2.exe	John	00	2,704 K
acrotray.exe	John	00	3,148 K
GrooveMonitor.exe	John	00	6,680 K
UltraMon.exe	John	00	1,272 K
VPTray.exe	John	00	8,908 K
SMax4.exe	John	00	4,416 K
SMax4PNP.exe	John	00	4,524 K
TSVNCache.exe	John	00	7,984 K
iexplore.exe	John	00	4,940 K
searchindexer.exe	SYSTEM	00	25,212 K
ViewpointService.exe	SYSTEM	00	2,440 K
EXCEL.EXE	John	00	31,936 K
SMAgent.exe	SYSTEM	00	1,728 K
Rtvscan.exe	SYSTEM	00	38,520 K
jqs.exe	SYSTEM	00	1,396 K
explorer.exe	John	00	7,208 K
DefWatch.exe	SYSTEM	00	2,212 K
svchost.exe	LOCAL SERVICE	00	6,032 K
svchost.exe	LOCAL SERVICE	00	3,928 K
svchost.exe	NETWORK SERVICE	00	3,516 K
svchost.exe	SYSTEM	00	28,488 K
svchost.exe	NETWORK SERVICE	00	4,472 K
svchost.exe	SYSTEM	00	5,012 K
ati2evxx.exe	SYSTEM	00	2,380 K
lsass.exe	SYSTEM	00	1,724 K
services.exe	SYSTEM	00	4,364 K
winlogon.exe	SYSTEM	00	1,476 K
csrss.exe	SYSTEM	00	5,680 K
alg.exe	LOCAL SERVICE	00	3,544 K
smss.exe	SYSTEM	00	416 K
spoolsv.exe	SYSTEM	00	7,352 K
ati2evxx.exe	John	00	3,552 K
System	SYSTEM	00	220 K
System Idle Process	SYSTEM	98	16 K

☐ Show processes from all users   End Process

Processes: 48   CPU Usage: 2%   Commit Charge: 706M / 3943M

Windows Task Manager is now in compact mode.

Image Name	User Name	CPU	Mem Usage
Acrobat.exe	John	00	43,512 K
acrotray.exe	John	00	3,148 K
aim6.exe	John	00	67,484 K
alg.exe	LOCAL SERVICE	00	3,544 K
aolsoftware.exe	John	00	6,548 K
ati2evxx.exe	John	00	3,552 K
ati2evxx.exe	SYSTEM	00	2,380 K
csrss.exe	SYSTEM	00	5,748 K
ctfmon.exe	John	00	4,736 K
DefWatch.exe	SYSTEM	00	2,212 K
EXCEL.EXE	John	00	32,028 K
explorer.exe	John	01	13,152 K
GrooveMonitor.exe	John	00	6,684 K
hpwuschd2.exe	John	00	2,704 K
iexplore.exe	John	00	5,040 K
iexplore.exe	John	00	90,156 K
jqs.exe	SYSTEM	00	1,396 K
jusched.exe	John	00	7,424 K
lsass.exe	SYSTEM	00	1,156 K
Rtvscan.exe	SYSTEM	00	38,520 K
searchindexer.exe	SYSTEM	00	26,240 K
services.exe	SYSTEM	00	4,364 K
SMAgent.exe	SYSTEM	00	1,728 K
SMax4.exe	John	00	4,416 K
SMax4PNP.exe	John	00	4,524 K
smss.exe	SYSTEM	00	416 K
Snagit32.exe	John	00	28,004 K
SnagitEditor.exe	John	00	41,844 K
SnagPriv.exe	John	00	3,028 K
spoolsv.exe	SYSTEM	00	7,356 K

☐ Show processes from all users   End Process

Click **Image Name**.

Image Name	User Name	CPU	Mem Usage
WINWORD.EXE	John	00	61,268 K
winlogon.exe	SYSTEM	00	2,168 K
WindowsSearch.exe	John	00	11,048 K
VPTray.exe	John	00	8,908 K
ViewpointService.exe	SYSTEM	00	2,440 K
UltraMonTaskbar.exe	John	00	3,456 K
UltraMon.exe	John	00	1,272 K
TSVNCache.exe	John	00	7,996 K
TscHelp.exe	John	00	3,432 K
taskmgr.exe	John	02	6,100 K
System Idle Process	SYSTEM	98	16 K
System	SYSTEM	00	220 K
svchost.exe	LOCAL SERVICE	00	6,032 K
svchost.exe	LOCAL SERVICE	00	3,928 K
svchost.exe	NETWORK SERVICE	00	3,512 K
svchost.exe	SYSTEM	00	28,468 K
svchost.exe	NETWORK SERVICE	00	4,484 K
svchost.exe	SYSTEM	00	5,012 K
spoolsv.exe	SYSTEM	00	7,356 K
SnagPriv.exe	John	00	3,028 K
SnagitEditor.exe	John	00	43,684 K
Snagit32.exe	John	00	28,020 K
smss.exe	SYSTEM	00	416 K
SMax4PNP.exe	John	00	4,524 K
SMax4.exe	John	00	4,416 K
SMAgent.exe	SYSTEM	00	1,728 K
services.exe	SYSTEM	00	4,364 K
searchprotocolhost.exe	SYSTEM	00	6,688 K
searchindexer.exe	SYSTEM	00	26,716 K
searchfilterhost.exe	LOCAL SERVICE	00	4,880 K

☐ Show processes from all users   End Process

Click **Image Name** again.

What effect does this have on the columns?

Image Name	User Name	CPU	Mem Usage
System Idle Process	SYSTEM	99	16 K
System	SYSTEM	00	220 K
smss.exe	SYSTEM	00	416 K
UltraMon.exe	John	00	1,272 K
jqs.exe	SYSTEM	00	1,396 K
SMAgent.exe	SYSTEM	00	1,728 K
lsass.exe	SYSTEM	00	2,048 K
winlogon.exe	SYSTEM	00	2,168 K
DefWatch.exe	SYSTEM	00	2,212 K
ati2evxx.exe	SYSTEM	00	2,380 K
ViewpointService.exe	SYSTEM	00	2,440 K
hpwuschd2.exe	John	00	2,704 K
SnagPriv.exe	John	00	3,028 K
acrotray.exe	John	00	3,148 K
TscHelp.exe	John	00	3,432 K
UltraMonTaskbar.exe	John	00	3,456 K
svchost.exe	NETWORK SERVICE	00	3,516 K
alg.exe	LOCAL SERVICE	00	3,544 K
ati2evxx.exe	John	00	3,552 K
svchost.exe	LOCAL SERVICE	00	3,928 K
services.exe	SYSTEM	00	4,364 K
SMax4.exe	John	00	4,416 K
svchost.exe	NETWORK SERVICE	00	4,484 K
SMax4PNP.exe	John	00	4,524 K
ctfmon.exe	John	00	4,736 K
searchfilterhost.exe	LOCAL SERVICE	00	4,920 K
svchost.exe	SYSTEM	00	5,012 K
iexplore.exe	John	00	5,080 K
csrss.exe	SYSTEM	00	5,764 K
svchost.exe	LOCAL SERVICE	00	6,032 K

☐ Show processes from all users   End Process

Click **Mem Usage**.

What affect does this have on the columns?

Double-click the outside border again for tabs mode.

Step 2

Open a browser.

NOTE: Firefox is used in this lab. However, any browser will work. Just substitute your browser name whenever you see the word Firefox.

Return to the **Windows Task Manager**.

Click **Image Name** so the list is in alphabetical order and select **firefox.exe**.

Right-click **firefox.exe > Set Priority**.

What is the default priority for the browser?

Set the priority to **Above Normal**.

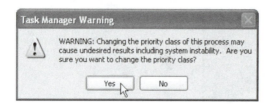

Click **Yes** in the Task Manager Warning window.

Step 3

Expand the width of the **Windows Task Manager** window.

Click **View > Select Columns**.

Place a check mark next to **Base Priority** and click **OK**.

Click **Base Pri**.

Which image name has a base priority of N/A?

List one image name that has a base priority of Above Normal?

Step 4

Reset Firefox.exe base priority to **Normal > Yes**.

Click **View > Select Columns > ** uncheck **Base Priority > OK**.

Close **Firefox**.

Is Firefox listed as a process?

Step 5

Click **Start > Control Panel > Regional and Language Options**.

The **Regional and Language Options** window appears.

What regional options format is being used?

Click **Customize**.

What are the tabs that can be customized?

Click **Cancel**.

Click the dropdown menu in **Standards and formats** area. Select **Belarusian**.

Notice the changes to the output in the **Samples** fields.

Click the dropdown menu in the **Standards and formats** area.

Return the setting to the original format.

Click **Details** on the **Language** tab.

What is the default input language?

Click **Cancel > Cancel** to close the **Regional and Language Options** window.

Step 6

Right-click the **Taskbar**.

Select **Toolbars > Language bar** to ensure that the **Language bar** is shown in the **Taskbar**.

Right-click the **Language bar** in the **Taskbar.**

Select **Settings**.

What is the Default input language?

Part 4: Managing Windows XP System Performance

In this part of the lab, you will manage and monitor Windows XP system performance.

Recommended Equipment

*   A computer running Windows XP Professional

Step 1

Log on to Windows as an administrator.

Click **Start > Control Panel > Administrative Tools > Computer Management >** expand **Services and Applications**.

Select **Services**.

Expand the **Computer Management** window so you see the **Help and Support** service.

What is the Status of the service?

Right-click the **Help and Support** service. Select **Properties**.

The **Help and Support Properties (Local Computer)** window appears.

Click **Stop**.

When disabling a service, to free up system resources, it is important to understand how the overall system operation will be affected.

When the **Service Control** window closes, set the **Startup type** field to **Disabled**, and click **Apply**.

Click **Start > Help and Support**.

The **Help and Support Error** window appears.

Help and Support Error ☒

Windows cannot open Help and Support because a system service is not running.

To fix this problem, start the service named 'Help and Support'.

OK

Why will Help and Support not start?

What must be done to correct the error?

Click **OK**.

What steps must be followed to start the Help and Support service?

Start the Help and Support service.

Click **OK**.

Click **Start > Help and Support**.

Did the **Help and Support Center** window appear?

Close the **Help and Support Center** window.

Step 2

Make sure the Computer Management window is open.

Expand **Event Viewer**. Select **System**.

Double-click the most recent Error event. Error events are displayed as a white X in a red circle icon.

The **Event Properties** window appears.

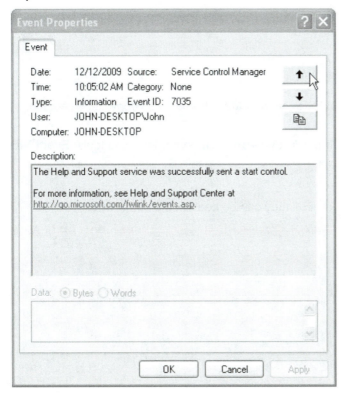

Why was helpsvc not started?

Click the **up arrow** button.

What has happened to the Help and Support service?

Click the **up arrow** button.

What has happened to the Help and Support service?

Close all open windows.

Step 3

Press **Ctrl-Alt-Delete**. When the **Windows Task Manager** window appears, select the **Performance** tab.

Click **Start > Control Panel > Administrative Tools**. Open the following tools: **Event Viewer** and **Performance**.

Close the **Administrative Tools** window.

Resize and position all three windows so they can be seen at the same time.

Step 4

Select the **Performance window**.

Expand **Performance Logs and Alerts**. Right-click **Counter Logs > New Log Settings**.

In the Name field, type **Memory Counter**.

Click **OK**.

When the **Memory Counter** window appears, click **Add Counters**.

Set the **Performance object** field to **Memory**.

Set the **Select counters from list** field to **Available Mbytes**. Click **Add > Close**.

Change the **Interval** field to **5**.

Select the **LogFiles** tab.

Set the **Log file type** field to **Text File (Tab delimited)**.

Click **Configure**.

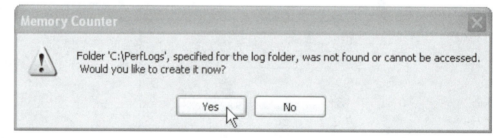

What is the default location for the log files?

Click **OK** to close the **Configure Log Files** window.

A folder not found information window appears. Click **Yes** to create the folder.

Select the **Schedule** tab.

Keep the default settings and click **OK**.

In the **Performance window**, click **Counter Logs**.

The Memory Counter log icon turns green once it has started.

Step 5

Select the Windows Task Manager window.

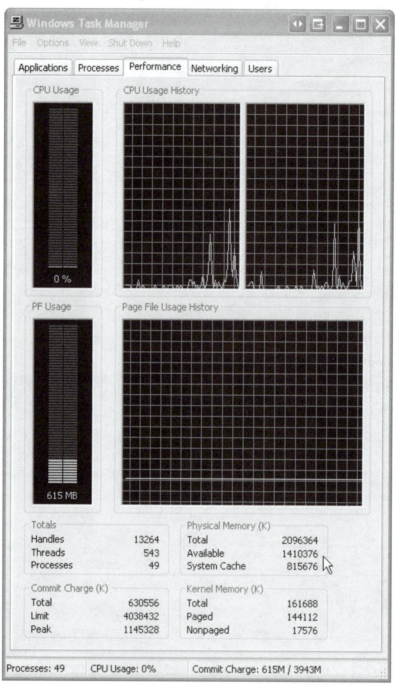

What amount of Physical Memory (K) is available?

Subtract about 10 MB of the available memory. Example: 1410376 – 10000 = 1400376.

How much available memory is left over?

Step 6

Make sure the **Performance** window is active.

Right-click **Alerts > New Alert Settings**.

In the Name field, type **Memory Alert**, then click **OK**.

When the **Memory Alert** window appears, click **Add**.

Set the **Performance object** field to **Memory**.

Set the **Select counters from list** field to **Available Mbytes**. Click **Add > Close**.

Set the following field values for the **General** tab:

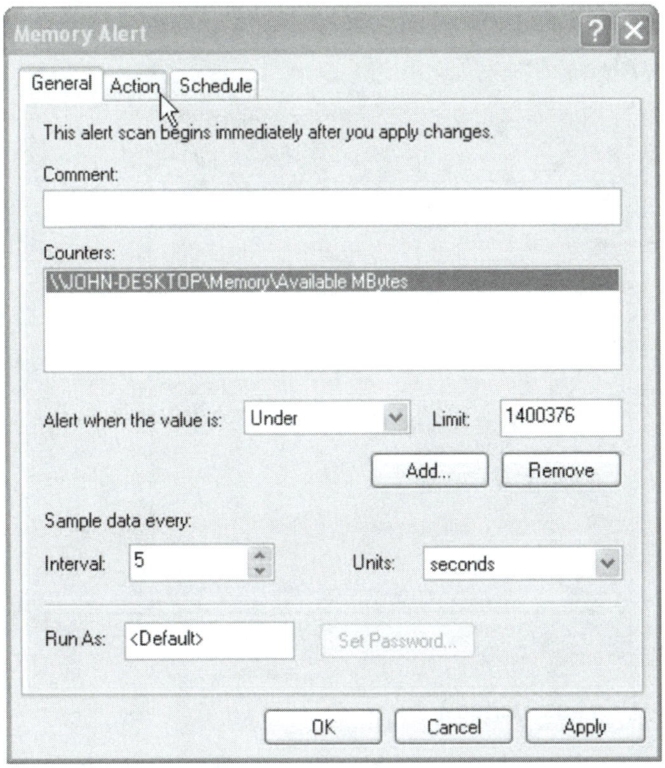

Alert when the value is: **Under**

Limit: **enter physical memory minus 10MB** (see step 5). Example – 1400376

Interval: **5**

Units: **seconds**

Select the **Action** tab.

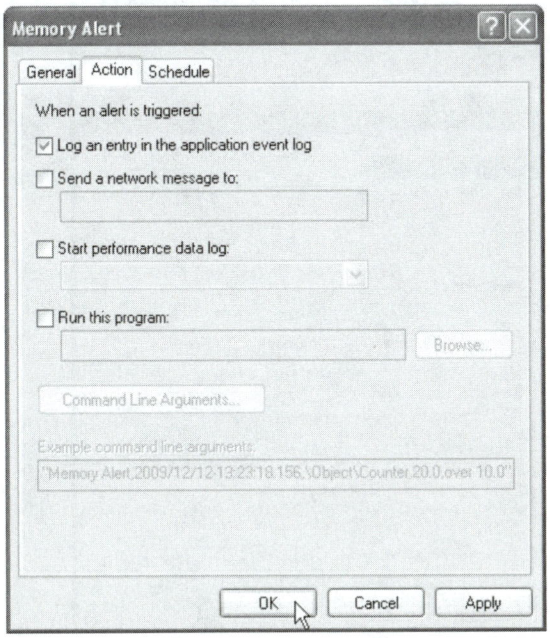

Click **OK** to keep default settings.

In the **Performance** window, click **Alerts**.

How can you tell that the Memory Alert has started?

Step 7

To force the computer to use some of the available memory, open and close a browser. Example: Internet Explorer or FireFox.

Right-click the **Memory Alert** icon **> Stop**.

Notice the Memory Alert icon has changed to a red color.

Select **Counter Logs**.

Right-click the **Memory Counter** icon and select **Stop**.

How can you tell the Memory Counter has stopped?

Step 8

Make sure the **Event Viewer** window is active.

Select **Application**, and double-click the event at the top of the list.

Does the event indicate that the available MBytes has tripped the alert threshold?

If you answered yes to the above question, what was the counter value that tripped the alert event?

If you answered no, click the down arrow a few times until you find the alert event. If you do not find an alert event ask the instructor for assistance.

Close the **Event Properties** window, click **OK**.

Step 9

Click **Start > My Computer >** double-click drive **C: > PerfLogs**.

Double-click **Memory Counter** file.

What does the column on the right show?

Step 10

Close the Memory Counter file, PerfLogs folder, and Windows Task Manager.

In the **Event Viewer** window click **Application > Action > Clear All Events.** Click **No** when you are asked to save the events to a file.

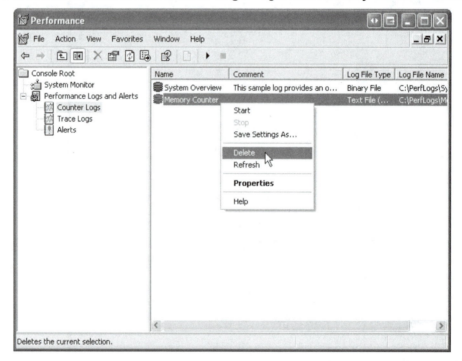

In the **Performance** window, click **Counter Logs** > right-click **Memory Counter > Delete**.

Select **Alerts > Memory Alert >** right-click **Memory Alert > Delete**.

Open drive **C:**.

Right-click the **PerfLogs** folder.

Click **Delete > Yes**.

Close all open windows.

Part 5: Managing Windows XP Remote Access

In this part of the lab, you will remotely connect to a computer, examine device drivers, and provide remote assistance.

Recommended Equipment

*   Two computers running Windows XP that are directly connected to each other or through a switch or hub.

*   The two computers must be part of the same Workgroup and on the same subnet.

Step 1

Log on to Computer2 as a member of the administrator group. Ask your instructor for the user name.

Click **Start > Control Panel > System**.

When the **System Properties** window appears, select the **Remote** tab.

In the **Remote Desktop** area, place a check mark in the box next to **Allow users to connect remotely to this computer**, and click **Apply**.

In the **Remote Desktop** area, click **Select Remote Users**.

Which user already has remote access?

Since you will use this account to gain remote access, you do not need to add any users, click **Cancel**.

Close the **Control Panel** window.

Move to Computer1.

Step 2

Log on to Computer1 as a member of the administrator group. Ask your instructor for the user name.

Click **Start > All Programs > Accessories > Remote Desktop Connection**.

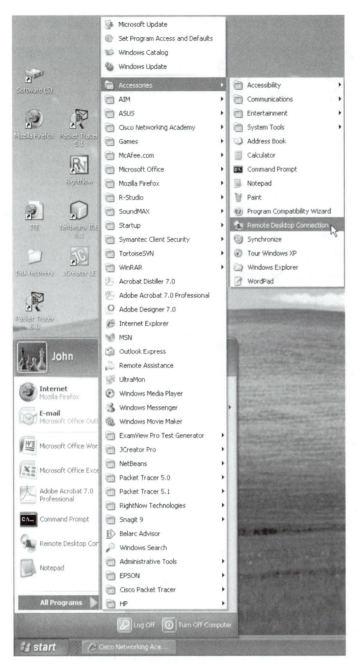

When the **Remote Desktop Connection** window appears, type **Computer2** in the **Computer** field and click **Connect**.

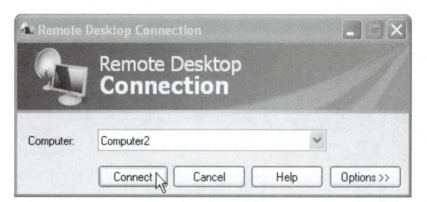

In the **User name** field, type in the account name you used to log on to Computer2. For example: **John_Computer2**.

In the **Password** field, type the password for **John_Computer2**.

NOTE: The user account must have a password.

Click **OK**.

What happened to the desktop of Computer2?

What happened to the desktop of Computer1?

Step 3

On Computer1, right-click the desktop of **Computer2 > New > Folder >** name the folder **Remote Permission**.

Right-click the **Remote Permission** folder **> Sharing and Security**.

Click the **Share this folder** radio button. Click **Apply**.

Click the **Security** tab. Make sure the user name from Computer1 is listed in Computer2. If it is not, create and add the user name.

Click **OK**.

Click **Start > Disconnect**.

When the **Disconnect Windows** window appears, click **Disconnect**.

When the **Your Remote Desktop session has ended** message appears, click **OK**.

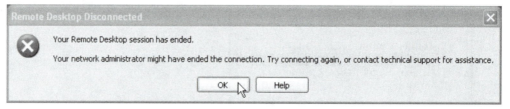

Click **Close** to exit the **Remote Desktop Connection** window.

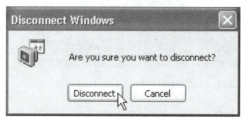

Step 4

Log on to Computer2.

Select the **System Properties** window.

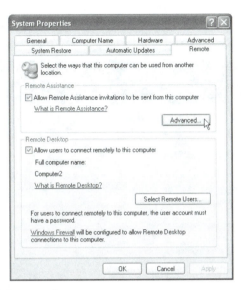

Click **Advanced**.

The **Remote Assistance Settings** window appears.

Make sure there is a check mark in the **Remote control** checkbox, set the invitation to **1 Hours**, and then click **OK**.

When the **System Properties** window appears, click **Apply**.

Step 5

On Computer2, click **Start > All Programs > Remote Assistance**.

The **Help and Support Center** window appears.

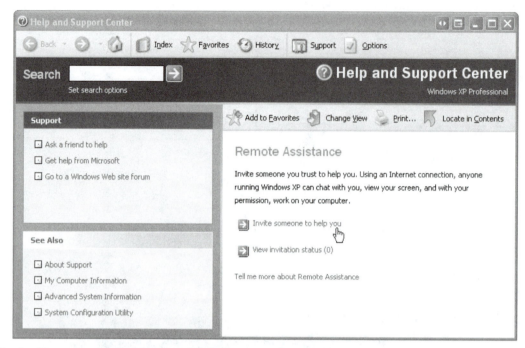

Click the **Invite someone to help you** link.

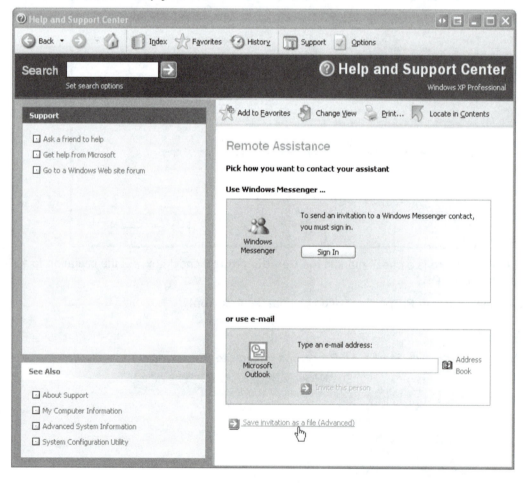

Which methods can you use to contact someone for assistance?

Click the **Save invitation as a file (Advanced)** link.

The **Remote Assistance – Save Invitation** window appears.

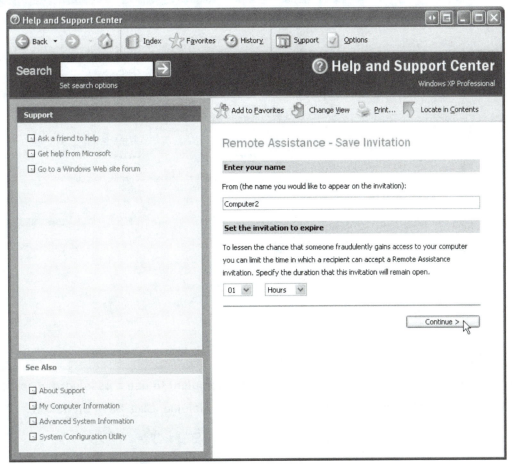

Type **Computer2** in the **Enter your name** field.

How long will the invitation remain open?

Click **Continue**.

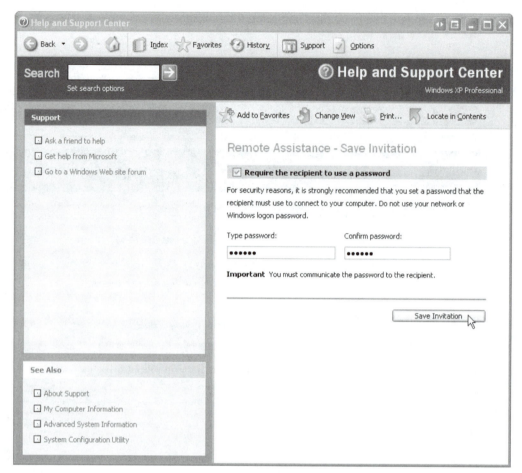

Make sure there is a check mark in the **Require the recipient to use a password** checkbox.

Type the password **HelpMe** and confirm the password **HelpMe**. Click **Save Invitation**.

Navigate to the folder **Remote Permission**.

What is the default file name?

What file type extension does the file have?

Click **Save**.

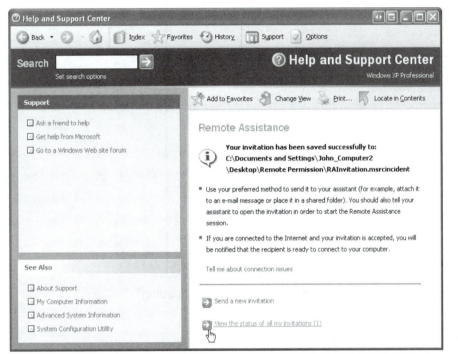

When the **Remote Assistance** window appears, click the **View the status of my invitation (1)** link.

The **View or change your invitation** window appears.

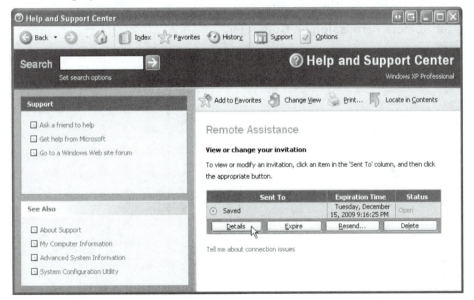

Click the **Saved** radio button. Click **Details**.

What advice is provided below the **Password Protected?** heading?

Click **Close**.

Close the **Help and Support Center** window.

Step 6

On Computer1, click **Start > My Network Place**.

Open the folder **Remote Permission on Computer2**.

Open the file **RAInvitation**.

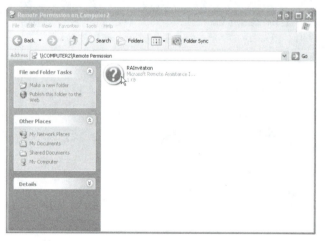

When the **Remote Assistance** window appears, type in the password **HelpMe**, and click **Yes**.

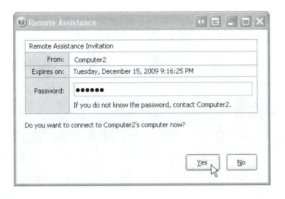

Step 7

On Computer2, answer **Yes** to allow access to the computer.

Read the message in the **Connection Status** area.

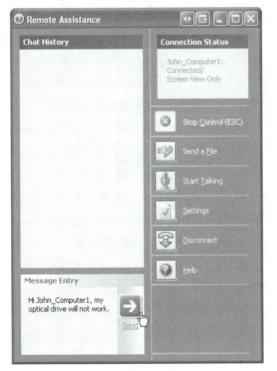

What is the connection status?

In the **Message Entry** field, type **Hi John_ Computer1, my optical drive will not work. >** click
Send.

Step 8

On Computer1, click the **Take Control** button in the **Remote Assistance** main menu.

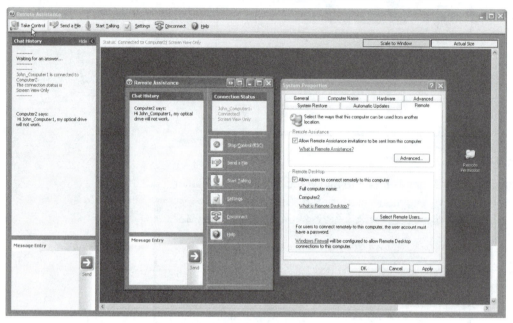

Step 9

On Computer2, click **Yes**.

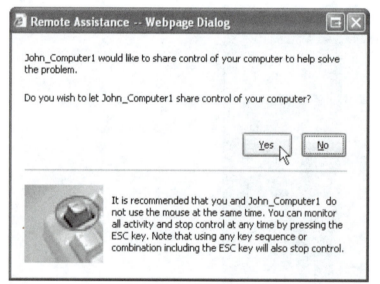

Step 10

Computer1:

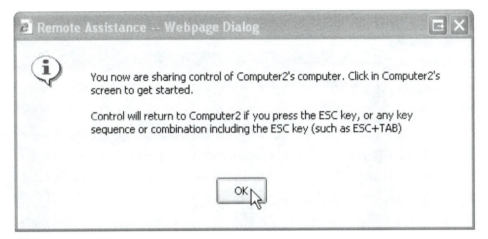

What must you do to activate the screen for Computer2?

What key must you press to return control back to Computer2?

Click **OK**.

Select the **System Properties** window for Computer2.

NOTE: If the Computer2 System Properties window is closed, you need to open it before you continue.

On the **Hardware** tab, click **Device Manager**.

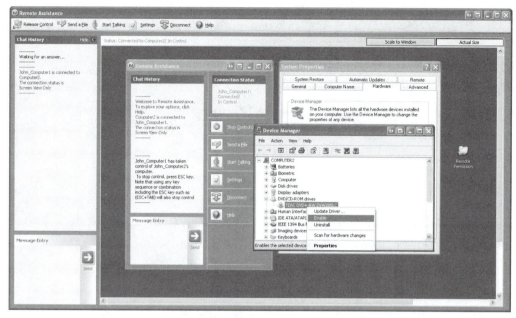

Right-click the **optical drive** with a red **X > Enable**.

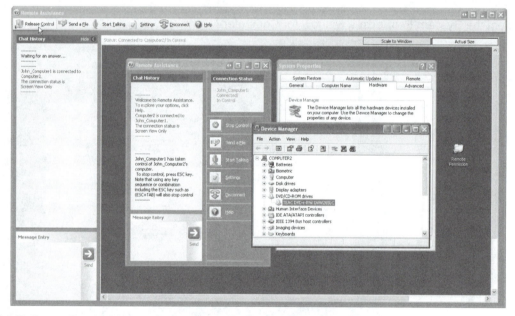

Click the **Release Control** button in the **Remote Assistance** main menu.

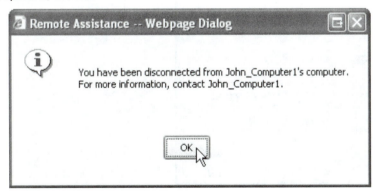

Click the **Disconnect** button in **Remote Assistance** main menu.

Click **OK**.

Close all open windows.

Step 11

On Computer2, click **OK**.

Click on the **Device Manager** window.

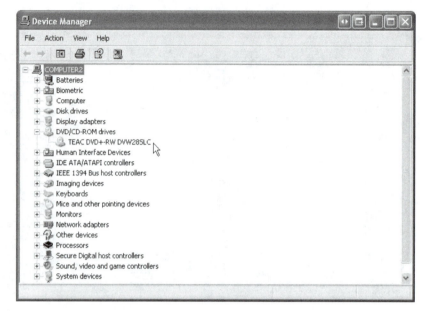

Does the optical drive have a red **X**?

Close the **Device Manager** window and the **Remote Assistance** window.

Delete the **Remote Permission** folder.

Select the **System Properties** window.

Remove the check mark from **Allow users to connect remotely to this computer > OK**.

12.2.4 Optional Lab: Customize Settings in Windows Vista

Introduction

This lab is comprised of five parts. This lab is designed to be completed in multiple lab sessions.

Part 1: Managing Virtual Memory, Startup Options, and Windows Update in Windows Vista

In this part of the lab, you will customize Virtual Memory settings. You will customize the Startup Folder and RunOnce Key in the Registry. You will change the default Windows Update option.

Recommended Equipment

- A computer running Windows Vista
- Internet access

Step 1

Log on to Windows as an Administrator.

Click **Start > Computer**.

The **Computer** window appears.

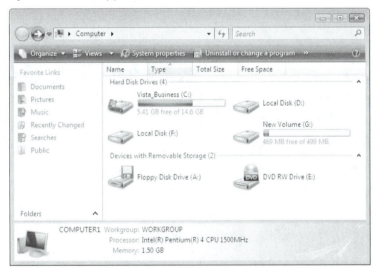

Step 2

Double-click the **Local Disk (D:)** drive.

Click **Format disk > Continue** to confirm the drive D: is to be formatted.

Step 3

The **Format Local Disk (D:)** window appears.

Select **NTFS** in the **File system** drop-down menu.

Click **Start**.

A warning window appears.

Click **OK**.

Windows formats the drive.

When the **Format Complete** message appears, click **OK**.

The **Format Local Disk (D:)** window re-appears.

Click **Close**.

Close all open windows.

Step 4

Click **Start > Control Panel > System > Advanced system settings**.

The **System Properties** window appears.

Select the **Advanced** tab and then click **Settings** in the **Performance** area.

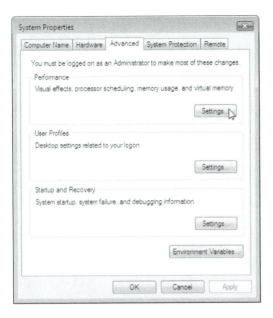

Step 5

The **Performance Options** window appears.

Click the **Advanced** tab.

What is the current size of the Virtual Memory (paging file)?

Click **Change** in the **Virtual Memory** area.

The **Virtual Memory** window appears.

Remove the check mark from **Automatically manage paging file size for all drives**.

What **Drive [Volume Label]** contains the paging file?

Choose the **D:** drive.

Click the **Custom size** radio button.

Look at the recommended size in the **Total paging file size for all drives** section of the **Virtual Memory** window.

Type the recommended file size in the **Initial size (MB):** field.

Type the recommended file size again in the **Maximum size (MB):** field.

Click **Set**.

Select the **C:** drive.

Click the **No paging file** radio button, and then click **Set**.

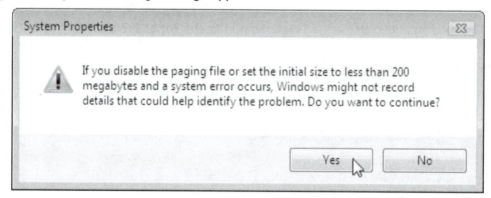

The **System Properties** warning message appears.

Click **Yes** to continue.

Click **OK** to accept the new virtual memory settings.

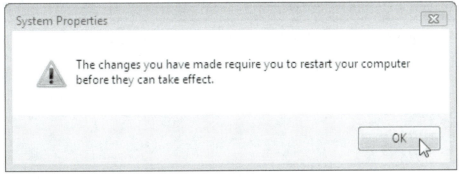

The **System Properties** restart warning message appears.

Click **OK**.

The **Performance Options** message window appears.

Click **OK**.

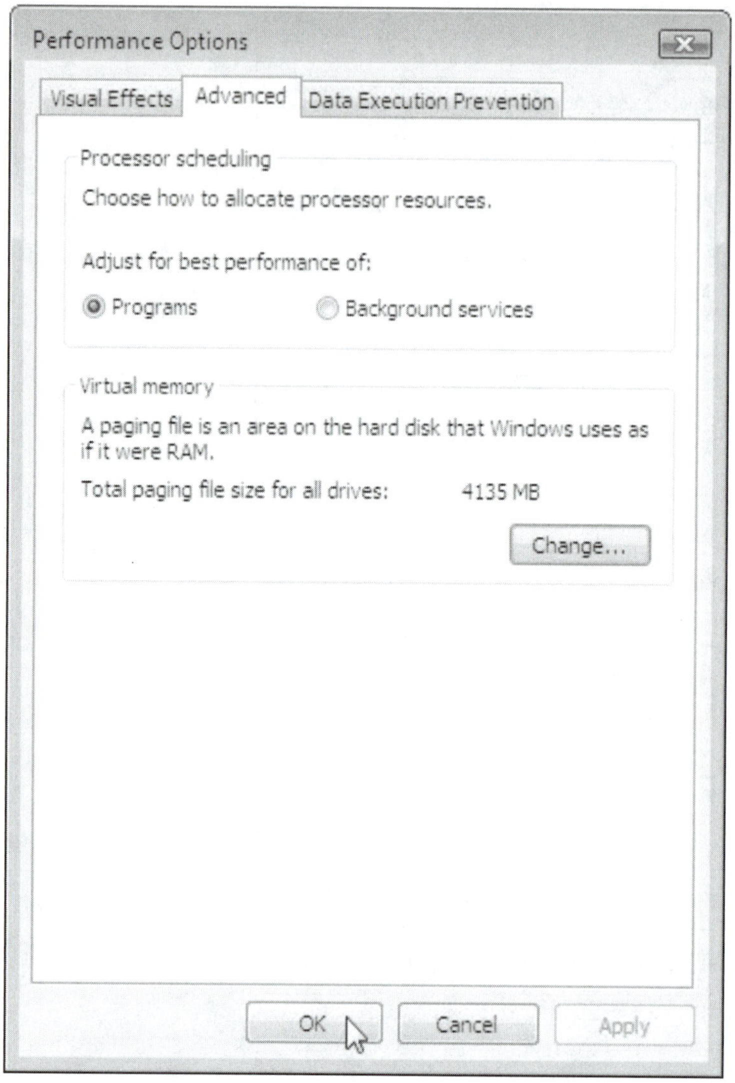

The **System Properties** message window appears.

Click **OK**.

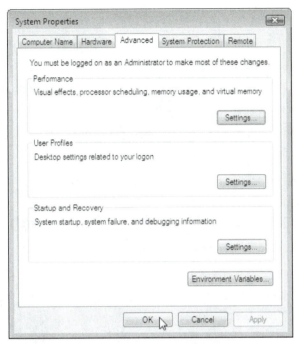

The **You must restart your computer to apply these changes** message appears, click **Restart Now**.

Step 6

Log on to Windows as an Administrator.

Open the **Virtual Memory** window.

What **Drive [Volume Label]** contains the paging file?

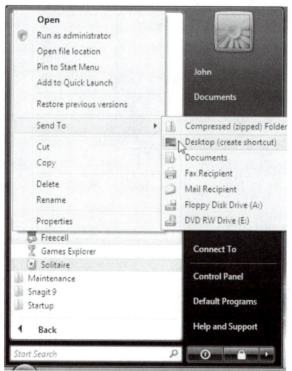

Click **Cancel** to close all open windows.

Step 7

Click **Start > All Programs > Games >** right-click **FreeCell > Send To > Desktop (create shortcut)**.

Step 8

Click and drag the shortcut **FreeCell** icon to the **Start** button.

The **Start menu** appears.

Do not release the shortcut icon.

Drag the icon to **All Programs**.

The **All Programs** menu appears.

Drag the icon to the bottom of the **Startup** folder.

When a blue arrow appears next to the FreeCell shortcut icon, release the icon.

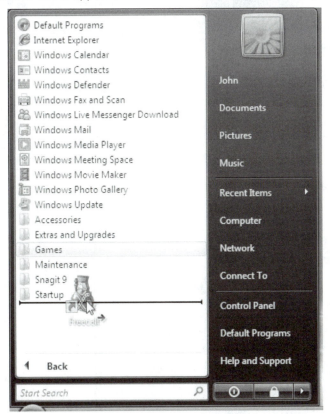

Click **Startup**.

You should see the FreeCell icon listed below Startup.

Step 9

Log off Windows.

Log on to Windows as an Administrator.

What happens when you log in?

Close the Freecell application.

Step 10

Click **Start > Start Search** > type **run**.

Type **regedit** In the Open: field > **OK > Continue**.

CAUTION: Incorrect changes to the registry can cause system errors and/or system instability.

The **Registry Editor** window appears.

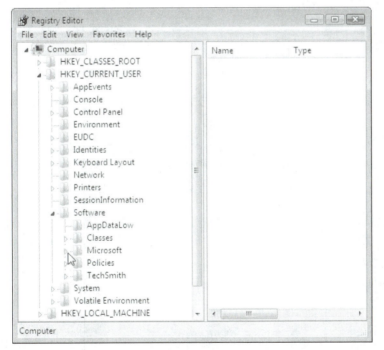

Expand the **HKEY_CURRENT_USER** Key.

Expand the **Software** Key.

Expand the **Microsoft** Key.

Expand the **Windows** Key.

Expand the **CurrentVersion** Key.

Select the **RunOnce** Key.

Right-click anywhere in the white space on the right side of the window.

Hover over **New** and select **String Value**.

Click anywhere in the white space of the window.

Right-click **New Value #1 > Rename**.

Type **Solitaire** and press **Enter**.

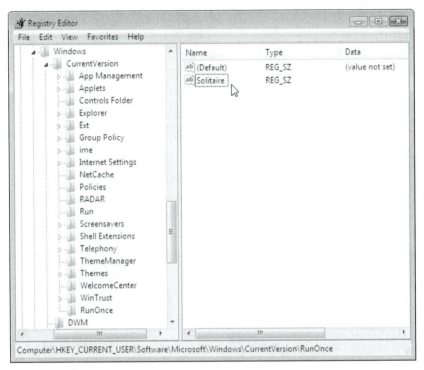

Right-click **Solitaire > Modify**.

Type **C:\Program Files\Microsoft Games\Solitaire\Solitaire.exe** in the Value data field.

Click **OK**.

Close the **Registry Editor** window.

Step 11

Log off Windows.

Log on to Windows as an Administrator.

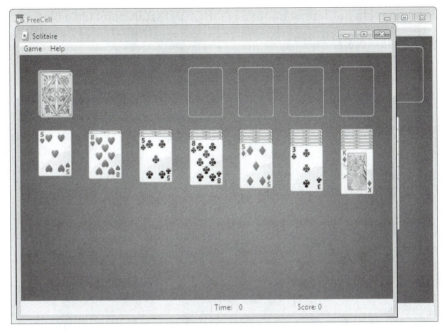

What happens when you log in?

Close all open Windows.

Step 12

Click **Start > Control Panel** > double-click **Windows Update > Change settings**.

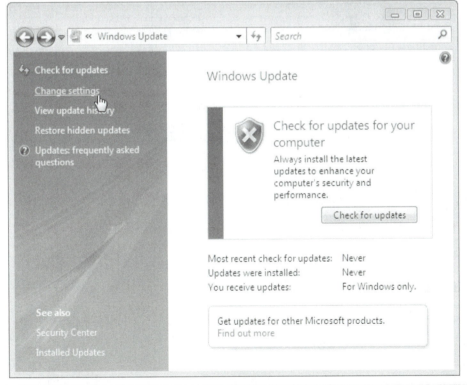

NOTE: The newest Windows Vista Update program has a different user interface. Both the original and new user interface are shown here.

Click the **Download updates but let me choose whether to install them** radio button.

Original Windows Vista Update program

New Windows Vista Update program

Click **OK > Continue**.

Step 13

Windows checks for updates.

The **New updates are available** balloon appears.

Double-click the **shield** icon in the system tray.

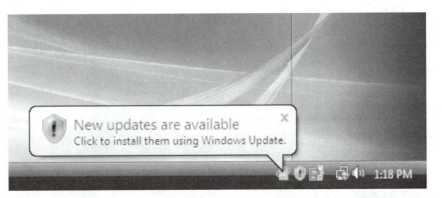

Click the link that shows how many updates have been downloaded. Example: **50 important updates are available**.

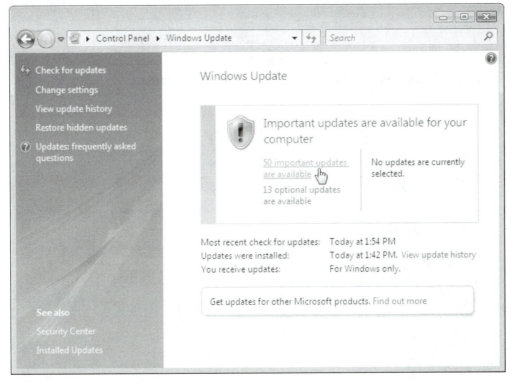

The **Select updates to install** window appears.

Place a check mark next to the important and optional updates to be installed, and then click **OK**.

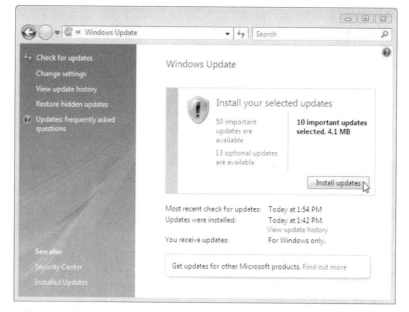

When the **Windows Update** window appears click **Install updates**.

The **Installing updates...** balloon appears.

You have successfully completed this part of the lab once the **Installing updates...** balloon appears.

Reboot the computer.

Part 2: Windows Vista Hard Drive Maintenance

In this part of the lab, you will examine the results after using Disk Check and Disk Defragmenter on a hard drive.

Recommended Equipment

- A computer running Windows Vista

Step 1

Log on to Windows as an administrator.

Start > Computer > double-click **New Volume (G:)**.

Right-click anywhere in the white space of the folder area for drive **G: > Properties > Tools** tab > **Check Now > Continue**.

The **Check Disk New Volume (G:)** window appears. Make sure there is not a check mark in either check box then click **Start**.

When the **Your device or disc was successfully scanned** screen appears, click the expand button next to **See details**.

Checking Disk New Volume (G:)

Your device or disc was successfully scanned

No problems were found on the device or disc. It is ready to use.

If you removed the device or disc before all files were fully written to it, parts of some files might still be missing. If so, go back to the source and recopy those files to your device or disc.

⌃ Hide details
Close

Volume label is New Volume.

CHKDSK is verifying files (stage 1 of 3)...
64 file records processed.

File verification completed.
0 large file records processed.

0 bad file records processed.

0 EA records processed.

0 reparse records processed.

CHKDSK is verifying indexes (stage 2 of 3)...
88 index entries processed.

Index verification completed.
0 unindexed files processed.

CHKDSK is verifying security descriptors (stage 3 of 3)...
64 security descriptors processed.

Security descriptor verification completed.
12 data files processed.

Windows has checked the file system and found no problems.

511999 KB total disk space.
328788 KB in 8 files.
16 KB in 14 indexes.
5099 KB in use by the system.
4608 KB occupied by the log file.
178096 KB available on disk.

4096 bytes in each allocation unit.

How many stages were processed?

Click **Close**.

Select the **Tools** tab, click **Check Now > Continue**. Remove the check mark next to **Automatically fix file system errors**. Place a check mark in the check box next to **Scan for and attempt recovery of bad sectors > Start**.

Check Disk New Volume (G:)

Check disk options

☐ Automatically fix file system errors
☑ Scan for and attempt recovery of bad sectors

Start   Cancel

When the **Your device or disc was successfully scanned** screen appears click the expand button next to **See details**.

Checking Disk New Volume (G:)

Your device or disc was successfully scanned

No problems were found on the device or disc. It is ready to use.

If you removed the device or disc before all files were fully written to it, parts of some files might still be missing. If so, go back to the source and recopy those files to your device or disc.

ⓐ Hide details   Close

Volume label is New Volume.

CHKDSK is verifying files (stage 1 of 5)...
  64 file records processed.

File verification completed.
  0 large file records processed.

  0 bad file records processed.

  0 EA records processed.

  0 reparse records processed.

CHKDSK is verifying indexes (stage 2 of 5)...
  88 index entries processed.

Index verification completed.
  0 unindexed files processed.

CHKDSK is verifying security descriptors (stage 3 of 5)...
  64 security descriptors processed.

Security descriptor verification completed.
  12 data files processed.

CHKDSK is verifying free space (stage 5 of 5)...
  44524 free clusters processed.

Free space verification is complete.
Windows has checked the file system and found no problems.

  511999 KB total disk space.
  328788 KB in 8 files.
      16 KB in 14 indexes.
    5099 KB in use by the system.
    4608 KB occupied by the log file.
  178096 KB available on disk.

What stages were processed?

Click **Close**.

Select the **Tools** tab, click **Check Now**.

Place a check mark in both check boxes then click **Start**.

Check Disk New Volume (G:)

Check disk options
  ☑ Automatically fix file system errors
  ☑ Scan for and attempt recovery of bad sectors

              Start   Cancel

An information window opens.

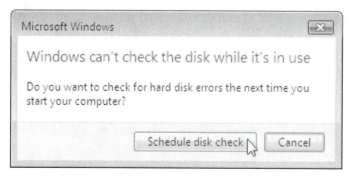

Why will Check Disk not start?

NOTE: This message is displayed because a boot partition will be scanned, or a non-boot partition that is going to be scanned is open.

Click **Schedule disk check** and then **OK** to close the **New Volume (G:) Properties** window.

Make sure drive **G:** stays open.

NOTE: To force CHKDSK to create a log file, when it scans a non-boot partition with no bad sectors, the non-boot partition drive must be open.

Click **Start >** hover over the **right arrow** button **> Restart**.

Step 2

The **Checking file system on G:** screen appears.

```
Checking file system on G:
The type of the file system is NTFS.
Volume label is New Volume.

A disk check has been scheduled.
Windows will now check the disk.

CHKDSK is verifying files (stage 1 of 5)...
  64 file records processed.
File verification completed.
  0 large file records processed.
  0 bad file records processed.
  0 EA records processed.
  0 reparse records processed.
CHKDSK is verifying indexes (stage 2 of 5)...
  88 index entries processed.
Index verification completed.
  0 unindexed files processed.
CHKDSK is verifying security descriptors (stage 3 of 5)...
  64 security descriptors processed.
Security descriptor verification completed.
  12 data files processed.
CHKDSK is verifying file data (stage 4 of 5)...
  48 files processed.
File data verification completed.
CHKDSK is verifying free space (stage 5 of 5)...
  121324 free clusters processed.
Free space verification is complete.
Windows has checked the file system and found no problems.

    511999 KB total disk space.
     21588 KB in 7 files.
        16 KB in 14 indexes.
         0 KB in bad sectors.
      5099 KB in use by the system.
      4608 KB occupied by the log file.
    485296 KB available on disk.

      4096 bytes in each allocation unit.
    127999 total allocation units on disk.
    121324 allocation units available on disk.
Windows has finished checking the disk.
. . . . .
```

How many stages in the scan are there?

What is being verified in each of the stages?

Were any problems found with the volume?

If so what are they?

Step 3

Log on to Windows as an administrator.

Start > Control Panel > Administrative Tools > Event Viewer > Continue. In the left pane expand **Windows Logs** > select **Application**.

Double-click the top event in the right pane. Click the black down arrow until the Disk Check event appears.

Which stages are shown as completed?

Close all open windows.

Step 4

Start > My Computer > right-click **drive (C:) > Properties >** select **Tools** tab > click **Defragment Now** button > **Continue**.

The **Disk Defragmenter** window appears.

Click **Defragment now**.

The **Disk Defragmenter: Defragment Now** window appears. Make sure there is a check mark only next to drive **(C:)**.

Click **OK**.

Windows starts defragmenting hard drive (C:).

When defragmenting is completed close all windows.

NOTE: It is not possible to view the detail of the defragmented hard drive through the GUI version of defragmenter.

Part 3: Managing Processes, and Regional and Language Settings in Windows Vista

In this part of the lab, you will examine regional and language settings, and explore how to manage processes in Task Manager.

Recommended Equipment

- A computer running Windows Vista

Step 1

Log on to Windows as an administrator.

Press keys **Ctrl-Alt-Delete** > click **Start Task Manager > Processes** tab.

Click **Show processes from all users**.

Double-click the border around the tabs.

Windows Task Manager is now in compact mode.

Click **Image Name**.

Click **Image Name** again.

What effect does this have on the columns?

Click **Memory (Private Working Set)**.

What affect does this have on the columns?

Double-click the outside border again to return to tabs mode.

Step 2

Open a browser.

NOTE: Firefox is used in this lab. However, any browser will work. Just substitute your browser name whenever you see the word Firefox.

Return to the **Windows Task Manager**.

Click **Image Name** so the list is in alphabetical order, then locate and select **firefox.exe**.

Right-click **firefox.exe > Set Priority**.

What is the default priority for the browser?

Set the priority to **Above Normal**.

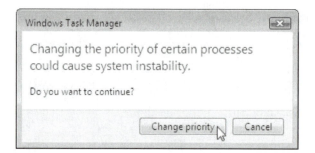

Click **Change priority** to the Windows Task Manager warning message.

Step 3

Expand the width of the **Windows Task Manager** window.

Click **View > Select Columns**.

Place a check mark next to **Base Priority** > click **OK**.

Click **Base Pri**.

Which image name has a base priority of N/A?

List one image name that has a base priority of Above Normal.

Step 4

Reset Firefox.exe base priority to **Normal > Change priority**.

Click **View > Select Columns** > uncheck **Base Priority > OK**.

Close Firefox.

Is Firefox listed as a process?

Step 5

Click **Start > Control Panel > Regional and Language Options**.

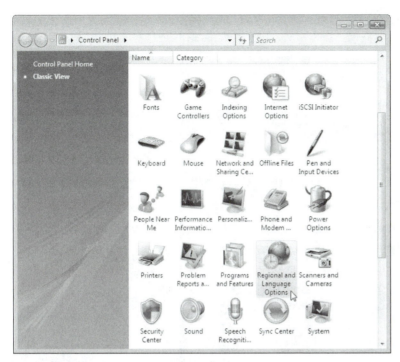

The **Regional and Language Options** appears.

What regional options format is being used?

Click **Customize**.

What are the tabs that can be customized?

Click **Cancel**.

Click the dropdown menu in **Current formats** area. Select **Belarusian**.

Notice the changes to the output in the **Example of how data is displayed using this format:** fields.

Click the dropdown menu in the **Current format** area.

Return the setting to the original format.

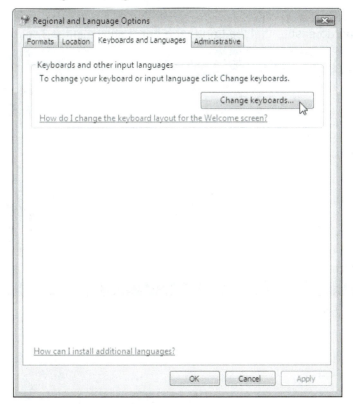

Click **Keyboard and Languages** tab > **Change keyboards**.

What is the default input language?

Click **Cancel > Cancel** to close **Regional and Language Options** window.

Step 6

Right-click the **Taskbar**.

Select **Toolbars > Language bar** to ensure that the **Language bar** is shown in the **Taskbar**.

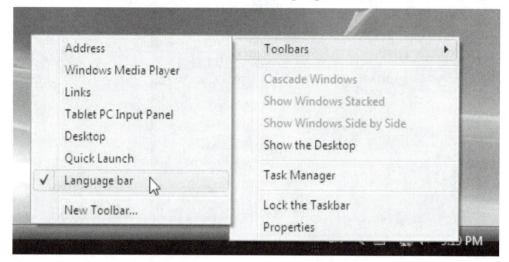

Right-click the **Language bar** in the **Taskbar.**

Select **Settings**.

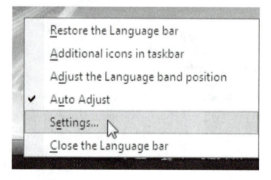

What is the Default input language?

Part 4: Managing Windows Vista System Performance

In this part of the lab, you will manage and monitor Windows Vista system performance.

Recommended Equipment

- A computer running Windows Vista

Step 1

Log on to Windows as an administrator.

Click **Start > Control Panel > Administrative Tools > Windows Defender**.

Click **Start > Control Panel > Administrative Tools > Computer Management > Continue >** expand **Services and Applications >** select **Services**.

Close the **Administrative Tools** window.

Resize and position both windows so they can be seen at the same time.

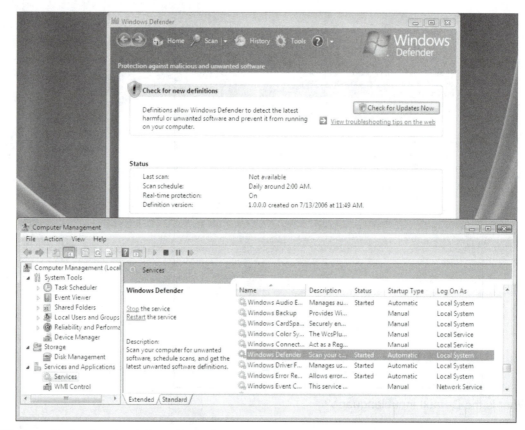

Can Windows Defender check for updates?

Scroll the **Computer Management** window so you see the **Windows Defender** service.

What is the Status of the service?

Right-click **Windows Defender** service > select **Stop**.

NOTE: The reason this service will be stopped is so you can easily see the results. When stopping a service, to free up system resources the service uses, it is important to understand how the overall system operation will be affected.

The **Service Control** window appears and closes.

Select the **Windows Defender** window so it is active.

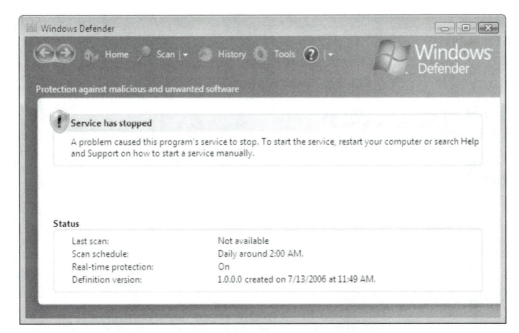

What must be done so Windows Defender can run?

What step must be followed to start the **Windows Defender** service?

Start the **Windows Defender** service.

Select the **Windows Defender** window so it is active.

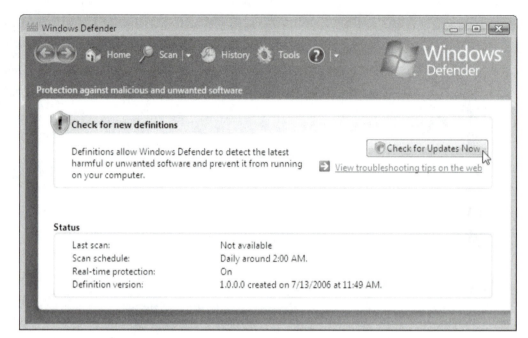

Can Windows Defender check for updates?

Close the **Windows Defender** window.

Step 2

Make sure the Computer Management window is open.

Expand **Event Viewer > Windows Logs >** select **System**.

Select the second event in the list.

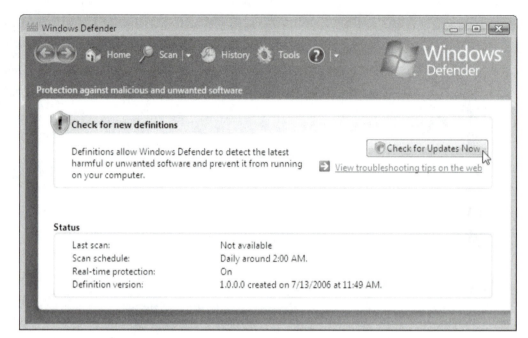

Look below the General tab then explain what has happened to the **Windows Defender** service.

Click the **up arrow** button on the keyboard or select the event above this one.

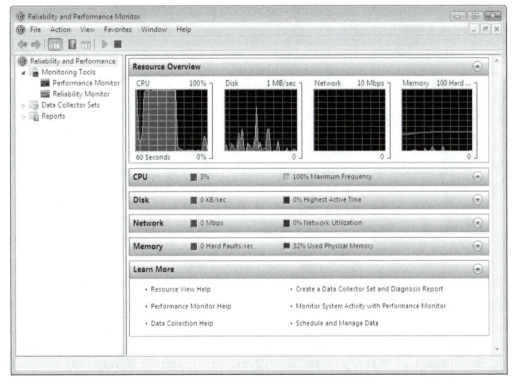

Look below the General tab then explain what has happened to the **Windows Defender** service.

Close all opened windows.

Step 3

Click **Start > Control Panel > Administrative Tools > Reliability and Performance Monitor > Continue**.

Expand **Data Collector Sets** > right-click **User Defined > New > Data Collector Set**.

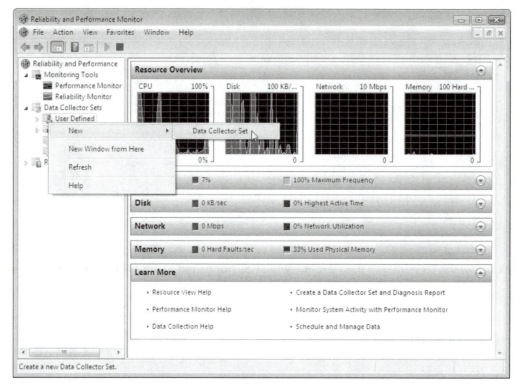

The Create new Data Collector Set window appears.

In the Name field, type **Memory Logs**. Select the **Create manually (Advanced)** radio button > **Next**.

Select **Performance counter > Next**.

Click **Add**.

From the list of available counters locate and expand **Memory**. Select **Available MBytes > Add**.

Click **OK**.

Set the Sample interval field to **4** seconds. Click **Next**.

Click **Browse**.

Select drive **(C:) > Make New Folder >** type **PerfLogs > OK**.

The **Create new Data Collector Set** window appears.

Click **Next**.

Click **Finish**.

Step 4

Expand **User Defined** > select **Memory Logs** > right-click **Data Collector01** > click **Properties**.

The **DataCollector01 Properties** window appears.

Change the **Log format:** field to **Comma Separated**.

Select the **File** tab.

What is the full path name to the example file name?

Click **OK**.

Step 5

Select the **Memory Logs** icon in the left pane of the **Reliability and Performance Monitor** window.

Click the **green arrow** icon to start the data collection set.

Step 6

To force the computer to use some of the available memory, open and close a browser.

Click the **black box** icon to stop the data collection set.

What change do you notice for the Memory Logs icon?

Step 7

Click **Start > Computer** > double-click drive **C:** > **PerfLogs > 00001 > Continue**.

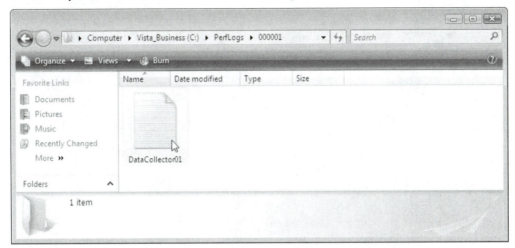

Double-click **DataCollector01** text file.

```
DataCollector01 - Notepad

File   Edit   Format   View   Help
"(PDH-CSV 4.0) (Pacific Standard Time)
(480)","\\COMPUTER1\Memory\Available MBytes"
"12/14/2009 18:28:35.016","1012"
"12/14/2009 18:28:38.937","1012"
"12/14/2009 18:28:42.937","1012"
"12/14/2009 18:28:46.937","1012"
"12/14/2009 18:28:50.937","1012"
"12/14/2009 18:28:54.937","1008"
"12/14/2009 18:28:58.937","1008"
"12/14/2009 18:29:02.937","1005"
"12/14/2009 18:29:06.937","1007"
"12/14/2009 18:29:10.937","1007"
"12/14/2009 18:29:14.937","1007"
"12/14/2009 18:29:18.937","1007"
"12/14/2009 18:29:22.937","1007"
"12/14/2009 18:29:26.937","1007"
"12/14/2009 18:29:30.937","1008"
"12/14/2009 18:29:34.937","1008"
"12/14/2009 18:29:38.937","1008"
"12/14/2009 18:29:42.937","1008"
"12/14/2009 18:29:46.937","1008"
"12/14/2009 18:29:50.937","1010"
"12/14/2009 18:29:54.937","1010"
"12/14/2009 18:29:58.937","1010"
```

What does the column farthest to the right show?

Step 8

Close the DataCollector01 text file and the window with the PerfLogs folder.

Select the **Reliability and Performance Monitor** window. Right-click **Memory Logs > Delete**.

Open drive **C: >** right-click the **PerfLogs** folder **> Delete > Yes**.

Close all open windows.

Part 5: Managing Windows Vista Remote Access

In this part of the lab, you will remotely connect to a computer, examine device drivers, and provide remote assistance.

Recommended Equipment

- Two computers running Windows Vista that are directly connected to each other or through a switch or hub.
- The two computers must be part of the same Workgroup and on the same subnet.

Step 1

Log on to Computer2 as a member of the administrator group. Ask your instructor for the user name.

Click **Start > Control Panel > System > Remote Settings**.

In the **Remote Desktop** area, select the radio button next to **Allow connections only from computers running Remote Desktop with Network Level Authentication (more secure)**.

If a message appears warring the computer is set to go to sleep, click the **Power Option** link and then change the settings to **Never > Save changes**.

Click **OK** to close the warning message.

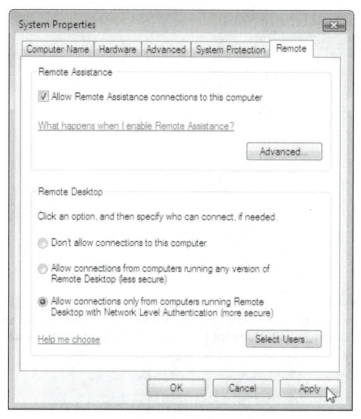

Click **Apply** in the **System Properties** window.

In the **Remote Desktop** area, click the **Select Users** button.

Which user already has remote access?

Since you will use this account to gain remote access, you do not need to add any users, click **Cancel**.

Click **Start > Control Panel > Windows Firewall > Change Settings**.

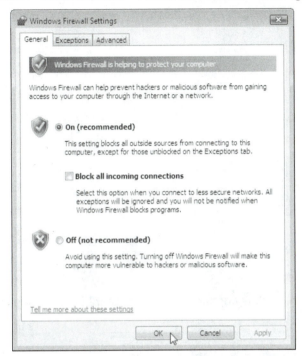

Make sure the **On (recommended)** radio button is selected then click **OK**.

Close the **Control Panel** window, the **Windows Firewall** window, and move to Computer1.

Step 2

Log on to Computer1 as an administrator or a member of the administrator group. Ask your instructor for the user name.

Click **Start > All Programs > Accessories > Remote Desktop Connection**.

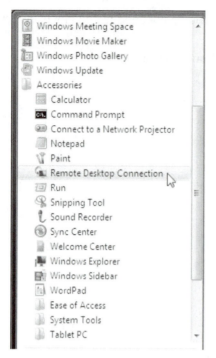

When the **Remote Desktop Connection** window appears, type **Computer2** in the **Computer** field and click **Connect**.

In the **User name** field, type the account name you used to log on to Computer2. For example: **John_Computer2**.

In the **Password** field, type the password for the user.

NOTE: The user account must have a password.

Click **OK**.

What happened to the desktop of Computer2?

What happened to the desktop of Computer1?

Step 3

From Computer1, right-click the desktop of **Computer2 > New > Folder >** name the folder
Remote Permission.

Right-click the **Remote Permission** folder **> Sharing > Advanced Sharing > Share this folder**
checkbox > keep the default name **Remote Permission > OK**.

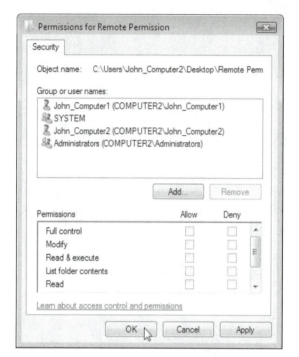

Click the **Security** tab. Make sure the user name from Computer1 is listed in Computer2. If it is not, create and add the user name.

Click **OK > Close**.

Click **Start > Disconnect**.

Step 4

Log on to Computer2.

Select the **System Properties** window.

Notice **Remote Assistance** is activated by default.

Click **Advanced**.

The **Remote Assistance Settings** window appears.

Make sure there is a check mark in the **Allow this computer to be controlled remotely** checkbox, set the invitation to **1 Hours**, place a check mark in the **Create invitations that can only be used from computers running Windows Vista or later** checkbox, and then click **OK**.

When the **System Properties** window appears, click **Apply**.

Step 5

On Computer2, click **Start > All Programs > Maintenance > Windows Remote Assistance**.

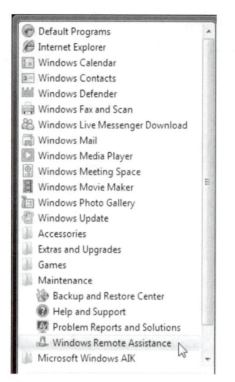

The **Do you want to ask for or offer help?** screen appears.

Click **Invite someone you trust to help you**.

The **How do you want to invite someone to help you?** screen appears.

Which methods can you use to contact someone for assistance?

Click the **Save invitation as a file**.

When the **Save the invitation as a file** screen appears, click **Browse**.

Locate the shared **Remote Permission** folder, and name the file **Invitation to Computer1.**

What type of extension does the file have?

Click **Save**.

When the **Save the invitation as a file** screen appears, type the password **HelpMe** and confirm the password **HelpMe**. Click **Finish**.

When the **Waiting for incoming connection** screen appears click **Settings**.

What key must you press to stop sharing control?

Which features are disabled with a Medium bandwidth usage?

Click **OK**.

Step 6

On **Computer1**, click **Start > Network >** double-click **Computer2**.

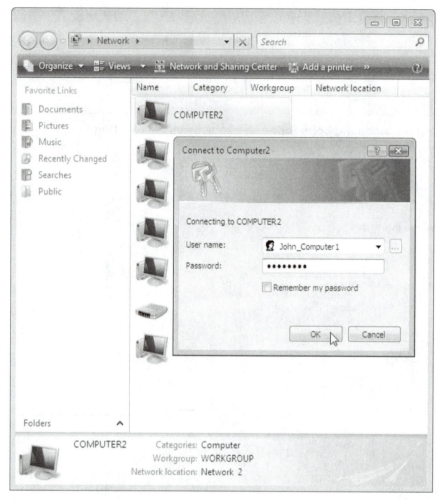

Log on with the user account from **Computer1**. Double-click the folder **Remote Permission** on **Computer2**. Double-click the file **Invitation to Computer1**.

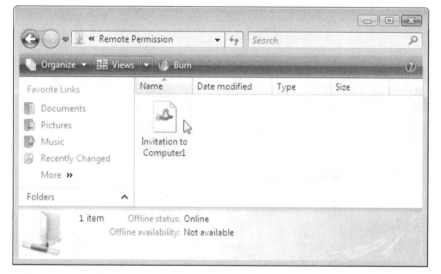

When the **Remote Assistance** window appears, type in the password **HelpMe**.

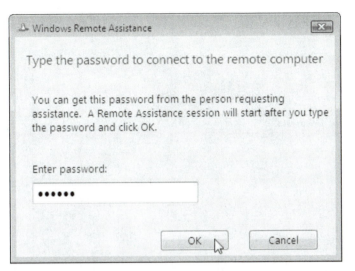

Click **OK**.

Step 7

From Computer2, answer **Yes** to allow access to the computer.

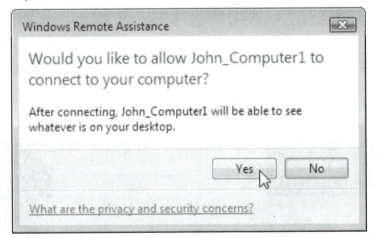

Select the **Windows Remote Assistance – Being helped by John_Computer1** window so it is activated.

Click **Chat**.

In the chat field type **Hi John_ Computer1, my optical drive will not work**. Click **Send**.

Step 8

From Computer1, click the **Request control** button in **Windows Remote Assistance** main menu.

Step 9

From Computer2, click the **Allow John_Computer1 to respond to User Account Control prompts** checkbox. Click **Yes**.

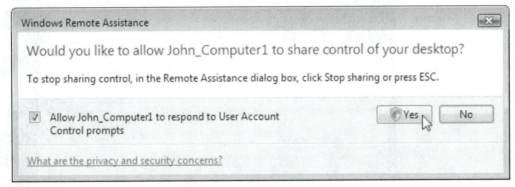

Step 10

From **Computer1**, select **System Properties** window for **Computer2**.

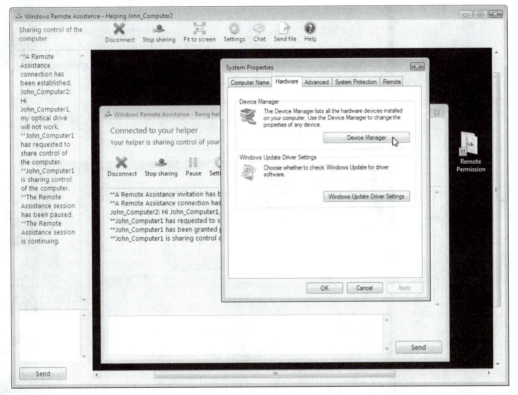

NOTE: If the **Computer2** System Properties window is closed, you need to open it before you continue.

Click **Hardware** tab > **Device Manager**.

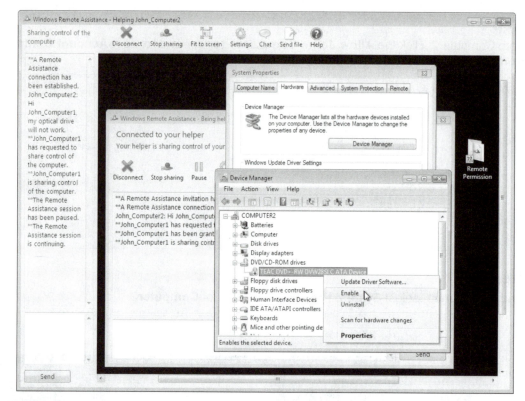

Right-click the **optical drive** that has a black down arrow. Select **Enable**.

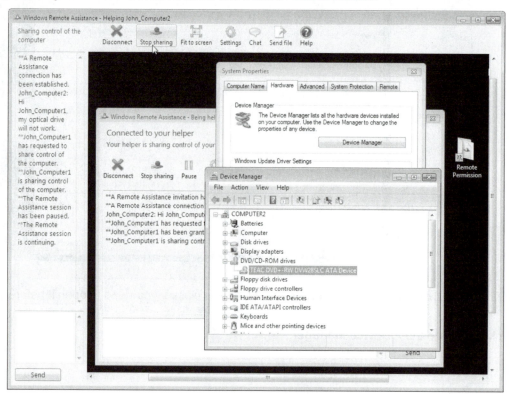

Click the **Stop Sharing** button in **Windows Remote Assistance** main menu.

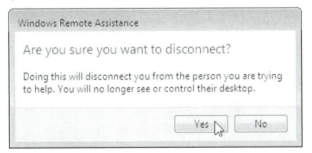

Click the **Disconnect** button in **Windows Remote Assistance** main menu.

Click **Yes**.

Close all open windows and log off **Computer1**.

Step 11

On **Computer2**, click **Yes**.

Click on **Device Manager** so it is activated.

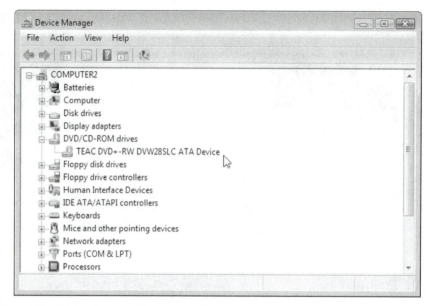

Does the optical drive have a black arrow?

Close the **Device Manager** window and the **Windows Remote Assistance** window.

Delete the **Remote Permission** folder.

Select the **System Properties** window. Place a check mark next to **Don't allow connection to this computer > OK**.

Log off **Computer2**.

12.2.5 Optional Lab: Install an Alternate Browser

Introduction

In this lab, you will install the Mozilla Firefox Web Browser.

Recommended Equipment

- A computer running Windows
- Internet access

Step 1

Click **Start > All Programs > Internet Explorer**.

In the **Address** field, type **www.mozilla.com**.

Press **Enter**.

Click the **Download Firefox – Free** link.

Step 2

The **File Download – Security Warning** window appears.

Click **Run**.

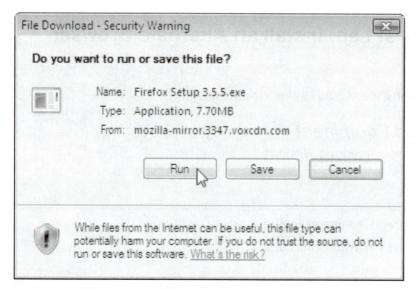

The Internet Explorer download window appears.

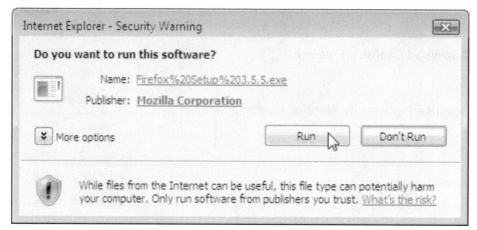

The Internet Explorer – Security Warning window may appear.

Click **Run > Continue**.

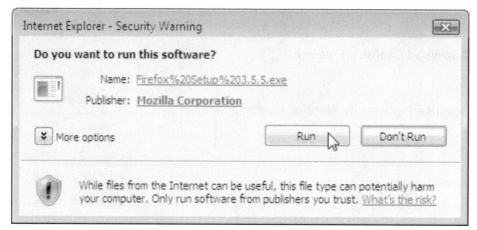

Step 3

The **Mozilla Firefox Setup** window appears.

Click **Next**.

The **Setup Type** window appears. The default is **Standard**.

Click **Next**.

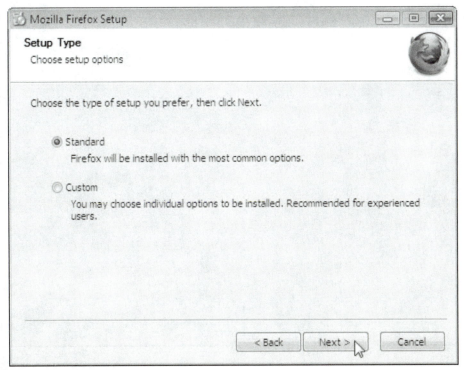

The **Summary** window appears.

Remove the check mark **from Use Firefox as my default web browser**, and then click **Install**.

The **Installing** window appears.

The **Completing the Mozilla Firefox Setup Wizard** window appears. The default is **Launch Mozilla Firefox now**.

Click **Finish**.

Step 4

The **Import Wizard** window appears. The default is **Microsoft Internet Explorer**.

Click **Next**.

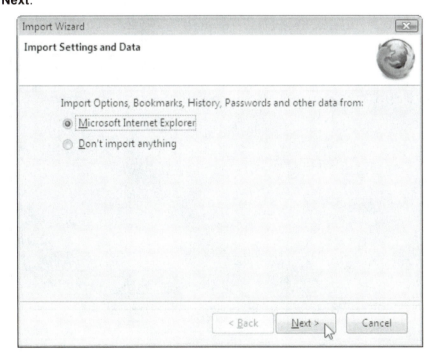

The **Home Page Selection** window appears. The default is **Firefox Start, a fast home page with built-in search**.

Click **Next**.

The **Import Wizard** window will appear.

Click **Finish**.

Step 5

The **Default Browser** window appears. The default is **Always perform this check when starting Firefox**.

Click **No**.

Click **Tools > Options**.

The **Options** window appears.

Click **Browse** in the **Downloads** area.

The **Browse For Folder** window appears.

Choose **Documents**, and then click **OK**.

The **Browse For Folder** window closes.

Click **OK**.

Note the Mozilla Firefox icon on your desktop.

12.4.1 Lab: Schedule Task Using GUI and "at" Command in Windows XP

Introduction

In this lab, you will schedule a task using the Windows XP GUI and schedule a task in a cmd window using the **at** command.

Recommended Equipment

- A computer running Windows XP

Step 1

Log on to Windows as an administrator.

Choose **start > Control Panel**.

Step 2

The "Control Panel" window appears.

Click **Performance and Maintenance**.

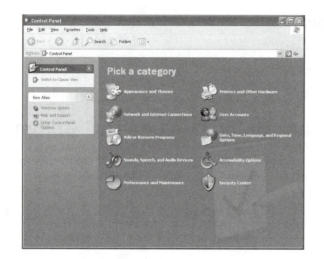

Step 3

The "Performance and Maintenance" window appears.

Click **Scheduled Tasks**.

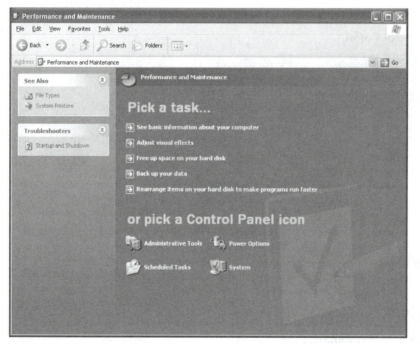

Step 4

The "Scheduled Tasks" window appears.

Double-click **Add Scheduled Task**.

Step 5

The "Scheduled Task Wizard" appears.

Click **Next**.

Scroll down the Application window, and then select **Disk Cleanup**.

Click **Next**.

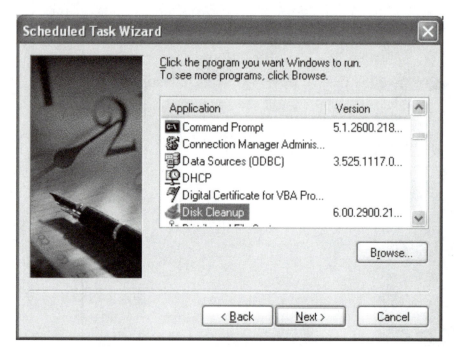

Type **Disk Cleanup** in the "Type a name for this task." field.

Click the **Weekly** radio button, and then click **Next**.

Use the scroll buttons in the "Start time:" field to select "6:00 PM".

Use the scroll buttons in the "Every _ weeks" field to select "1".

Check the "Wednesday" check box, and then click **Next**.

Enter your username and password in the appropriate fields.

Click **Next**.

The "You have successfully scheduled the following task:" window appears.

Click **Finish**.

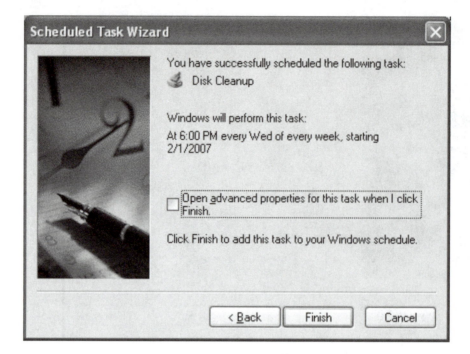

Step 6

The scheduled task that you created appears in the "Scheduled Tasks" window.

Step 7

Choose **Start > Run**.

Type **cmd**, and then click **OK**.

The "C:\WINDOWS\System32\cmd.exe" window appears.

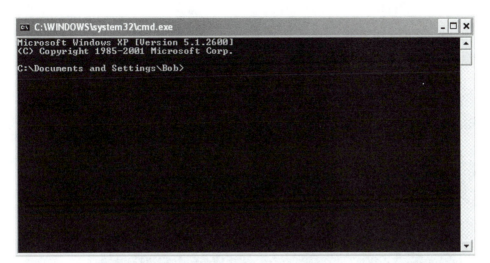

Type **at/?**, and then press the **Enter** key.

The options for the **at** command are displayed.

Type **at 20:00 /every:W backup**.

Note that the time must be military time.

"Added a new job with job ID = 1" is displayed.

Type **at \\computername**. For example **at \\labcomputer**.

The scheduled job appears.

Which command would you enter to get the backup to run every Tuesday and Wednesday at 3:00 PM?

Type **exit**, and then press the **Return** key.

Step 8

Open the Scheduled Tasks window.

The task created using the **at** command is listed in the window.

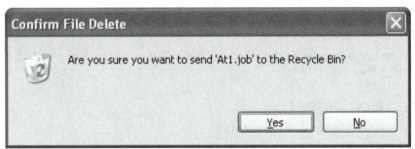

Step 9

Right-click your scheduled task.

Choose **File > Delete**.

The "Confirm File Delete" window appears.

Click **Yes**.

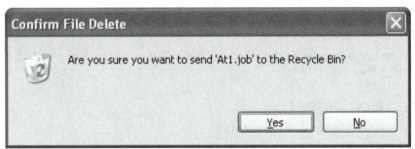

The task created using the **at** command is removed from the scheduled tasks window.

12.4.1 Optional Lab: Schedule Task Using GUI and "at" Command in Windows Vista

Introduction

In this lab, you will schedule a task using the Windows Vista GUI and schedule a task in a command window using the **at** command.

Recommended Equipment

- A computer running Windows Vista

Step 1

Log on to Windows as an Administrator.

Click **Start > Control Panel > Administrative Tools > Task Scheduler > Continue**.

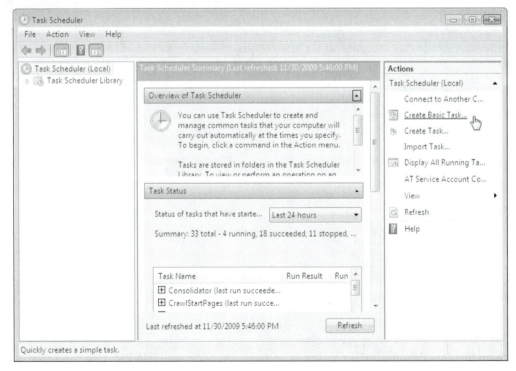

Step 2

The **Task Scheduler** window appears.

Click **Create Basic Task** in the Actions area.

Step 3

The **Create Basic Task Wizard** appears.

Type **Disk Cleanup** in the **Name** field, and then click **Next**.

Click the **Weekly** radio button, and then click **Next**.

Click on the time field and select the hour, minute, seconds, and AM/PM. Use the scroll buttons in the **Start:** field to set the time to **6:00:00 PM**.

Set the **Recur every _ weeks on:** field to **1**.

Check the **Wednesday** check box, and then click **Next**.

The **Action** screen opens.

Make sure **Start a program** is selected then click **Next**.

The **Start a Program** screen opens.

Click **Browse**.

Type **cle** in the **File name** field, select **cleanmge.exe**, and then click **Open**.

When the **Start a Program** screen re-opens, click **Next**.

The **Summary** screen appears.

Click **Finish**.

Step 4

The **Task Scheduler** window appears.

Drag the center screen scroll bar to the bottom of the screen.

Next drag the **Task Name** scroll bar down until you see the task **Disk Cleanup** you created.

Minimize the **Task Scheduler** window and close all other windows.

Step 5

Click **Start**, and then in the **Start Search** field type **cmd**.

Right-click **cmd > Run as administrator > Continue**.

The **Administrator: C:\Windows\System32\cmd.exe** window appears.

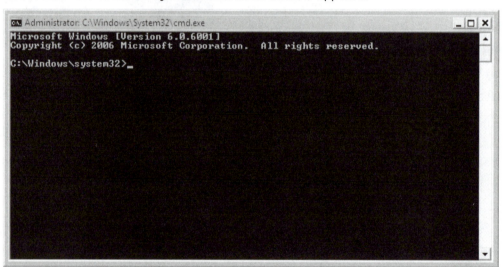

Type **at/?**, and then press the **Enter** key.

The options for the **at** command are displayed.

Type **at 20:00:00 /every:W backup**.

Note that the time must be military time.

Press **Enter**.

Added a new job with job ID = 1 is displayed.

Type **at** \\computername. For example **at \\computer1**.

The scheduled job appears.

Which command would you enter to get the backup to run every Tuesday and Wednesday at 3:00 PM?

Type **exit**, and then press the **Enter** key.

Step 6

Open the **Scheduled Tasks** window.

Click **Task Scheduler Library**.

The task created using the **at** command is listed in the window.

Step 7

For the scheduled tasks that you have created, right-click the scheduled task and then click **Delete**.

Click **Yes** to confirm you want to delete the task.

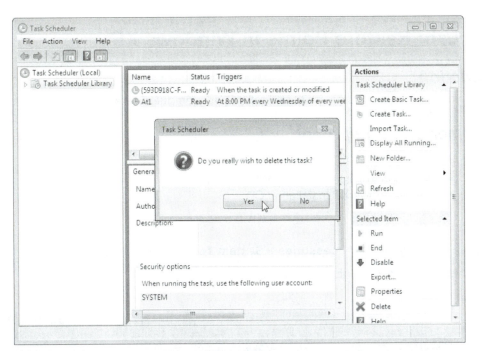

Both scheduled tasks created are removed from the scheduled tasks window.

12.4.2 Lab: Restore Points in Windows XP

Introduction

In this lab, you will create a restore point and return your computer back to that point in time.

Recommended Equipment

The following equipment is required for this exercise:

- A computer system running Windows XP
- The Windows XP installation CD

Step 1

Click **Start > All Programs > Accessories > System Tools > System Restore**.

Click the **Create a restore point** radio button.

Click **Next**.

Step 2

In the "Restore point description" field, type **Application Installed**.

Click **Create**.

Step 3

The "Restore Point Created" window appears.

Click **Close**.

Step 4

Click **Start > Control Panel > Add or Remove Programs**.

Click the **Add or Remove Programs** icon.

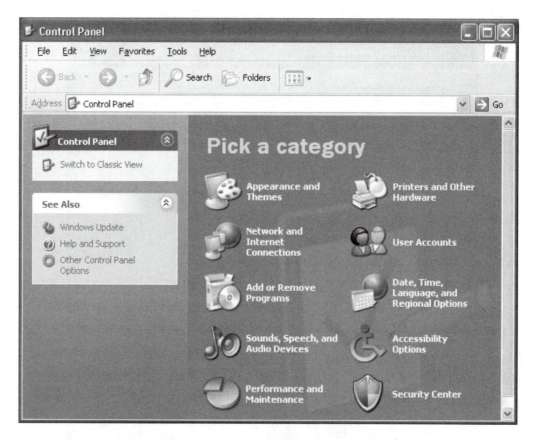

Step 5

Click **Add/Remove Windows Components**.

Step 6

Click the Internet Information Services (IIS) checkbox.

Click Next.

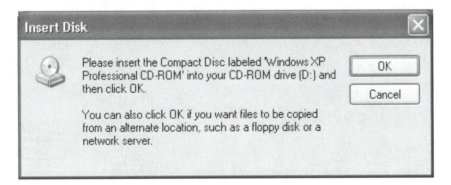

Step 7

Place the Windows XP installation CD into the optical drive.

Click **OK**.

Step 8

The "Files Needed" window appears.

Click **OK**.

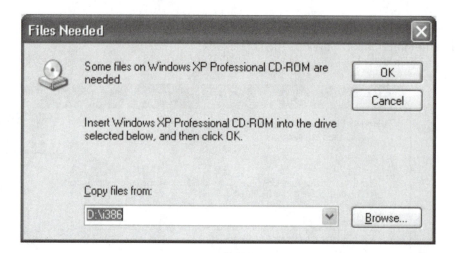

The "Configuring Components" progress window appears.

Step 9

The "Completing the Windows Components Wizard" window appears.

Click **Finish**.

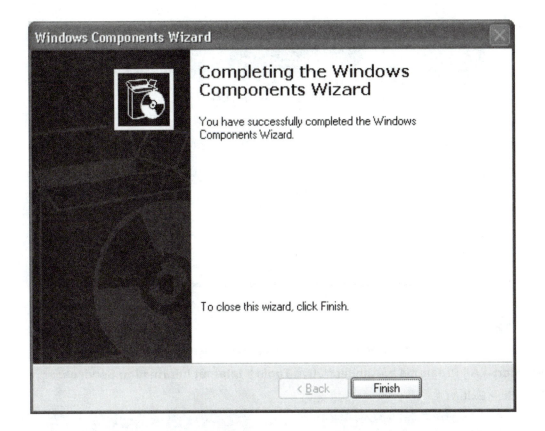

Step 10

The "System Settings Change" dialog box appears.

Remove the Windows XP installation disk from the optical drive.

Click **Yes**.

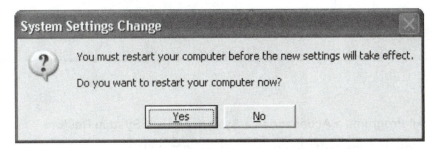

Step 11

Log on to Windows as yourself.

Open the Notepad application by clicking **Start > All Programs > Accessories > Notepad**.

Type **This is a test of the Restore Points** in the Notepad application.

Click **File > Save As…**.

Click **My Documents.**

Type **Restore Point Test file** in the "File Name:" field.

Click **Save.**

Click **File > Exit**.

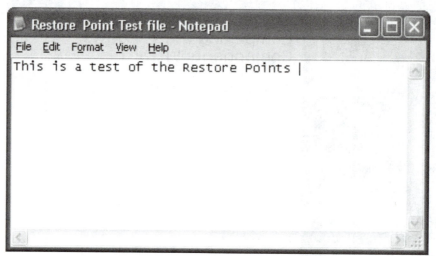

Step 12

Open IIS to confirm that you have successfully installed this service.

Click **Start > All Programs > Administrative Tools > Internet Information Services**.

Click **File > Exit**.

Step 13

Click **Start > All Programs > Accessories > System Tools > System Restore**.

Select the **Restore my computer to an earlier time** radio button.

Click **Next**.

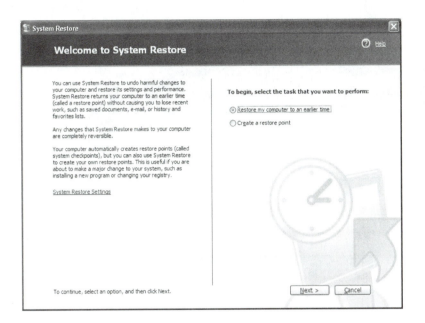

Step 14

Select today's date from the calendar on the left.

Select **Application Installed** from the list on the right.

Click **Next**.

Step 15

The "Confirm Restore Point Selection" window appears.

NOTE: When you click Next, Windows will restart the computer. Close all applications before you click Next.

Click **Next**.

The operating system restores to the point before the IIS application was installed.

Step 16

The "Restoration Complete" window appears. Click **OK**.

Step 17

Click **Start > All Programs > Administrative Tools**.

Is the Internet Information Services application listed?

Step 18

Navigate to the "My Documents" folder.

Open the "Restore Point Test file.txt" file.

Are the contents the same?

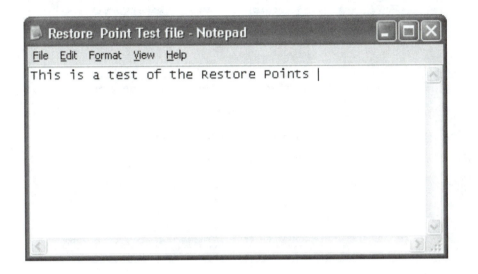

12.4.2 Optional Lab: Restore Points in Windows Vista

Introduction

In this lab, you will create a restore point and return your computer back to that point in time.

Recommended Equipment

The following equipment is required for this exercise:

- A computer system running Windows Vista

Step 1

Click **Start > All Programs > Accessories > System Tools > System Restore**.

Click **Continue** if asked for permission.

The "System Restore" window appears.

To create a restore point, click **open System Protection**.

Step 2

The "System Properties" window appears.

In the "System Protection" tab, click **Create**.

Step 3

In the "Create a restore point" description field, type **Application Installed**.

Click **Create**.

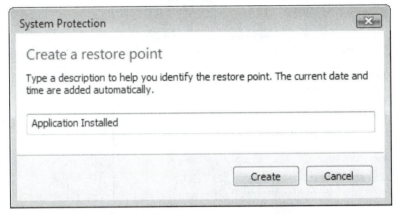

Step 4

After a period of time, a "The restore point was created successfully" message appears.

Click **OK**.

Step 5

The "System Properties" window with the "System Protection" tab selected appears. Notice in "Available Disks" area the new date below "Most recent restore point".

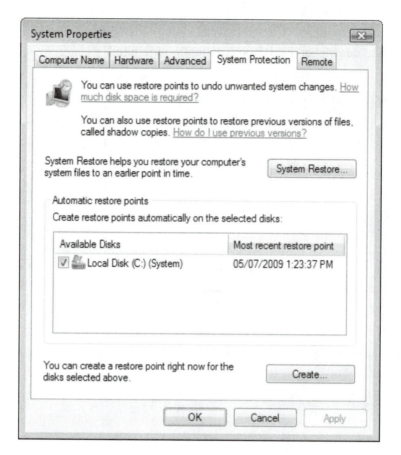

Click **OK**.

Close all open windows.

Step 6

Click **Start > Control Panel > Programs and Features**.

Click the **Turn Windows features on or off** link.

Click **Continue** if asked for permission.

Step 7

The "Windows Features" window appears.

Click the **Internet Information Services** checkbox.

Click **OK**.

Step 8

The configuring features progress window appears.

The progress windows will close on its own when the configuration is completed.

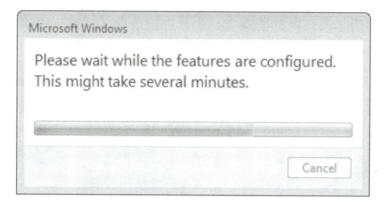

Step 9

When you navigate in a browser to localhost, you will see the new IIS default page.

Click **Start >** in **Start Search** type **http://localhost**.

Close the browser.

Step 10

Open the Notepad application by clicking **Start > All Programs > Accessories > Notepad**.

Type **This is a test of the Restore Points** in the Notepad application.

Click **File > Save As…**.

Click **Documents**.

Type **Restore Point Test file** in the "File Name:" field.

Click **Save**.

Click **File > Exit**.

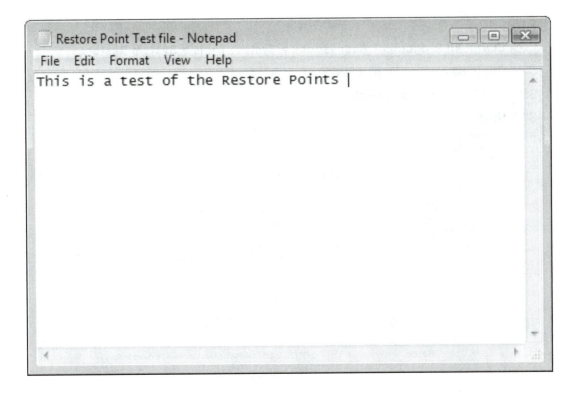

Step 11

Open IIS to confirm that you have successfully installed this service.

Click **Start > All Programs > Administrative Tools > IIS Manager**.

Click **Continue** if asked for permission.

Click **File > Exit**.

Step 12

Click **Start > All Programs > Accessories > System Tools > System Restore**.

Click **Continue** if asked for permission.

Select the **Recommended Restore** radio button.

Click **Next**.

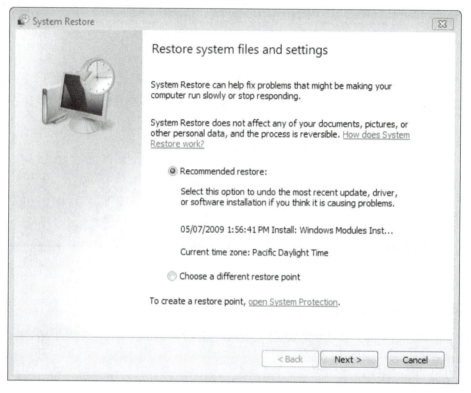

Step 13

The "Confirm your restore point" window appears.

NOTE: When you click Finish, Windows will restart the computer. Close all applications before you click Finish.

Click **Finish**.

Click **Yes** to confirm "System Restore".

The operating system restores to the point before the IIS application was installed. This can take several minutes to complete.

Step 14

The "Restoration Complete" window appears. Click **Close**.

Step 15

Click **Start > Control Panel > Administrative Tools**.

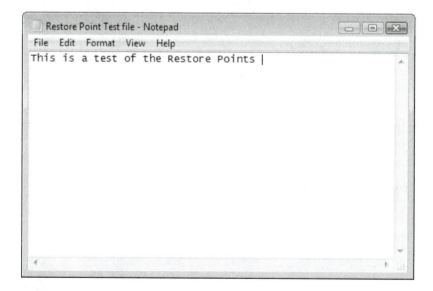

Is the IIS Manager application listed?

Step 16

Navigate to the "Documents" folder.

Open the "Restore Point Test file.txt" file.

Are the contents the same?

12.5.3 Lab: Fix Operating System Problem

Introduction

In this lab, you will troubleshoot and fix a computer that does not connect to the network.

Recommended Equipment

- A computer running Windows
- Linksys 300N wireless router
- Ethernet patch cable

Scenario

The computer will not connect to the Internet, network shares, or network printers.

Step 1

Open a command line and use command line tools to determine the ip address, subnet mask, and default gateway of the computer.

Step 2

Use Windows tools to determine the status of the Ethernet NIC.

Step 3

Repair the Ethernet connection by restoring the computer.

Step 4

What steps did you perform to fix the network?

12.5.3 Lab: Remote Technician: Fix an Operating System Problem

(Student Technician Sheet)

In this lab, you will gather data from the customer, and then instruct the customer on how to fix a computer that does not connect to the network. Document the customer's problem in the work order below.

Company Name: Main Street Stoneworks
Contact: Karin Jones
Company Address: 4252 W Main St.
Company Phone: 1-888-7744

Work Order

Category Operating System Closure Code ____   Status Open _____

Type: _____   Escalated Yes   Pending _____

Item _____   Pending Until Date _____

Business Impacting? X Yes   O No

Summary Customer cannot connect to the network or the Internet. _____
_____
_____

Case ID#_____   Connection Type Ethernet _____
Priority _____2_____   Environment _____
User Platform Windows XP Pro_____

Problem Description: Computer boots correctly. Network cable connected. Link lights not working. Network icon not visible in tray. _____
_____
_____
_____

Problem Solution _____
_____
_____
_____
_____
_____
_____

(Student Customer Sheet)

Use the contact information and problem description below to report the following information to a level-two technician:

Contact Information

Company Name: Main Street Stoneworks

Contact: Karin Jones

Company Address: 4252 W. Main St.

Company Phone: 1-888-7744

Problem Description

When I came into the office today, I could not get my email. The Internet does not work either. I tried to restart my computer, but that did not help. None of the files that I need are available to me either. It is like someone pulled the plug, but the plug is still there. I need to get some files from my folder that I was working on yesterday. It is very important for me to get my files so that I can send them to my client. I do not know how to get the files or send them because my computer cannot find them. What do I do?

(NOTE: Once you have given the level-two tech the problem description, use the Additional Information to answer any follow up questions the technician may ask.)

Additional Information

- Windows XP Pro
- Computer has not had any new hardware installed recently
- There is no wireless network available at work
- Computer detected new hardware at boot-up
- Computer could not install new hardware

12.5.3 Lab: Troubleshooting Operating System Problems in Windows XP

Introduction

In this lab, the instructor will introduce various operating system problems. The student will diagnose the causes and solve the problems.

Recommended Equipment

The following equipment is required for this exercise:

- Computer running Windows XP

Scenario

You must solve operating system problems for a customer. Make sure you document and solve the problems, and then document the solutions.

There are several errors. Solve one problem at a time until you can successfully boot the computer, the desktop contains the appropriate open programs, and the display is set to the native resolution or the resolution given to you by your instructor.

Step 1

Start the computer.

Does the computer boot to the desktop?

If the computer started Windows XP, log on to the computer with the Administrator account.

If the computer did not start Windows XP, troubleshoot the operating system until the computer successfully boots. Because all hardware is correctly connected, you do not need to troubleshoot hardware in this lab.

If the operating system is missing the required files to boot the computer, you can replace these files by booting the computer with the Windows XP installation media. Start the Recovery Console and copy the missing files to the root of the C: drive.

Does the Performance Monitor start automatically?

If the Performance Monitor does not start automatically, configure Windows to start the Performance Monitor every time Windows starts.

Is the resolution of the screen the native resolution or the resolution chosen by your instructor?

If the screen resolution is not native or the resolution chosen by your instructor, configure Windows to display the desktop at the native resolution of the monitor or the resolution chosen by your instructor.

If the computer successfully started, the desktop contains the appropriate open programs, and the display is set to the native resolution you have successfully solved all operating system problems. Hand the lab into your instructor.

If you could not successfully start the computer, the desktop does not contain the appropriate open programs, and the display is not set to the native resolution, continue troubleshooting the problems.

Students start by troubleshooting the computer for problems. Answer the following questions after each problem is solved.

What problem did you find?

What steps did you take to determine the problem?

What is causing the problem?

List the steps taken to fix the problem.

12.5.3 Optional Lab: Troubleshooting Operating System Problems in Windows Vista

Introduction

In this lab, the instructor will introduce various operating system problems. The student will diagnose the causes and solve the problems.

Recommended Equipment

The following equipment is required for this exercise:

- Computer running Windows Vista

Scenario

You must solve operating system problems for a customer. Make sure you document and solve the problems, and then document the solutions.

There are several errors. Solve one problem at a time until you can successfully boot the computer, the desktop contains the appropriate open programs, and the display is set to the native resolution or the resolution given to you by your instructor.

Step 1

Start the computer.

Does the computer boot to the desktop?

If the computer started Windows Vista, log on to the computer with the Administrator account.

If the computer did not start Windows Vista, troubleshoot the operating system until the computer successfully boots. Because all hardware is correctly connected, you do not need to troubleshoot hardware in this lab.

If the operating system is missing the required files to boot the computer, you can replace these files by booting the computer with the Windows Vista installation media. Use the Startup Repair option to replace any missing files.

Does the Performance Monitor start automatically?

If the Performance Monitor does not start automatically, configure Windows to start the Performance Monitor every time Windows starts.

Is the resolution of the screen the native resolution or the resolution chosen by your instructor?

If the screen resolution is not native or the resolution chosen by your instructor, configure Windows to display the desktop at the native resolution of the monitor or the resolution chosen by your instructor.

If the computer successfully started, the desktop contains the appropriate open programs, and the display is set to the native resolution you have successfully solved all operating system problems. Hand the lab into your instructor.

If you could not successfully start the computer, the desktop does not contain the appropriate open programs, and the display is not set to the native resolution, continue troubleshooting the problems.

Students start by troubleshooting the computer for problems. Answer the following questions after each problem is solved.

What problem did you find?

What steps did you take to determine the problem?

What is causing the problem?

List the steps taken to fix the problem.

Chapter 13: Advanced Laptops and Portable Devices

13.2. Worksheet: Investigating Repair Centers

For this worksheet, you will investigate the services provided by a computer repair center. Use the Internet or a local phone directory to locate a repair center. Once you have found a repair center, use their web site to obtain information and answer the following questions. If a web site is not available, contact the local repair center.

1. What laptop and desktop computers can be repaired at this repair center?

2. What type(s) of warranty is offered at this repair center?

3. Does the staff have industry certifications? If so, what are the certifications?

4. Is there a guaranteed completion time for repairs? If so, what are the details?

5. Does the repair center offer remote technical services?

13.3.1 Worksheet: Laptop Batteries

In this activity, you will use the Internet, a newspaper, or a local store to gather information and then enter the specifications for a laptop battery onto this worksheet.

1. List the specifications for an _____ laptop battery. Please ask your instructor for the laptop model to research.

2. Shop around, and in the table below list the features and cost for a generic and an _____ laptop battery.

Battery Specifications	Generic	
Voltage requirements		
Battery cell configuration- ex: 6-Cell, 9-Cell		
Compatibiltiy		
Dimensions		
Hours of life		
Approxmate cost		

3. Based on your research, which battery would you select? Be prepared to discuss your decisions regarding the battery you select.

13.3.2 Worksheet: Docking Station

In this activity, you will use the Internet, a newspaper, or a local store to gather information and then enter the specifications for a laptop docking station onto this worksheet. Be prepared to discuss your decisions regarding the docking station you select.

1. Research a docking station compatible with a(n) _____ laptop. What is the model number of the docking station?

2. What is the approximate cost?

3. What are the dimensions of the docking station?

4. How does the laptop connect to the docking station?

5. List the features available with this docking station.

6. Is this docking station compatible with other laptop models?

13.3.3 Worksheet: Research DVD Drives

In this activity, you will use the Internet, a newspaper, or a local store to gather information about DVD rewritable (DVD-RW) drive for an _____ laptop.

1. Shop around and in the table below list the features and costs for an internal DVD/RW drive and an external DVD/RW drive.

	Internal DVD/RW Drive	External DVD/RW Drive
Connection Type		
Write Speed		
Cost		

2. List the advantages of an internal drive.

3. List the advantages of an external drive.

4. Which DVD drive would you purchase based on your research? Write a brief explanation supporting your answer.

13.3.4 Worksheet: Laptop RAM

In this activity, you will use the Internet, a newspaper, or a local store to gather information about expansion memory for a(n) _____ laptop.

1. Research the manufacturer specifications for the memory in the _____. List the specifications in the table below:

Memory Specifications	IBM T-43 Laptop Expansion Memory
Form Factor	
Type	
Size (MB)	
Manufacturer	
Speed	
Slots	

2. Shop around, and in the table below list the features and costs for expansion memory for a _____.

Memory Specifications	Expansion Memory
Form Factor	
Type	
Size (MB)	
Manufacturer	
Speed	
Retail Cost	

3. In your research, did you find any reason to select a particular type of expansion memory over another?

4. Is the new expansion memory compatible with the existing memory installed in the laptop? Why is this important?

13.5.3 Worksheet: Verify Work Order Information

In this worksheet, a level-two call center technician will find creative ways to verify information that the level-one tech has documented in the work order.

A customer complains that the network connection on the laptop is intermittent. The customer states that they are using a wireless PC card for network connectivity. The customer believes that the laptop may be too far from the wireless access point; however, he does not know where the wireless access point is located.

As a level-two technician, you need to be able to verify information from the work order without repeating the same questions previously asked by the level-one technician. In the table below, re-word the level-one technician's question with a new question or direction for the customer.

Level-One Tech	Level-Two Tech
1. What are the problems that you are experiencing with the laptop?	
2. What is the manufacturer and model of the laptop?	
3. Which operating system is installed on the laptop?	
4. How is the laptop getting power?	
5. What were you doing when the problem occurred?	
6. Were there any system changes on the laptop recently?	
7. Does your laptop have a wireless network connection?	
8. Is your PC Card installed securely?	
9. How much RAM does your laptop have?	

13.5.3 Worksheet: Investigating Support Websites and Repair Companies

For this worksheet, you will investigate the services provided by a local laptop repair company or a laptop manufacturer support website. Use the Internet or a local phone directory to locate a local laptop repair company or laptop manufacturer support website. Answer the following questions:

Local Laptop Repair Company

1. What different types of services are offered by the repair company?

2. What brand(s) of laptop computers can be repaired at this repair company?

3. What type(s) of warranty is offered at this repair company?

4. Does the staff have industry certifications? If so, what are the certifications?

5. Is there a guaranteed completion time for repairs? If so, what are the details?

6. Does the repair company offer remote technical services?

Laptop Manufacturer Support Website

1. What steps are required for locating device drivers for a laptop?

2. What type(s) of support are offered for troubleshooting laptops?

3. Does the manufacturer website offer remote technical services, if so what type(s)?

4. What method(s) are used to located parts?

5. What steps are required for locating manuals for a laptop?

13.5.3 Optional Lab: Troubleshooting Laptop Problems in Windows XP

Introduction

In this lab, the instructor will introduce various laptop problems. The student will diagnose the causes and solve the problems.

Recommended Equipment

The following equipment is required for this exercise:

- A laptop computer running Windows XP

Scenario

You have been sent out to solve laptop problems for a customer. You may need to troubleshoot both software and hardware used by the laptop. Make sure you document and solve the problems, and then document the solutions.

There are several possible errors. Solve one problem at a time until the laptop boots without errors, plays audio, and the touchpad functions correctly.

NOTE: It is important that you solve only one problem at a time. Troubleshoot, solve, and document only one problem before moving onto the next problem.

Students start by troubleshooting the laptop for problems. Answer the following questions after each problem is solved.

What problem did you find?

What steps did you take to determine the problem?

What caused the problem?

List the steps taken to fix the problem.

Validate that each problem has been solved with these steps.

13.5.3 Optional Lab: Troubleshooting Laptop Problems in Windows Vista

Introduction

In this lab, the instructor will introduce various laptop problems. The student will diagnose the causes and solve the problems.

Recommended Equipment

The following equipment is required for this exercise:

- A laptop computer running Windows Vista

Scenario

You have been sent out to solve laptop problems for a customer. You may need to troubleshoot both software and hardware used by the laptop. Make sure you document and solve the problems, and then document the solutions.

There are several possible errors. Solve one problem at a time until the laptop boots without errors, plays audio, and the touchpad functions correctly.

NOTE: It is important that you solve only one problem at a time. Troubleshoot, solve, and document only one problem before moving onto the next problem.

Students start by troubleshooting the laptop for problems. Answer the following questions after each problem is solved.

What problem did you find?

What steps did you take to determine the problem?

What caused the problem?

List the steps taken to fix the problem.

Validate that each problem has been solved with these steps.

Chapter 14: Advanced Printers and Scanners

14.2.4 Lab: Install an All-in-one Printer/Scanner

Introduction

In this lab, you will check the Windows XP Hardware Compatibility List (HCL) for your All-in-one Printer/Scanner, install the all-in-one printer/scanner, upgrade the driver and any associated software, and test the printer and scanner.

Recommended Equipment

- A computer with the Windows XP operating system
- An available USB port on the computer
- All-in-one Printer/Scanner
- Printer/scanner installation CD
- An Internet connection

Step 1

Open Internet Explorer.

Search the Microsoft Website for "windows xp hcl".

Choose "Windows XP".

Choose "Devices".

Choose the processor type used by the computer.

Select "Printers & Scanners".

Choose "Start".

Search the HCL for your All-in-one Printer/Scanner.

What Company manufactures this component?

For what operating system(s) was this component designed?

For what operating system(s) has this component been certified?

Step 2

Carefully unpack and assemble the printer/scanner if necessary. Follow the manufacturer's instructions.

Plug the printer/scanner into a grounded wall outlet and turn on the unit. Do not attach the USB cable to the computer until instructed to do so.

Step 3

Insert the manufacturer's software CD into the optical drive. If the installation program does not start automatically, select **Start > My Computer,** and then double-click the **Epson CD-ROM** icon.

The "Install Menu" window appears.

Click **Install**.

Connect the USB cable when instructed.

The "License Agreement" window appears.

Click **Yes**.

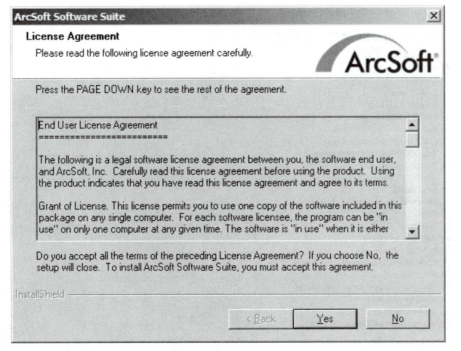

The "Epson Product Registration" window appears.

Click **Cancel**.

Step 4

Go to the All-in-one Printer/Scanner manufacturer's website and download the newest drivers for the All-in-one Printer/Scanner.

Click **Start**, and then right-click **My Computer**. Choose **Manage > Device Manager**.

The Device Manager appears in the right column.

```
☐ 🖳
   ☐ 🔋 Batteries
   ☐ 💻 Computer
   ☐ 💾 Disk drives
   ☐ 🖵 Display adapters
   ☐ 💿 DVD/CD-ROM drives
   ☐ 🎮 Human Interface Devices
   ☐ 🔌 IDE ATA/ATAPI controllers
   ☐ 🔗 IEEE 1394 Bus host controllers
   ☐ 🖼 Imaging devices
         🖼 EPSON Stylus CX
   ☐ ⌨ Keyboards
   ☐ 🖱 Mice and other poin     devices
   ☐ 📠 Modems
   ☐ 🖥 Monitors
   ☐ 🖧 Network adapters
   ☐ 📇 PCMCIA adapters
   ☐ 📇 PCMCIA and Flash memory devices
   ☐ 🔲 Processors
   ☐ 🔊 Sound, video and game controllers
   ☐ 💾 Storage volumes
   ☐ 🖳 System devices
   ☐ 🔌 Universal Serial Bus controllers
```

Double-click the **All-in-one Printer/Scanner**, and then select the **Driver** tab.

Choose **Update Driver**.

General	Driver	Details

EPSON Stylus

Driver Provider: EPSON

Driver Date: 3/11/2004

Driver Version: 2.3.0.0

Digital Signer: Microsoft Windows Hardware Compatibility Publ

Driver Details...	To view details about the driver files.
Update Driver...	To update the driver for this device.
Roll Back Driver	If the device fails after updating the driver, roll back to the previously installed driver.
Uninstall	To uninstall the driver (Advanced).

OK   Cancel

Follow the instructions to install the driver that was downloaded.

Choose **Start > Printers and Faxes**.

Right-click **All-in-one Printer/Scanner,** and then click **Properties**.

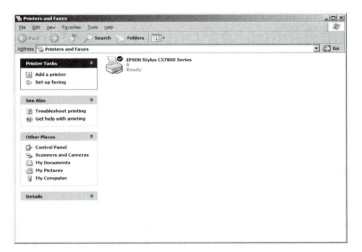

Click the **Print Test Page** button.

Step 5

Place a picture or document in the upper left corner of the scanner, face down.

Double-click the **Epson Scan** icon on the desktop or open the **Epson SmartPanel** using the **Start** menu.

Scan the image.

Print the scanned image.

14.3.2 Lab: Share the All-in-one Printer/Scanner in Windows XP

Introduction

In this lab, you will share the All-in-one printer/scanner, configure the printer on a networked computer, and print a test page from the remote computer.

Recommended Equipment

- Two computers directly connected or connected through a hub or switch
- Windows XP installed on both computers
- An All-in-one Printer/Scanner installed on one of the computers

Step 1

Click **My Computer > Tools > Folder Options > View**, and then uncheck **Use Simple File Sharing (Recommended)**.

Click **OK**.

Step 2

Choose **Start > Printers and Faxes**.

Right-click the **All-in-one Printer/Scanner**, and then choose **Properties**.

Click the **Sharing** tab.

Choose **Share this printer**. Name the new share **Example**, and then click **Apply**.

Click **OK**.

Step 3

Log on to the computer without the printer/scanner connected, and then choose **Start > Printers and Faxes.**

Click **Add a printer**.

The "Add Printer Wizard" window appears.

Click **Next**.

The "Local or Network Printer" window appears.

Click the **A network printer, or a printer attached to another computer** radio button, and then click **Next**.

Type **\\computername\printer** in the **Connect to this printer (or to browse for a printer, select this option and click Next):** radio button, where computername is the name of the computer with the connected printer/scanner and printer is the name of the printer/scanner.

Step 4

Choose **Start > Printers and Faxes**.

Right-click the **All-in-one Printer/Scanner**, and then choose **Properties**.

Click the **Print Test Page** button.

14.3.2 Optional Lab: Share the All-in-one Printer/Scanner in Windows Vista

Introduction

In this lab, you will share the All-in-one printer/scanner, configure the printer on a networked computer, and print a test page from the remote computer.

Recommended Equipment

- Two computers directly connected or connected through a hub or switch
- Windows Vista installed on both computers
- An All-in-one Printer/Scanner installed on one of the computers

Step 1

Click **Start > Computer > Tools > Folder Options > View**, and then uncheck **Use Sharing Wizard (Recommended)** if it is checked.

Click **OK**.

Step 2

Click **Start > Network > Network and Sharing Center > Password protected sharing**, and then check **Turn off password protected sharing**.

Click **Apply**. If User Account Control appears, click **Continue**.

Step 3

Choose **Start > Control Panel** > double click **Printers**.

Right-click the **All-in-one Printer/Scanner**, and then choose **Properties**.

Click the **Sharing** tab.

Click **Change sharing options**. If User Account Control appears, click **Continue**.

Choose **Share this printer**. Name the new share **Example**, and then click **OK**.

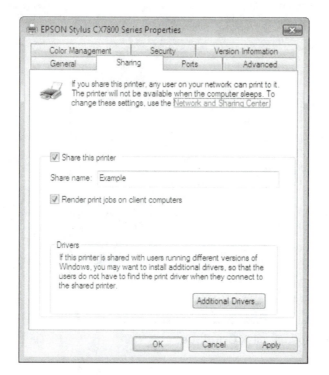

Step 4

Log on to the computer without the printer/scanner connected, and then choose **Start > Control Panel > Printers.**

Click **Add a printer**.

The "Add Printer" window appears.

Click **Add a network, wireless or Bluetooth printer**.

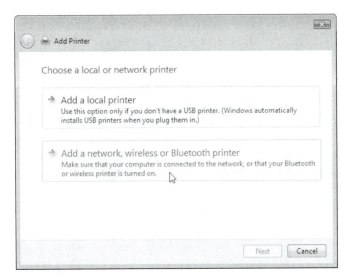

The "Searching for available Printers ..." page appears.

If displayed in the search list select *Printer* **on** *Computername* and then click **Next.**

Or to find a printer by name or TCP/IP address, select **The printer that I want isn't listed**.

Select the radio button **Select a shared printer by name** and type **\\computername\printer**, where computername is the name of the computer with the connected printer/scanner and printer is the name of the printer/scanner.

Click **Next**.

If prompted to install drivers click **Install driver**. If User Account Control appears, click **Continue**.

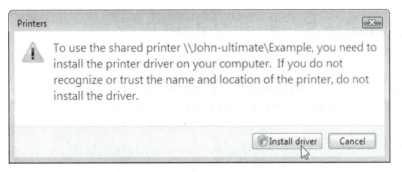

Accept all default settings, click **Next** and then click **Finish**.

Step 5

Choose **Start > Control Panel >** double click **Printers**.

Right-click the **All-in-one Printer/Scanner**, and then choose **Properties**.

Click the **Print Test Page** button.

14.4.2 Lab: Optimize Scanner Output

Introduction

In this lab, you will scan a picture at two different levels of DPI. The results will be displayed and compared on your monitor, as two saved files, and as two printed images.

Recommended Equipment

The following equipment is required for this exercise:

- A computer with Windows installed
- An All-in-One Printer/Scanner installed

Step 1

Scan the image supplied by your instructor at 300 DPI, and then save it as a file named SCAN1.

Right-click the SCAN1 file, and then select **Properties**.

What is the size of the image?

Print the image.

Step 2

Scan the same image at 72 DPI, and then save it as a file named SCAN2.

Right-click the SCAN2 file, and then select **Properties**.

What is the size of the image?

Print the image.

Step 3

Did it take longer to scan SCAN2 than it did to scan SCAN1?

Why?

Step 4

Is there a difference between the sizes of the image files?

Why?

Step 5

Open both image files.

Which image, in your opinion, looks better?

Which of the printed images, in your opinion, looks better?

Step 6

What DPI setting would work best when scanning an image to be used on a Website?

Why did you choose this DPI setting?

Which DPI setting would work best when printing an image?

Why did you choose this DPI setting?

14.5.1 Worksheet: Search for Certified Printer Technician Jobs

In this activity, you will use the Internet to gather information about becoming a certified printer technician.

In the table below, list the name of three printer manufacturers, any certification programs available, the required skills of the certification, and make and model of the printers that require a certified technician. An example has been provided for you. Be prepared to discuss your answers.

Printer Manufacturer	Certification Programs	Required Skills	Printer make/model
HP	Accredited Platform Specialist (APS): • HP LaserJet Solutions • HP Designjet Solutions	Fundamental architectures and technologies of electro photographic printers Troubleshooting of LaserJet products and solutions Drivers LaserJet components fundamentals	All

14.6.3 Lab: Fix a Printer Problem

In this lab, you will troubleshoot and fix a printer that does not print documents for a user.

Recommended Equipment

- At least two computers running Windows XP
- All-in-one printer connected and installed on one of the computers
- All-in-one printer installed as a network printer on other computer(s)
- Computers networked using switch, hub, or wireless router

Scenario

The printer will not print documents for a user.

Step 1

Verify printer hardware.

Step 2

Verify network printer installation on client computer(s).

Step 3

Verify network connectivity for computer that will not print.

Step 4

Verify installation of printer on directly-connected computer.

Step 5

What steps did you perform to fix the printer?

14.6.3 Lab: Remote Technician: Fix a Printer Problem

(Student Technician Sheet)

In this lab, you will gather data from the customer, and then instruct the customer on how to fix a printer that does not print documents for a user. Document the customer's problem in the work order below.

Company Name: Don's Delivery
Contact: Don Marley
Company Address: 11 E. Main Street
Company Phone: 1-800-555-0032

Work Order

Category Printer

Closure Code ____

Status Open

Type: _____

Escalated Yes

Pending _____

Item _____

Pending Until Date _____

Business Impacting? X Yes O No

Summary _____
_____
_____

Case ID#_____

Connection Type Ethernet

Priority _____2_____

Environment _____

User Platform Windows XP Pro

Problem Description: Printer is powered on. Cables are securely connected. Printer has ink and paper. Printer is installed as network printer on all client computers. Other users are able to print to the printer.
_____
_____
_____

Problem Solution: _____
_____
_____
_____
_____
_____
_____
_____

(Student Customer Sheet)

Use the contact information and problem description below to report the following information to a level-two technician:

Contact Information

Company Name: Don's Delivery

Contact: Don Marley

Company Address: 11 E. Main Street

Company Phone: 1-800-555-0032

Problem Description

I am not able to print documents on our printer. I tried turning the printer off and then back on, but I am still unable to print. The printer worked fine yesterday, but now, no documents print. Nobody has touched the printer since yesterday, and I do not understand why it will not print. What can I do to make my documents print?

(NOTE: Once you have given the level-two tech the problem description, use the Additional Information to answer any follow up questions the technician may ask.)

Additional Information

- Printer is hosted by dedicated computer on the network
- Printer is an all-in-one device
- Tech support fixed a similar problem for a user yesterday

14.6.3 Lab: Troubleshooting Printer Problems in Windows XP

Introduction

In this lab, the instructor will introduce various printer problems. The student will diagnose the causes and solve the problems.

Recommended Equipment

The following equipment is required for this exercise:

- A computer running Windows XP

- A printer connected to the computer

Scenario

You must solve printer problems for a customer. You may need to troubleshoot both the printer and computer. Make sure you document and solve the problems, and then document the solutions.

There are several possible errors. Solve one problem at a time until you can successfully print a document from Notepad.

Step 1

Log on to the computer with the Administrator account.

Click **Start > Run >** type **Notepad >** click **OK**.

In the Notepad document type **Printer problems solved by yourname**.

Save the document to the desktop as **Printer Works**.

Try printing the "Printer Works" document.

Did the document print?

Students start by troubleshooting the computer or printer for problems. Answer the following questions after each problem is solved.

Print the "Printer Works" document.

Did the document successfully print?

If the "Printer Works" document printed correctly, you have successfully solved all printer problems. Hand the "Printer Works" document into your instructor.

If the "Printer Works" document did not print correctly, continue troubleshooting the problem.

Problem 1

What problem did you find?

What steps did you take to determine the problem?

What is causing the problem?

List the steps taken to fix the problem.

Problem 2

What problem did you find?

What steps did you take to determine the problem?

What is causing the problem?

List the steps taken to fix the problem.

Problem 3

What problem did you find?

What steps did you take to determine the problem?

What is causing the problem?

List the steps taken to fix the problem.

Problem 4

What problem did you find?

What steps did you take to determine the problem?

What is causing the problem?

List the steps taken to fix the problem.

Problem 5

What problem did you find?

What steps did you take to determine the problem?

What is causing the problem?

List the steps taken to fix the problem.

Problem 6

What problem did you find?

What steps did you take to determine the problem?

What is causing the problem?

List the steps taken to fix the problem.

14.6.3 Optional Lab: Troubleshooting Printer Problems in Windows Vista

Introduction

In this lab, the instructor will introduce various printer problems. The student will diagnose the causes and solve the problems.

Recommended Equipment

The following equipment is required for this exercise:

- A computer running Windows Vista
- A printer connected to the computer

Scenario

You must solve printer problems for a customer. You may need to troubleshoot both the printer and computer. Make sure you document and solve the problems, and then document the solutions.

There are several possible errors. Solve one problem at a time until you can successfully print a document from Notepad.

Step 1

Log on to the computer with the Administrator account.

Click **Start > Start Search >** type **Notepad >** press **Enter**.

In the Notepad document type **Printer problems solved by yourname**.

Save the document to the desktop as **Printer Works**.

Try printing the "Printer Works" document.

Did the document print?

Students start by troubleshooting the computer or printer for problems. Answer the following questions after each problem is solved.

Print the "Printer Works" document.

Did the document successfully print?

If the "Printer Works" document printed correctly, you have successfully solved all printer problems. Hand the "Printer Works" document into your instructor.

If the "Printer Works" document did not print correctly, continue troubleshooting the problem.

Problem 1

What problem did you find?

What steps did you take to determine the problem?

What is causing the problem?

List the steps taken to fix the problem.

Problem 2

What problem did you find?

What steps did you take to determine the problem?

What is causing the problem?

List the steps taken to fix the problem.

Problem 3

What problem did you find?

What steps did you take to determine the problem?

What is causing the problem?

List the steps taken to fix the problem.

Problem 4

What problem did you find?

What steps did you take to determine the problem?

What is causing the problem?

List the steps taken to fix the problem.

Problem 5

What problem did you find?

What steps did you take to determine the problem?

What is causing the problem?

List the steps taken to fix the problem.

Problem 6

What problem did you find?

What steps did you take to determine the problem?

What is causing the problem?

List the steps taken to fix the problem.

Chapter 15: Advanced Networks

15.2.2 Worksheet: Protocols

In this worksheet, you will write the name of the protocol and the default port(s) for each protocol definition in the table.

Be prepared to discuss your answers.

Protocol Definition	Protocol	Default Port(s)
Provides connections to computers over a TCP/IP network		
Sends e-mail over a TCP/IP network		
Translates URLs to IP address		
Transports Web pages over a TCP/IP network		
Automates assignment of IP address on a network		
Securely transports Web pages over a TCP/IP network		
Transports files over a TCP/IP network		

15.3.2 Worksheet: ISP Connection Types

In this worksheet, you will determine the best ISP type for your customer.

Be prepared to discuss your answers.

Scenario 1

The customer lives in a remote area deep in a valley and cannot afford broadband.

Scenario 2

The customer can only receive television using satellite but lives in an area where high-speed Internet access is available.

Scenario 3

The customer is a sales person travels most of the time. A connection to the main office is required almost 24 hours a day.

Scenario 4

The customer works from home, needs the fastest possible upload and download speeds to access the company's FTP server, and lives in a very remote area where DSL and cable are not available.

Scenario 5

The customer wants to bundle television, Internet access and phone all through the same company, but the local phone company does not offer all the services.

15.4.2 Lab: Configure Browser Settings in Windows XP

Introduction

In this lab, you will configure browser settings in Microsoft Internet Explorer. You will select Internet Explorer as the default browser.

Recommended Equipment

- A computer with Windows XP installed
- An Internet connection
- Mozilla Firefox browser installed (from lab in chapter 12)

Step 1

Choose **Start > Run...**. Type **www.cisco.com**, and press **Return**.

Which browser was used to open the web page?

If you answered "Internet Explorer":

> Choose **Start > All Programs > Mozilla Firefox > Mozilla Firefox**.
>
> Choose **Tools** > **Options**, and click the "Main" tab.
>
> Click the **Always check to see if Firefox is the default browser on startup** check box, and then click **OK.**
>
> Restart your computer.
>
> Choose **Start > All Programs > Mozilla Firefox > Mozilla Firefox**.
>
> Click **Yes** to make Firefox the new default browser.

If you answered "Firefox":

> Choose **Start > All Programs > Internet Explorer**.
>
> Choose **Tools > Internet Options**, and then click the "Programs" tab.
>
> Click the "Internet Explorer should check to see whether it is the default browser", and then click **OK**.
>
> Restart your computer.
>
>
> Choose **Start > All Programs > Internet Explorer**.
>
> Click **Yes** to make Internet Explorer the new default browser.

Step 2

Choose **Start > Run...**. Type **www.cisco.com**, and press **Return**.

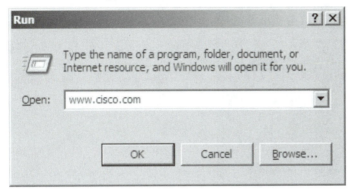

Which browser was used to open the web page this time?

Make Internet Explorer your default browser.

Open Internet Explorer, and then choose **Help > About Internet Explorer**.

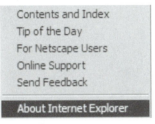

Which version of Internet Explorer is installed on your computer?

Step 3

Choose **Tools > Internet Options**.

The "Internet Options" window appears.

Click the **Settings** button, and then click the **View Files** button.

How many temporary Internet files were listed?

Close the "Temporary Internet Files" window.

Close the "Settings" window.

Choose **Delete Files**.

A confirmation window appears.

Click the **OK** button.

Click the **Settings** button, and then click the **View Files** button.

How many temporary Internet files were listed?

Step 4

Click the **down** arrow at the right end of the "address" field to view previously visited sites.

How many sites are listed in the drop-down box?

To clear the browser history, choose **Tools > Internet Options**, and then click the **Clear History** button.

A confirmation window appears. Click **Yes**.

Click the **down** arrow at the right end of the "address" field to view previously visited sites.

How many sites are now found in the drop-down box?

Step 5

Use this path to change Security settings:

Choose **Tools > Internet Options**, and then click the **Security** tab.

Click the **Custom Level** button.

The "Security Settings" window appears.

Select the options in the list that you wish to change, and then click **OK**.

15.4.2 Optional Lab: Configure Browser Settings in Windows Vista

Introduction

In this lab, you will configure browser settings in Microsoft Internet Explorer. You will select Internet Explorer as the default browser.

Recommended Equipment

- A computer with Windows Vista
- An Internet connection
- Mozilla Firefox browser installed (from lab in chapter 12)

Step 1

Choose **Start > Start Search**. Type **www.cisco.com**, and click **Search the Internet**.

Which browser was used to open the web page?

If you answered "Internet Explorer":

Choose **Start > All Programs > Mozilla Firefox > Mozilla Firefox**.

Choose **Tools** > **Options > Advanced**, and click the "General" tab.

Click the **Always check to see if Firefox is the default browser on startup** check box, and then click **OK.**

Restart your computer.

Choose **Start > All Programs > Mozilla Firefox > Mozilla Firefox**.

Click **Yes** to make Firefox the new default browser.

If you answered "Firefox":

Choose **Start > All Programs > Internet Explorer**.

Choose **Tools > Internet Options**, and then click the "Programs" tab.

Click the "Tell me if Internet Explorer is not the default web browser", and then click **OK**.

Restart your computer.

Choose **Start > All Programs > Internet Explorer**.

Click **Yes** to make Internet Explorer the new default browser.

Step 2

Choose **Start > Start Search**. Type **www.cisco.com**, and click **Search the Internet**.

Which browser was used to open the web page this time?

Make Internet Explorer your default browser.

Open Internet Explorer, and then choose **Help > About Internet Explorer**.

Which version of Internet Explorer is installed on your computer?

Step 3

Choose **Tools > Internet Options**.

The "Internet Options" window appears.

Click the **Settings** button in Browsing history.

Click the **View Files** button.

How many temporary Internet files were listed?

Close the "Temporary Internet Files" window.

Close the "Temporary Internet Files and History Settings" window.

Choose **Delete** in Browser History. The "Delete Browser History" window appears.

Make sure the following are selected: **Preserve Favorites website data, Temporary Internet files, Cookies** and **History**.

Click **Delete**.

Click the **Settings** button in Browser History, and then click the **View Files** button.

How many temporary Internet files were listed?

Step 4

Click the **down** arrow at the right end of the "address" field to view previously visited sites.

How many sites are listed in the drop-down box?

To clear the browser history, choose **Tools > Internet Options** >select **Delete browsing history on exit > OK**.

Close the browser.

Open the browser, click the **down** arrow at the right end of the "address" field to view previously visited sites.

How many sites are now found in the drop-down box?

Step 5

Use this path to change Security settings:

Choose **Tools > Internet Options**, and then click the **Security** tab.

Click the **Custom Level** button.

The "Security Settings – Internet Zone" window appears.

Select the options in the list that you wish to change, and then click **OK**.

15.4.2 Lab: Share a Folder, Share a Printer, and Set Share Permissions in Windows XP

Introduction

In this lab, you will create and share a folder, share a printer, and set permissions for the shares.

Recommended Equipment

- Two computers running Windows XP that are directly connected to each other or through a switch or hub

- A printer installed on one of the two computers

Step 1

Choose **My Computer > Tools > Folder Options**.

Click the **View** tab.

Uncheck the "Use Simple File Sharing (Recommended)" checkbox, and then click **OK**.

Step 2

Right-click the **desktop**, and then choose **New > Folder**.

Type **Example**, and then press the **Return** key.

Open WordPad. Type "This is an example document.".

Save the file in the "Example" folder with the name "Brief.doc", and then close WordPad.

Step 3

Right-click the **Example** folder, and then choose **Sharing and Security**

Click the **Share this folder** radio button, and then click **OK**.

What is the icon of the "Example" folder?

On the computer with the shared folder, right-click **My Computer**, and then click the **Computer Name** tab.

What is the name of the computer?

Step 4

On the other computer, choose **Start > Run**.

Type **\\computername\Example**, where computername is the name of the computer with the "Example" folder, and then press the **Enter** key.

Open the "Brief.doc" file.

Delete the text in the "Brief.doc" file, and then choose **File > Save**.

What happens?

Click **OK**.

Close WordPad, and then choose **NO** when prompted to save changes to the file.

Step 5

Return to the computer with the shared folder.

Right-click **Example folder** > **Sharing and Security**, and then click **Permissions**.

What are the default permissions?

Step 6

Open the Control Panel on the computer with the attached printer.

Choose **Printers and Other Hardware** > **Printers and Faxes**.

Right-click the icon of the installed printer, and then choose **Sharing...**.

Click the **Share this printer** radio button, and then click **OK**.

Step 7

Return to the computer that is not directly connected to a printer.

Open the Control Panel. Choose **Printers and Other Hardware** > **Printers and Faxes**.

Choose **File** > **Add Printer** on the screen below.

The "Add Printer Wizard" window appears.

Click **Next**.

The Local or Network Printer of the Add Printer Wizard window appears. Click the **A network printer, or a printer attached to another computer** radio button, and then click **Next**.

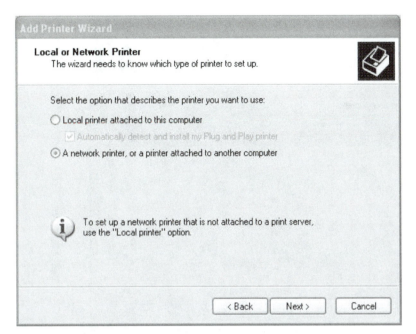

The "Specify a Printer" window appears.

Click the **Connect to this printer** radio button, and then click **Next**.

The Browse for a Printer window appears.

Expand "Shared printers".

Choose the printer from the list, and then click **Next**.

The "Default Printer" screen of the "Add Printer Wizard" appears.

Click **Next**.

The "Completing the Add Printer Wizard" window appears.

Click **Finish**.

Step 8

Choose **Start > Printers and Faxes**.

Right-click the printer you installed, and then choose **Properties**.

The "Printer Properties" window appears.

Choose the **General** tab, and then click **Print Test Page**.

Click **OK** in the confirmation dialog box, and then click **OK** to close the printer properties window.

15.4.2 Optional Lab: Share a Folder, Share a Printer, and Set Share Permissions in Windows Vista

Introduction

In this lab, you will create and share a folder, share a printer, and set permissions for the shares.

Recommended Equipment

- Two computers running Windows Vista that are directly connected to each other or through a switch or hub

- A printer installed on one of the two computers

Step 1

Click **Start > Control Panel >** double-click **Folder Options**.

Click the **View** tab.

Uncheck the "Use Sharing Wizard (Recommended)" checkbox, and then click **OK**.

Step 2

Right-click the **desktop**, and then choose **New > Folder**.

Type **Example**, and then press the **Return** key.

Open WordPad. Type "This is an example document.".

Save the file in the "Example" folder with the name "Brief.doc", and then close WordPad.

Step 3

Right-click the **Example** folder, and then choose **Sharing > Advanced Sharing > Continue**.

Click the **Share this folder** radio button, and then click **OK**.

What is the icon of the "Example" folder?

On the computer with the shared folder, click **Start >** right-click **Computer > Properties**.

What is the name of the computer?

Step 4

On the other computer, choose **Start > Start Search**.

Type **\\computername\Example**, where computername is the name of the computer with the "Example" folder, and then press the **Enter** key.

Open the "Brief.doc" file.

Delete the text in the "Brief.doc" file, and then choose **File > Save**.

What happens?

Click **OK**.

Close WordPad, and then choose **Don't Save** when prompted to save changes to the file.

Step 5

Return to the computer with the shared folder.

Right-click **Example** folder **> Sharing**, and then click **Advanced Sharing > Continue > Permissions**.

What are the default permissions?

Step 6

Open the **Control Panel** on the computer with the attached printer.

Double click **Printers**.

Right-click the icon of the installed printer, and then choose **Run as administrator > Sharing > Continue**.

Click the **Share this printer** radio button, and then click **OK**.

Step 7

Return to the computer that is not directly connected to a printer.

Open the **Control Panel**. Double click **Printers**.

Choose **Add Printer** on the screen below.

The "Add Printer" window appears.

The "Choose a local or network printer" of the "Add Printer" window appears. Click **Add a network, wireless or Bluetooth printer**.

The "Searching for available Printers …" page appears.

Select **Printer on computername** if it is displayed in the search list.

If the printer was not in the search list, find a printer by name or TCP/IP address.

Select **The printer that I want isn't listed** and select the radio button **Select a shared printer by name** and type **\\computername\printer**.

Click **Next**.

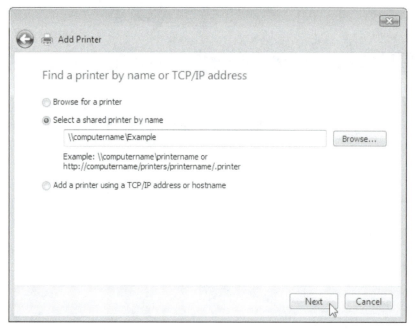

If prompted to install drivers click **Install drivers**. If User Account Control appears, click **Continue**.

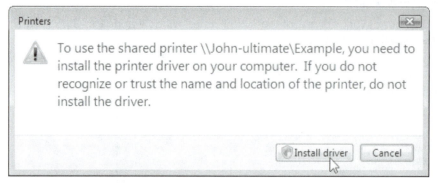

Accept all default setting, click **Next** then click **Finish**.

Step 8

Choose **Start > Control Panel > Printers**.

Right-click the printer you installed, and then choose **Properties**.

The "Printer Shared Properties" window appears.

Choose the **General** tab, and then click **Print Test Page**.

Click **OK** in the confirmation dialog box, and then click **OK** to close the printer properties window.

15.5.1 Lab: Install a Wireless NIC in Windows XP

Introduction

In this lab, you will install and configure a wireless NIC.

Recommended Equipment

- A computer with Windows XP installed
- Empty PCI slot on the motherboard
- A wireless access point or router
- A wireless PCI NIC
- An antistatic wrist strap

Step 1

Turn off your computer. If a switch is present on the power supply, set the switch to "0" or "off". Unplug the computer from the AC outlet. Remove the side panels from the case.

Put on the antistatic wrist strap and attach it to an unpainted metal surface of the computer case.

Choose an appropriate slot on the motherboard to install the new wireless NIC.

You may need to remove the metal cover near the slot on the back of the case.

Make sure the wireless NIC is properly lined up with the slot. Push down gently on the wireless NIC.

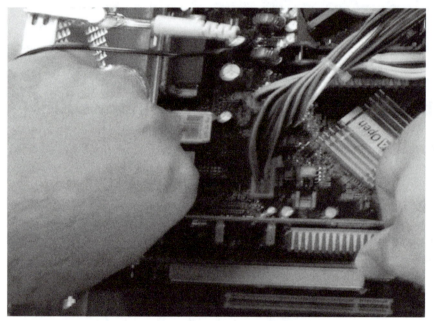

Secure the wireless NIC mounting bracket to the case with a screw.

Attach the antenna to the antenna connector on the back of the computer.

Disconnect the antistatic wrist strap. Replace the case panels. Plug the power cable into an AC outlet. If a switch is present on the power supply, set the switch to "1" or "on".

Step 2

Boot your computer, and then log on as an administrator.

The wireless NIC will be detected by Windows. The "Found New Hardware Wizard" window will appear.

Click the **Yes, this time only** radio button, and then click **Next**.

Insert the manufacturer's CD.

Click the **Install the software automatically (Recommended)** radio button, and then click **Next**.

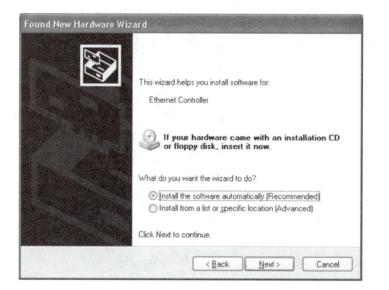

Step 3

Right-click **My Computer**, and choose **Manage**.

Choose **Device Manager**, and then expand "Network Adapters".

What network adapters are installed in the computer?

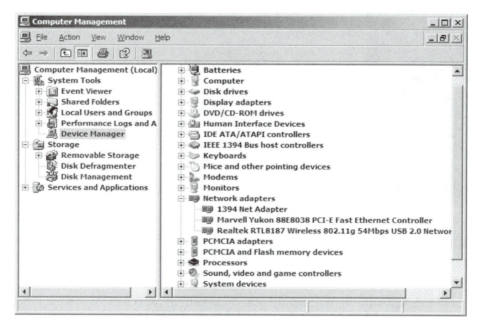

Close the "Computer Management" window.

Step 4

Choose **Start**.

Right-click **My Network Places**, and then choose **Properties.**

Double-click the wireless NIC, and then click the **Properties** button.

Choose **Internet Protocol (TCP/IP)**, and then click the **Properties** button.

Click the **Obtain an IP address automatically** radio button.

Click the **Obtain DNS server address automatically** radio button.

Click **OK**.

Step 5

Choose **Start** > **Run**.

Type **cmd**, and then press the **Enter** key.

Type **ipconfig /all**, and then press the **Enter** key.

What is the IP address of the computer?

What is the subnet mask of the computer?

What is the default gateway of the computer?

What are the DNS servers for the computer?

What is the MAC address of the comptuer?

Is DHCP Enabled?

What is the IP address of the DHCP server?

Step 6

A wireless NIC may also be configured with a static IP address.

Choose **Start**.

Right-click **My Network Places**, and then choose **Properties.**

Double-click the wireless NIC, and then click the **Properties** button.

Choose **Internet Protocol (TCP/IP)**, and then click the **Properties** button.

Click the **Use the following IP address** radio button. Type the IP address, subnet mask and default gateway addresses from step 5.

Click the **Use the following DNS server address** radio button. Type the DNS address from step 5.

Click **OK**.

Step 7

Choose **Start** > **Run**.

Type **cmd**, and then press the **Enter** key.

Type **ipconfig /all**, and then press the **Enter** key.

Is DHCP Enabled?

Step 8

Return the NIC to original settings.

Choose **Start**.

Right-click **My Network Places**, and then choose **Properties.**

Double-click the wireless NIC, and then click the **Properties** button.

Choose **Internet Protocol (TCP/IP)**, and then click the **Properties** button.

Click the **Obtain an IP address automatically** radio button.

Click the **Obtain DNS server address automatically** radio button.

Click **OK**.

15.5.1 Optional Lab: Install a Wireless NIC in Windows Vista

Introduction

In this lab, you will install and configure a wireless NIC.

Recommended Equipment

- ∞ A computer with Windows Vista installed
- ∞ Empty PCI slot on the motherboard
- ∞ A wireless access point or router
- ∞ A wireless PCI NIC
- ∞ An antistatic wrist strap

Step 1

Turn off your computer. If a switch is present on the power supply, set the switch to "0" or "off". Unplug the computer from the AC outlet. Remove the side panels from the case.

Put on the antistatic wrist strap and attach it to an unpainted metal surface of the computer case.

Choose an appropriate slot on the motherboard to install the new wireless NIC.

You may need to remove the metal cover near the slot on the back of the case.

Make sure the wireless NIC is properly lined up with the slot. Push down gently on the wireless NIC.

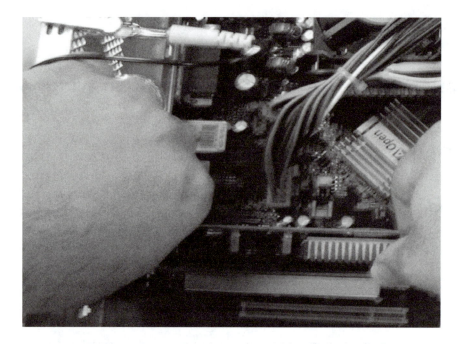

Secure the wireless NIC mounting bracket to the case with a screw.

Attach the antenna to the antenna connector on the back of the computer.

Disconnect the antistatic wrist strap. Replace the case panels. Plug the power cable into an AC outlet. If a switch is present on the power supply, set the switch to "1" or "on".

Step 2

Boot your computer, and then log on as an administrator.

The wireless NIC will be detected by Windows. The "Found New Hardware" window will appear.

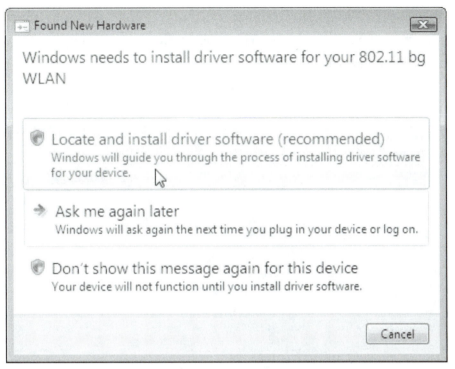

Click **Locate and install driver software (recommended)**. Click **Continue**.

You will be prompted to insert the manufacturer's CD.

Insert the CD.

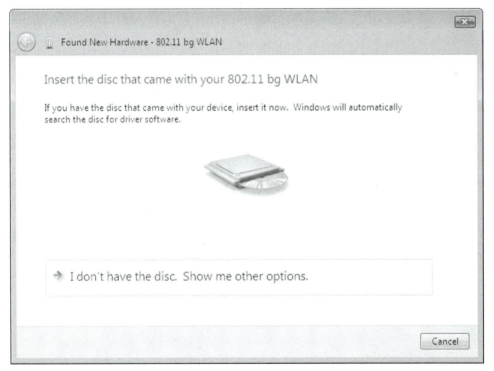

Once the drivers are installed click **Close** to complete the driver installation process.

Step 3

Click **Start** > right-click **Computer**, and choose **Manage** > **Continue**.

Choose **Device Manager**, and then expand "Network Adapters".

What network adapters are installed in the computer?

Close the "Computer Management" window.

Step 4

Choose **Start**.

Right-click **Network** > **Properties** > select **Manage network connections.**

Double-click the wireless NIC, and then click the **Properties** button > **Continue**.

Choose **Internet Protocol Version 4 (TCP/IPv4)**, and then click the **Properties** button.

Click the **Obtain an IP address automatically** radio button.

Click the **Obtain DNS server address automatically** radio button.

Click **OK**.

Step 5

Choose **Start > Start Search**.

Type **cmd**, and then press the **Enter** key.

Type **ipconfig /all**, and then press the **Enter** key.

What is the IP address of the computer?

What is the subnet mask of the computer?

What is the default gateway of the computer?

What are the DNS servers for the computer?

What is the MAC address of the comptuer?

Is DHCP Enabled?

What is the IP address of the DHCP server?

Step 6

A wireless NIC may also be configured with a static IP address.

Choose **Start**.

Right-click **Network > Properties >** select **Manage network connections.**

Double-click the wireless NIC, and then click the **Properties** button **> Continue**.

Choose **Internet Protocol Version 4 (TCP/IPv4)**, and then click the **Properties** button.

Click the **Use the following IP address** radio button. Type the IP address, subnet mask and default gateway addresses from step 5.

Click the **Use the following DNS server address** radio button. Type the DNS address from step 5.

Click **OK**.

Step 7

Choose **Start > Start Search**.

Type **cmd**, and then press the **Enter** key.

Type **ipconfig /all**, and then press the **Enter** key.

Is DHCP Enabled?

Step 8

Return the NIC to original settings.

Choose **Start**.

Right-click **Network > Properties >** select **Manage network connections.**

Double-click the wireless NIC, and then click the **Properties** button **> Continue**.

Choose **Internet Protocol Version 4 (TCP/IPv4)**, and then click the **Properties** button.

Click the **Obtain an IP address automatically** radio button.

Click the **Obtain DNS server address automatically** radio button.

Click **OK**.

15.5.2 Lab: Configure Wireless Router

Introduction

In this lab, you will configure and test the wireless settings on the Linksys WRT300N.

Recommended Equipment

- A computer with Windows XP Professional or Windows Vista
- A Wireless NIC installed
- An Ethernet NIC installed
- Linksys WRT300N Wireless Router
- Ethernet patch cable

Step 1

Ask the instructor for the following information that is used during the lab.

Router Static IP Information:

IP address _____

Subnet mask _____

Gateway _____

DNS _____

SSID Values:

New SSID _____

Wireless Security:

Pre-shared key _____

Important: Only use configurations assigned by the instructor.

Step 2

Connect the computer to one of the **Ethernet** ports on the wireless router with an Ethernet patch cable.

Plug in the power of the wireless router. Boot the computer and log in as an administrator.

Step 3

Open the command prompt.

Type **ipconfig /renew**.

What is the default gateway for the computer?

Step 4

Open Internet Explorer. Type the IP address of your default gateway in the "Address" field, and then press **Return**.

The "Connect to" window appears.

Type "admin" in the "Password:" field.

The Setup screen appears.

Step 5

What is the Internet Connection Type assigned to the router?

To configure the router with a static IP address, click the dropdown menu **Internet Connection Type** and select **Static IP**.

Enter the following static IP information provided by the instructor (step 1): Internet IP Address, Subnet Mask, Default Gateway, and DNS 1.

Click **Save Settings**.

The "Settings are successful" screen appears.

Click **Continue**. Keep the router configuration page open.

Step 6

Open the command prompt again.

Type **ipconfig /all**, and record the following information.

Computer IP information:

IP address _____

Subnet mask _____

Gateway _____

DNS _____

Use this information to configure the wireless NIC with static IP information.

Save these settings.

Step 7

Click the "Wireless" tab.

Click Network Mode dropdown menu.

What 802.11 technologies are supported?

Choose "Mixed" in the "Network Mode:" drop-down box.

What is the default SSID for the wireless router?

Type "cisco#" in the "Network Name (SSID):" field, where # is the number assigned by your instructor.

Click **Save Settings > Continue**.

Close Internet Explorer.

Step 8

Unplug the Ethernet cable from the computer.

View wireless networks associated with the wireless adapter configured for the computer.

What wireless network(s) are available?

Choose **cisco#**, and then click the **Connect** button.

Open Internet Explorer. Type the IP address of your default gateway in the "Address" field, and then press **Return**.

The "Connect to" window appears.

Type "admin" in the "Password:" field.

The Setup screen appears.

Disable SSID broadcast.

Click **Save Settings > Continue**.

Why would you disable SSID broadcast?

View wireless networks associated with the wireless adapter configured to the computer.

What wireless network(s) are available?

Click on the router configuration page so it is activated.

Enable SSID broadcast.

Click **Save Settings > Continue**.

15.5.3 Lab: Test the Wireless NIC in Windows XP

Introduction

In this lab, you will check the status of your wireless connection, investigate the availability of wireless networks, and test connectivity.

Recommended Equipment

- A computer with Windows XP installed
- A wireless NIC installed
- An Ethernet NIC installed
- Linksys WRT300N Wireless Router
- Internet connectivity

Step 1

Disconnect the Ethernet patch cable from your computer.

A red "X" appears over the "Local Area Connection" icon.

Hover over the "Wireless Network Connection" icon in the tray.

What is the Speed and Signal Strength?

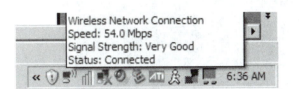

Open a command window.

Ping **127.0.0.1**.

How many Replies did you receive?

```
C:\WINDOWS\system32\cmd.exe

C:\>ping 127.0.0.1

Pinging 127.0.0.1 with 32 bytes of data:

Reply from 127.0.0.1: bytes=32 time<1ms TTL=128
Reply from 127.0.0.1: bytes=32 time<1ms TTL=128
Reply from 127.0.0.1: bytes=32 time<1ms TTL=128
Reply from 127.0.0.1: bytes=32 time<1ms TTL=128

Ping statistics for 127.0.0.1:
    Packets: Sent = 4, Received = 4, Lost = 0 (0% loss),
Approximate round trip times in milli-seconds:
    Minimum = 0ms, Maximum = 0ms, Average = 0ms

C:\>
```

Use the ipconfig command.

What is the IP address of the default gateway?

```
C:\WINDOWS\system32\cmd.exe

C:\>ipconfig

Windows IP Configuration


Ethernet adapter Local Area Connection:

        Media State . . . . . . . . . . . : Media disconnected

Ethernet adapter Wireless Network Connection:

        Connection-specific DNS Suffix  . :
        IP Address. . . . . . . . . . . . : 192.168.2.3
        Subnet Mask . . . . . . . . . . . : 255.255.255.0
        Default Gateway . . . . . . . . . : 192.168.2.1

C:\>
```

Ping the default gateway.

A successful ping indicates that there is a connection between the computer and the default gateway.

Step 2

Open a web browser.

Type **www.cisco.com** in the "Address" field, and then press **Return**.

Step 3

Open the **Network Connections** window.

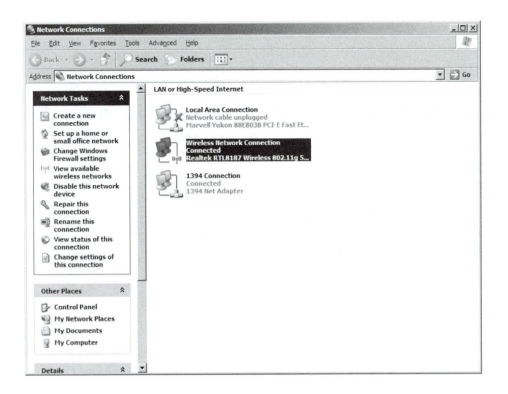

Right-click the wireless connection and choose **Properties**.

Click the **Wireless Networks** tab.

Click the **View Wireless Networks** button.

What are the names of the wireless networks that are available?

15.5.3 Optional Lab: Test the Wireless NIC in Windows Vista

Introduction

In this lab, you will check the status of your wireless connection, investigate the availability of wireless networks, and test connectivity.

Recommended Equipment

- A computer with Windows Vista installed
- A wireless NIC installed
- An Ethernet NIC installed
- Linksys WRT300N Wireless Router
- Internet connectivity

Step 1

Disconnect the Ethernet cable from your computer.

A red "X" appears over the "Local Area Connection" icon.

Connect to a wireless network.

Hover over the "Wireless Network Connection" icon in the tray.

What is the name of the wireless connection?

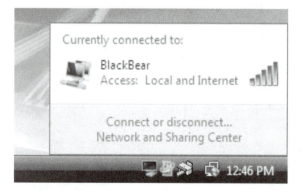

Open a command window.

Ping **127.0.0.1**.

How many Replies did you receive?

Use the ipconfig command.

What is the IP address of the default gateway?

Ping the default gateway.

A successful ping indicates that there is a connection between the computer and the default gateway.

Step 2

Open a web browser.

Type **www.cisco.com** in the "Address" field, and then press **Enter**.

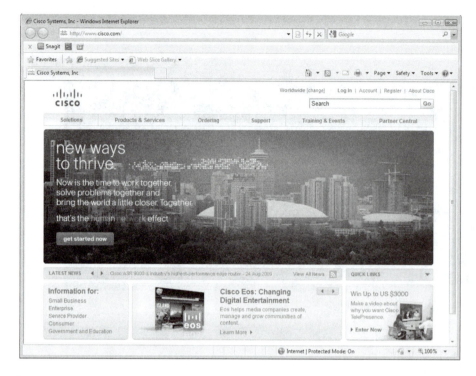

Step 3

Open the **Network Connections** window.

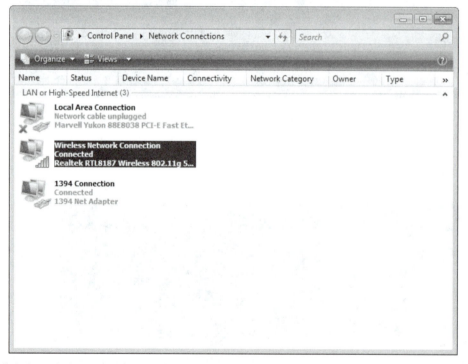

Right-click the wireless connection and choose **Connect / Disconnect**.

Select **All** from the Show dropdown menu. Press the **Refresh** button.

What are the names of the wireless networks that are available?

15.8.3 Lab: Fix Network Problem

Introduction

In this lab, you will troubleshoot and fix a computer that does not connect to the network.

Recommended Equipment

- A computer running Windows XP
- Linksys 300N wireless router
- Ethernet patch cable

Scenario

The computer will not connect to the Internet, network shares, or network printers.

Step 1

Open a command line and use command line tools to determine the ip address, subnet mask, and default gateway of the computer.

Step 2

Use command line tools to attempt to fix the network connection problem.

Step 3

Verify the settings in the wireless router configuration screens.

Step 4
What steps did you perform to fix the network?

15.8.3 Lab: Remote Technician: Fix Network Problem

(Student Technician Sheet)

In this lab, you will gather data from the customer, and then instruct the customer on how to fix a computer that does not connect to the network. Document the customer's problem in the work order below.

Company Name: <u>JH Paint Supply</u>
Contact: <u>Jill Henderson</u>
Company Address: <u>114 W. Main Street</u>
Company Phone: <u>1-888-555-2143</u>

Work Order

Generating a New Ticket

Category <u>Network</u>   Closure Code ____   Status <u>Open</u>

Type: _____   Escalated <u>Yes</u>   Pending _____

Item _____   Pending Until Date _____

Business Impacting? X Yes   O No

Summary <u>One computer cannot connect to the Internet, network shares, or</u>
<u>network printers.</u>

Case ID#_____   Connection Type <u>Wireless</u>
Priority _____2_____   Environment _____
User Platform <u>Windows XP Pro</u>

Problem Description: <u>All computers boot up properly. Computer does not</u>
<u>connect to shares or the Internet. Computer has not been moved. Cables are</u>
<u>securely connected. Link lights are blinking.</u>

Problem Solution:

(Student Customer Sheet)

Use the contact information and problem description below to report the following information to a level-two technician:

Contact Information

Company Name: JH Paint Supply

Contact: Jill Henderson

Company Address: 114 W. Main Street

Company Phone: 1-888-555-2143

Problem Description

Well, the problem does not always seem to be there. Typically, not all computers on the network are used all of the time, so everything seems to be fine. On some busy days, every computer is being used and there is always one computer that cannot connect. I cannot figure out what the problem is because it is not usually on the same computer. When a computer cannot make connectivity, I check to make sure all cables and connections are fine.

(NOTE: Once you have given the level-two tech the problem description, use the Additional Information to answer any follow up questions the technician may ask.)

Additional Information

- Windows XP Pro
- Computer has no new hardware
- Computer has not been moved recently
- A extra computer was added to the network recently
- Computer looks the same as it did yesterday

15.8.3 Lab: Troubleshooting Network Problems in Windows XP

Introduction

In this lab, the instructor will introduce various network problems. The student will diagnose the causes and solve the problems.

Recommended Equipment

The following equipment is required for this exercise:

- Two computers running Windows XP
- Linksys 300N wireless router
- Two Ethernet cables
- Internet access

Scenario

You must solve network problems for a customer. You may need to troubleshoot both the router and two computers. Make sure you document and solve the problems, and then document the solutions.

There are several possible errors. Solve one problem at a time until you can successfully establish a connection between the two computers.

Step 1

List the computer name used for computer one and computer two. Use these names whenever the lab refers to computer one and computer two.

Computer one name:

Computer two name:

Complete the following from computer one.

Log on to the computer with the Administrator account.

Click **Start > My Network Places > View workgroup computers**.

Do you see computer two?

If you answered yes, double click computer two.

Did the connection open?

Students start by troubleshooting the router or computers for problems. Answer the following questions after each problem is solved.

What problem did you find?

What steps did you take to determine the problem?

What is causing the problem?

List the steps taken to fix the problem.

Do you see computer two?

If you answered yes, double click computer two.

Did the connection open?

If you answered yes, what is the name of the shared folder?

Open the text file in the shared folder. What does the hidden message say?

If you opened and recorded the message from the shared folder, you have successfully solved all networking problems. Hand the lab into your instructor.

If you could not open the connection to computer two, continue troubleshooting the problem.

Problem 1

What problem did you find?

What steps did you take to determine the problem?

What is causing the problem?

List the steps taken to fix the problem.

Problem 2

What problem did you find?

What steps did you take to determine the problem?

What is causing the problem?

List the steps taken to fix the problem.

Problem 3

What problem did you find?

What steps did you take to determine the problem?

What is causing the problem?

List the steps taken to fix the problem.

15.8.3 Optional Lab: Troubleshooting Network Problems in Windows Vista

Introduction

In this lab, the instructor will introduce various network problems. The student will diagnose the causes and solve the problems.

Recommended Equipment

The following equipment is required for this exercise:

- Two computers running Windows Vista

- Linksys 300N wireless router

- Two Ethernet cables

- Internet access

Scenario

You must solve network problems for a customer. You may need to troubleshoot both the router and two computers. Make sure you document and solve the problems, and then document the solutions.

There are several possible errors. Solve one problem at a time until you can successfully establish a connection between the two computers.

Step 1

List the computer name used for computer one and computer two. Use these names whenever the lab refers to computer one and computer two.

Computer one name:

Computer two name:

Complete the following from computer one.

Log on to the computer with the Administrator account.

Click **Start > Network**.

Do you see computer two?

If you answered yes, double click computer two.

Did the connection open?

Students start by troubleshooting the router or computers for problems. Answer the following questions after each problem is solved.

What problem did you find?

What steps did you take to determine the problem?

What is causing the problem?

List the steps taken to fix the problem.

Do you see computer two?

If you answered yes, double click computer two.

Did the connection open?

If you answered yes, what is the name of the shared folder?

Open the text file in the shared folder. What does the hidden message say?

If you opened and recorded the message from the shared folder, you have successfully solved all networking problems. Hand the lab into your instructor.

If you could not open the connection to computer two, continue troubleshooting the problem.

Problem 1
What problem did you find?

What steps did you take to determine the problem?

What is causing the problem?

List the steps taken to fix the problem.

Problem 2
What problem did you find?

What steps did you take to determine the problem?

What is causing the problem?

List the steps taken to fix the problem.

Problem 3
What problem did you find?

What steps did you take to determine the problem?

What is causing the problem?

List the steps taken to fix the problem.

Chapter 16: Advanced Security

16.1.1 Worksheet: Answer Security Policy Questions

In this activity, you will answer security questions regarding the IT Essentials classroom.

1. List the person(s) responsible for each piece of network equipment that is used in your classroom (for example, routers, switches, and wireless access points).

2. List the person(s) responsible for the computers that are used in your classroom.

3. List the person(s) responsible for assigning permissions to use the network resources.

4. Which Internet web sites do you have permission to access?

5. What type of Internet web sites are not permitted to be accessed in the classroom?

6. List activities that could damage the network or the computers attached to the network with malware.

7. Should anyone, other than the network administrator, be be allowed to attach modems or wireless access points to the network? Please explain why or why not.

16.2.3 Worksheet: Research Firewalls

In this activity, you will use the Internet, a newspaper, or a local store to gather information about hardware and software firewalls.

1. Using the Internet, research two different hardware firewalls. Based on your research, complete the table below.

Company/Hardware Name	Website URL	Cost	Subscription Length (Month/Year/Lifetime)	Hardware Features
				∞

2. Which hardware firewall would you purchase? List reasons for your selection.

3. Using the Internet, research two different software firewalls. Based on your research, complete the table below.

Company/Software Name	Website URL	Cost	Subscription Length (Month/Year/Lifetime)	Software Features
				∞

4. Which software firewall would you purchase? List reasons for your selection.

16.3.1 Lab: Configure Wireless Security

Introduction

In this lab, you will configure and test the wireless settings on the Linksys WRT300N.

Recommended Equipment

- Two computers with Windows XP or Windows Vista
- An Ethernet NIC installed in computer 1
- A Wireless NIC installed in computer 2
- Linksys WRT300N Wireless Router
- Ethernet patch cable

Step 1

Ask the instructor for the following information that is used during the lab.

Default Login Information:

User Name (if any) _____

Password _____

Basic Wireless Settings:

Network Name (SSID) _____

Important: Only use configurations assigned by the instructor.

NOTE: use computer 1 for all lab instructions unless stated.

Step 2

Connect computer 1 to an **Ethernet** ports on the wireless router with an Ethernet patch cable.

Plug in the power of the wireless router. Boot the computer and log in as an administrator.

Step 3

Open the command prompt.

Type **ipconfig**.

What is the IP address for the computer?

What is the default gateway for the computer?

Step 4

Open Internet Explorer and connect to the wireless router.

Type "admin" in the "Password:" field.

The Setup screen appears. Click **Wireless** tab.

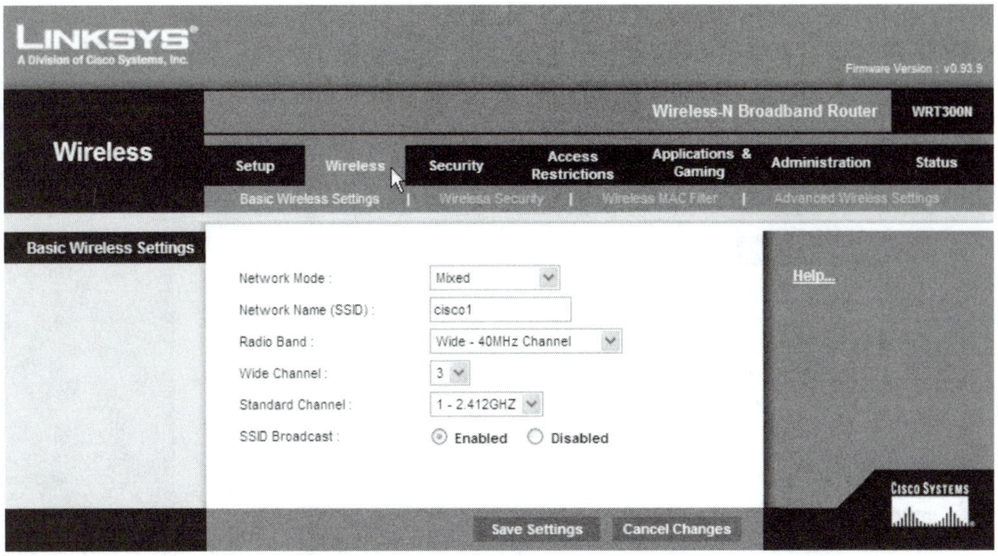

Step 5

Click **Wireless Security** tab, then for Security Mode select **WPA2 Personal**.

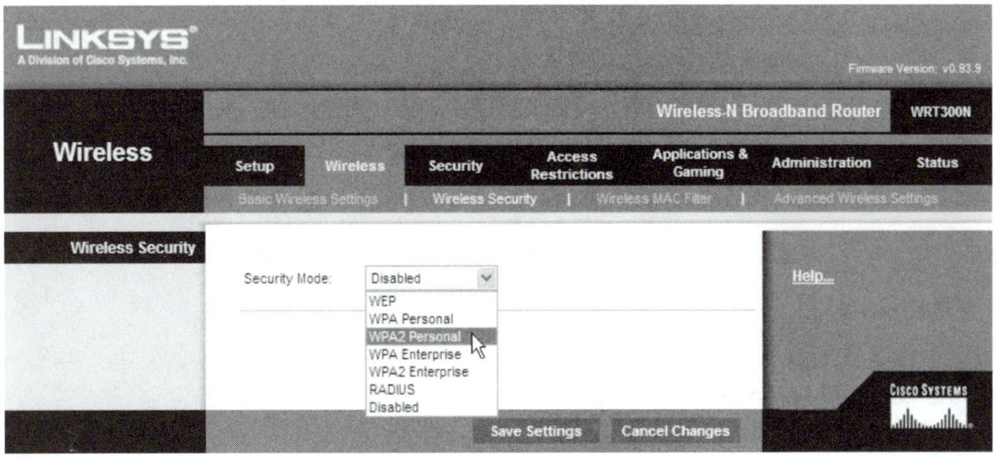

Set the following settings:

Encryption – AES

Pre-shared Key – c!scol&b1361

Key Renewal – 3600

Click **Save Settings > Continue**.

Keep Internet Explorer open to the Linksys router.

Step 6

Log in to computer 2, the wireless computer, as the administrator.

Connect to the wireless network. If asked for a security key or passphase enter: **c!scol&b1361**

Open the command prompt.

Type **ipconfig /all**.

What is the physical address of the wireless NIC?

Type **ping IPaddress**. Where IPaddress is the IP address of computer 1.

Was the ping successful?

Keep the command prompt window open.

Step 7

From computer 1, make sure Internet Explorer is active.

Under the Wireless tab click **Wireless MAC Filter**.

Select **Enabled** > **Prevent** > click **Wireless Client List** button.

Step 8

Select **Save to MAC Address Filter List** check box for computer 2.

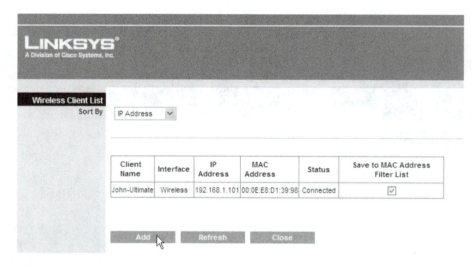

Click **Add**.

The Wireless MAC Filter window opens.

Click **Save Settings > Continue**.

Step 9

From computer 2:

In the command prompt window type **ping IPaddress**. Where IPaddress is the IP address of computer 1.

Was the ping successful?

Step 10

From computer 1, click **the browser** so it is activated.

Click **Administration** on the main tab bar.

Highlight the Router Password, type **lab1631**. Type the same password in Re-enter to confirm.

Click **Cancel Changes**. Do not save the new password.

Step 11

Click **Security** on the main tab bar.

By default SPI Firewall Protection is Enabled.

What Internet Filters are activated?

What Web Filters are activated?

Step 12

Click **Applications & Gaming** on the main tab bar.

Click Single Port Forwarding.

To forward an otherwise blocked port to a specific computer, select Application Name **FTP**.

Type the last octet of the IP address for the computer and then click **Enabled** checkbox.

Click **Cancel Changes**. Do not save the new setting.

Step 13

Click **Port Range Triggering**.

To open an otherwise blocked port, type in the application name **IRC**. Then type the Triggered Range **6660 to 7000**, Forwarded Range **113 to 113** and then click **Enabled** checkbox.

Click **Cancel Changes**. Do not save the new setting.

Step 14

From computer 1, click **Wireless** tab.

Click **Wireless MAC Filter** > **Disable**.

Click **Save Settings** > **Continue**.

16.3.2 Lab: Configure Windows XP Firewall

In this lab you will explore the Windows XP Firewall and configure some advanced settings.

Recommended Equipment

- Two computers directly connected or connected through a hub or switch
- Windows XP installed on both computers
- Computers are in the same workgroup and share the same subnet mask

Step 1

From computer 1, right-click the **Desktop**, select **New > Folder**. Name the folder Cisco. Share the folder, use the default name Cisco.

From computer 2 open **My Network Place >** select **View workgroup computers** and connect to computer 1.

Can you see the shared folder Cisco?

NOTE: If you answered no, ask the instructor for help.

Close **My Network Place**.

NOTE: Use computer 1 for the rest of the lab unless otherwise stated.

Step 2

Navigate to the Windows XP Firewall:

Click **Start > Control Panel > Security Center**.

The Firewall indicator shows the status of the firewall. The normal setting is "**ON**".

Access Windows firewall by clicking **Windows Firewall** at the bottom of the window.

Step 3

The Windows Firewall window opens.

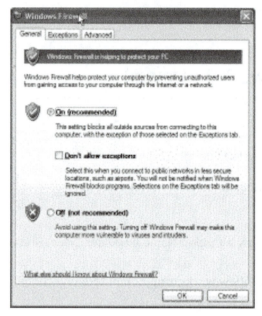

In the space below, state why turning off the Windows Firewall is not advised.

Step 4

From the Windows Firewall window select the **Exceptions** tab. Programs and services that Windows Firewall is not blocking will be listed with a checkmark.

You can add applications to this list. This may be necessary if your customer has an application that requires outside communications but for some reason the Windows Firewall cannot perform the configuration automatically. You must be logged on to this computer as an administrator to complete this procedure.

Click **What are the risks of allowing exceptions?**

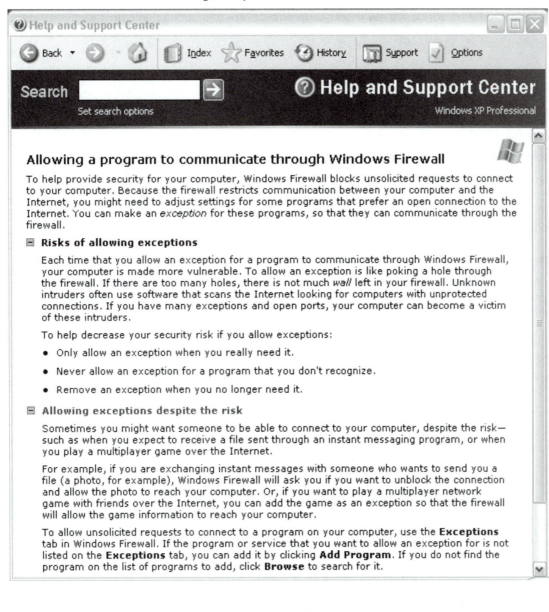

Creating too many exceptions in your Programs and Services file can have negative consequences. Describe a negative consequence to having too many exceptions.

Close the Help and Support Center window.

Step 5

From computer 1:

To turn off an exception, remove the check mark from **File and Printer Sharing > OK**.

From computer 2:

Open **My Network Place > View workgroup computers** and connect to computer 1.

Can you connect to computer 1?

From computer 1:

To turn on an exception, add a check mark to **File and Printer Sharing > OK**.

From computer 2:

Refresh **My Network Place** and connect to computer 1.

Can you connect to computer 1?

Log off computer 2. Use computer 1 for the rest of the lab.

Step 6

From the Windows Firewall control menu select the **Advanced** tab to view the **Network Connection Settings**. Network Connection Settings displays the different connections configured for your computer.

Click the **Settings** button in the Network Connection Settings area. The Advanced Settings window has two tabs: Services and ICMP. Click the **Services** tab.

In the space below, list the services that are available.

Step 7

There are many applications that users do not normally see that also need to get through the Windows Firewall to access your computer. These are the network level commands that direct traffic on the network and the Internet.

Under the ICMP heading, click the **Settings** button. You will see the menu where ICMP exceptions are configured.

In the example here, allowing incoming echo requests is what allows network users to ping your computer to determine if it is present on the network and how fast information travels to and from it.

In the space below, list the requests for information that your computer will respond to.

Close all windows.

16.3.2 Optional Lab: Configure Windows Vista Firewall

In this lab you will explore the Windows Vista Firewall and configure some advanced settings.

Recommended Equipment

- Two computers directly connected or connected through a hub or switch
- Windows Vista installed on both computers
- Computers are in the same workgroup and share the same subnet mask

Step 1

For computer 1, right-click the **desktop**, select **New > Folder**. Name the folder Cisco.

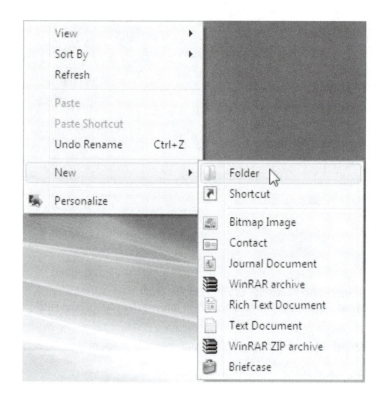

Right-click on the Cisco folder then select **Share > Continue**.

Share the folder, use the default name Cisco.

From computer 2 click **Start > Network** and connect to computer 1.

Can you see the shared folder Cisco?

NOTE: If you answered no, ask the instructor for help.

Close **Network**.

NOTE: Use computer 1 for the rest of the lab unless otherwise stated.

Step 2

Navigate to the Windows Vista Firewall:

Click **Start > Control Panel > Security Center**

The Firewall indicator shows the status of the firewall. The normal setting is "**ON**".

Access Windows firewall by clicking **Firewall** at the right side of the window.

Step 3

Click **Change settings > Continue**.

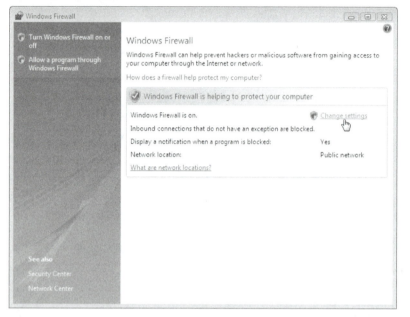

The Windows Firewall Settings window opens.

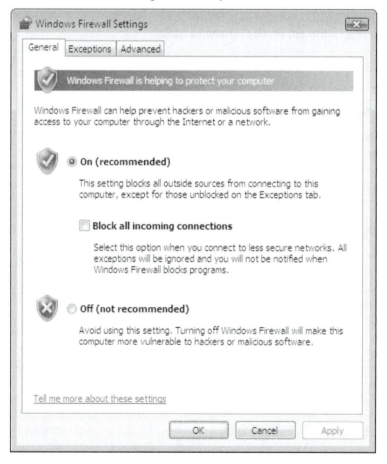

In the space below, state why turning off the Windows Firewall is not advised.

Step 4

From the Windows Firewall Settings window select the **Exceptions** tab. Programs and services that Windows Firewall is not blocking will be listed with a checkmark.

You can add applications to this list. This may be necessary if your customer has an application that requires outside communications but for some reason the Windows Firewall cannot perform the configuration automatically. You must be logged on to this computer as an administrator to complete this procedure.

Click **What are the risks of unblocking a program**?

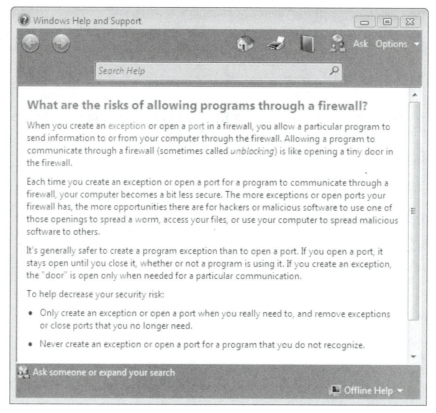

Creating too many exceptions in your Programs and Services file can have negative consequences. Describe a negative consequence to having too many exceptions.

Close Windows Help and Support window.

Step 5

From computer 1:

To turn off an exception, remove the check mark from **File and Printer Sharing > OK**.

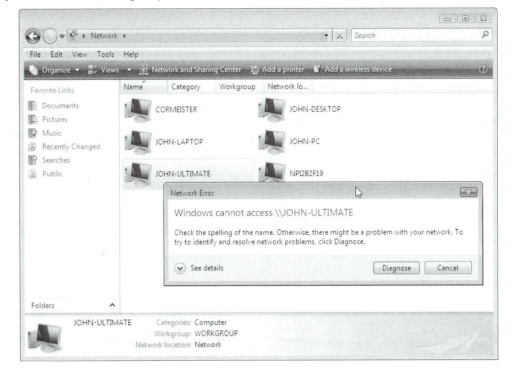

From computer 2:

Open **Network > Workgroup** and connect to computer 1.

Can you connect to computer 1?

From computer 1:

To turn on an exception add a check mark to **File and Printer Sharing > OK**.

From computer 2:

Refresh **Network** and connect to computer 1.

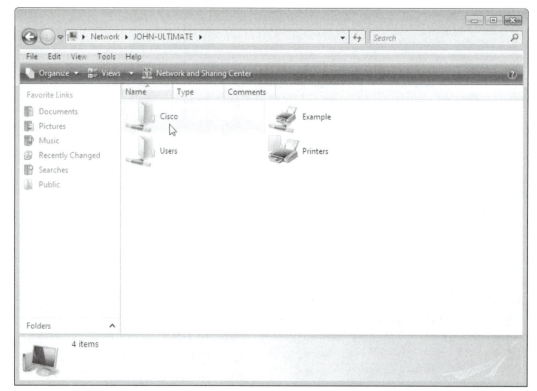

Can you connect to computer 1?

Log off computer 2. Use computer 1 for the rest of the lab.

Step 6

Click **Start > Control Panel > Administrative Tools > Windows Firewall with Advanced Security > Continue > Inbound Rules**.

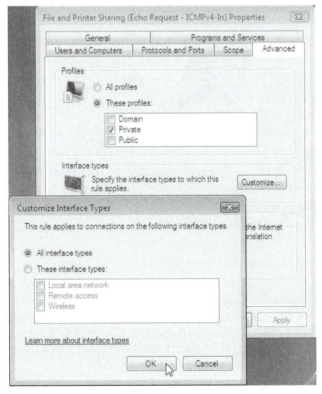

Expand the window so you can see the full name of the Inbound rules. Locate Files and Printer Sharing (Echo Request – ICMPv4-In).

Right-click on the rule and select **Properties > Advanced** tab **> Customize**. The Advance tab displays the profile(s) used by the computer and the Customize Interface Types window displays the different connections configured for your computer.

Click **OK**.

Click **Programs and Services** tab.

In the space below, list the short name of four services that are available.

Click **Cancel**.

Step 7

There are many applications that users do not normally see that also need to get through the Windows Firewall to access your computer. These are the network level commands that direct traffic on the network and the Internet.

Click **Protocols and Ports** tab. For the ICMP settings, click the **Customize** button. You will see the menu where ICMP exceptions are configured.

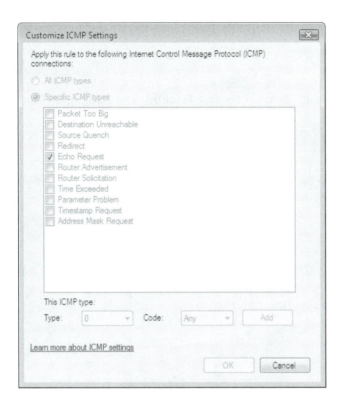

In the example here, allowing incoming echo requests is what allows network users to ping your computer to determine if it is present on the network and how fast information travels to and from it.

In the space below, list the requests for information that your computer will respond to.

Close all windows.

16.4.3 Lab: Data Backup and Recovery in Windows XP

Introduction

In this lab, you will back up data. You will also perform a recovery of the data.

Recommended Equipment

The following equipment is required for this exercise:

- A computer system running Windows XP is required for this exercise.

Step 1

Log on to the computer as an administrator.

Navigate to the location where backed up files will be stored. For example, use the external hard drive H:\. Create a folder called **Backup Location**.

Create a text file on the desktop called **Backup File One**. Open the file and type the text "The text in this file will not be changed."

Create another text file on the desktop called **Backup File Two**. Open the file and type the text "The text in this file will be changed."

Step 2

Click **Start > All Programs > Accessories > System Tools > Backup**. The **Backup or Restore Wizard** window appears.

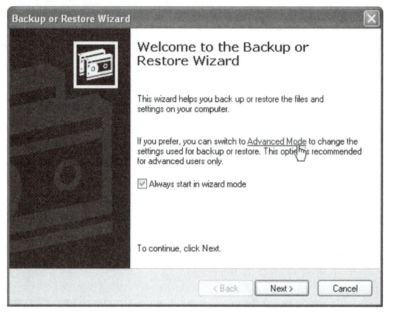

Click Advanced Mode.

Step 3

The Backup Utility window appears.

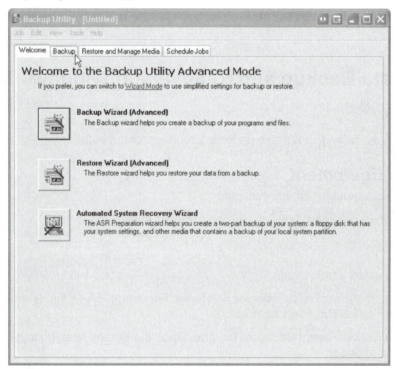

Click the **Backup** tab.

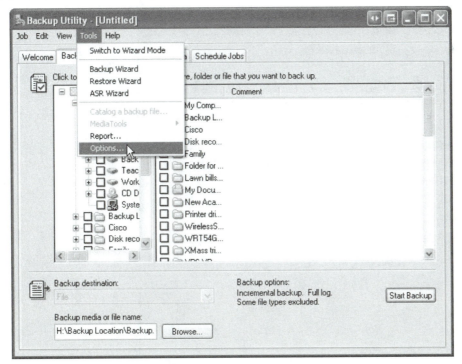

Step 4

From the menu select **Tools > Options**.

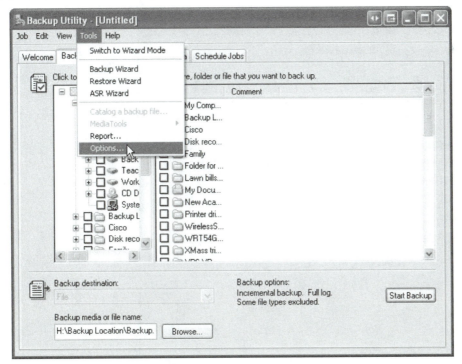

Select the default Backup Type to **Normal**.

What is the description of a normal backup?

Click **OK**.

Step 5

Click the **Desktop:** icon in the left panel. Then locate in the right panel the files named **Backup File One** and **Backup File Two**, and place a check mark next to the files.

Step 6

Click the **Browse** button. If asked to insert a disk into drive A, click **Cancel**.

Locate the **Drive H:** folder called **Backup Location**. Select the **Backup Location** folder and click **Open**. Click **Save**.

Step 7

Click **Start Backup** button.

The Backup Job Information window appears. Keep the default settings.

What is the default label for the backup file?

Click **Start Backup**.

The Backup Progress window appears.

When the backup is finished, click **Report**.

A backup log file opens. Scroll to the bottom of the file.

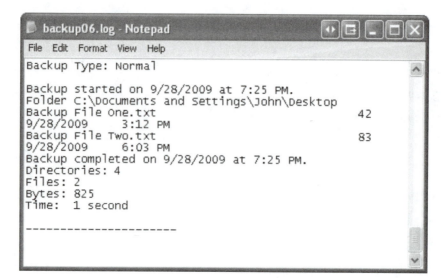

What files were backed up?

Close the notepad document.

Click **Close** to exit Backup Progress.

Step 8

Navigate to the Desktop. Delete **Backup File One** and **Backup File Two**.

Empty the Recycle Bin.

Step 9

Click on the **Backup Utility** window so it is activated.

Click the **Restore and Manage Media** tab.

In the left panel expand the most recent backup file. Place a check mark in the checkbox.

Make sure the Restore file to is set to Original location.

Click **Start Restore > OK**.

When the restore is finished, click Close.

Navigate to the desktop.

Are the two files restored to the desktop?

Step 10

Open file **Backup File Two**. Add the following text "More text added." to the file. Save the file.

Step 11

Click the **Backup Utility** window.

In the main menu select **Tools > Options > Backup Type** tab.

Change the default Backup Type to **Incremental**.

What is the description of an incremental backup?

Click **Ok**.

Step 12

Click the **Backup Tab**. Click the **Desktop** icon in the left panel. Locate in the right panel the file named **Backup File One** and **Backup File Two.** Place a check mark next to the files.

Click **Start Backup** button.

The Backup Job Information window appears. Keep the default settings.

What is the default label for the backup file?

Click **Start Backup**.

When the backup is finished, click **Report**.

Scroll to the bottom of the file.

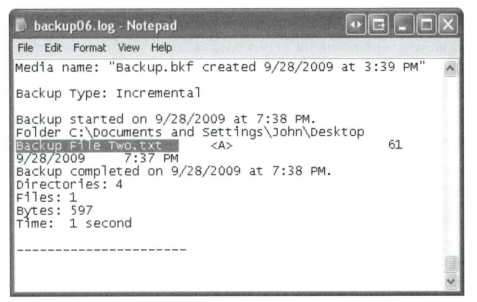

What file(s) were backed up?

Close the notepad document.

Click **Close** to exit Backup Progress.

Step 13

Click the **Schedule Job** tab.

Click **Add Job > Next**.

Select **Back up selected files, drivers, or network data**.

Click **Next**.

Locate and place a check mark next to files **Backup File One** and **Backup File Two**.

Click **Next**.

Click the **Browse** button, then locate and select the **Backup Location** folder. Click **Open > Save**.

Click **Next**.

Set backup type to **Daily**.

What is the description of a daily backup?

Click **Next > Next > Next**.

The When to Back Up window appears, select **Later**.

For Job name type **Daily Work Files**, then click **Set Schedule**.

Set Schedule Task to **Daily**, Start time to **2:00 AM**, Schedule Task Daily Every **1** day(s), and then click the **Advanced** button.

The Advanced Schedule Options window appears, click **Cancel**.

Click the **Settings** tab.

What is the default maximum time allowed to run a backup?

Click **OK**.

Enter the administrator password and confirm the password.

Click **OK**.

The **When to Back Up** screen appears with the new settings.

Click **Next > OK**.

Click **Cancel**. Do not save the scheduled backup. Close the **Backup Utility [Schedule Jobs]** window.

Step 14

Delete the following from the Desktop: **Backup File One,** and **Backup File Two**.

Delete the **Backup Location** folder from Drive H:.

Empty the trash.

16.4.3 Optional Lab: Data Backup and Recovery in Windows Vista

Introduction

In this lab, you will back up data. You will also perform a recovery of the data.

Recommended Equipment

The following equipment is required for this exercise:

- A computer system running Windows Vista is required for this exercise

Step 1

Log on to the computer as an administrator.

Create a text file on the desktop called **Backup File One**. Open the file and type the text "The text in this file will not be changed."

Create another text file on the desktop called **Backup File Two**. Open the file and type the text "The text in this file will be changed."

Step 2

Click **Start > All Programs > Accessories > System Tools > Backup Status and Configuration**. The Backup Status and Configuration window appears.

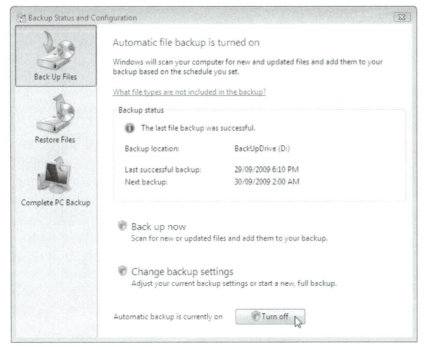

If automatic backup is turned on click **Turn Off > Continue**.

Step 3

Click **Change backup settings > Continue**.

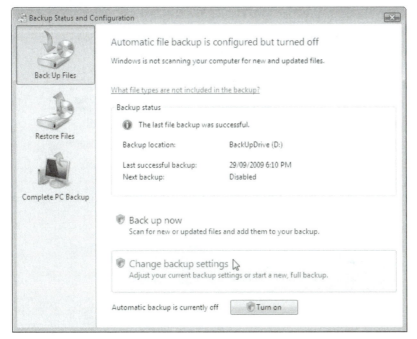

Select the location where the backup will be stored. In this example an external hard drive is used.

Click **Next**.

Step 4

What file type can be backed up?

What file types will not be backed up?

Only files on what type of disk can be backed up?

Make sure only file type **Documents** is selected.

Click **Next**.

Step 5
The **How often do you want to create a backup?** screen appears.

Set the following conditions:

How often – Daily

What day – blank

What time – 2:00 AM

Which files will be backed up?

Place a check mark in the checkbox **Create a new, full backup now in addition to saving settings**.

Click **Save settings and start backup**.

The **Creating a shadow copy** progress screen appears.

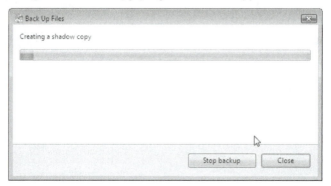

When the backup is finished, click **Close**.

Step 6

The **Backup Status and Configuration** window appears.

When will the next backup take place?

What is the state of automatic backup?

Step 7

Navigate to the Desktop. Delete **Backup File One** and **Backup File Two**.

Empty the Recycle Bin.

Step 8

Click on the **Backup Status and Configuration** window.

Click **Restore Files**.

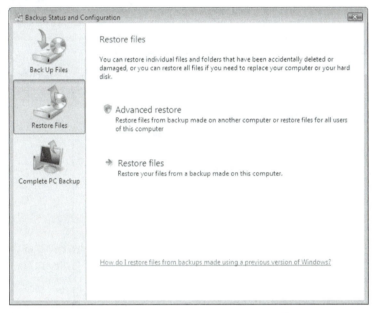

Step 9

Click **Restore files**.

Step 10

The **What do you want to restore?** screen appears.

Select **Files from the latest backup**, and then click **Next**.

Step 11

The **Select the files and folders to restore** screen appears.

Click **Add files**.

Navigate to the Desktop and locate files **Backup File One** and **Backup File Two**. Select both files by clicking **Backup File One** and then holding down the Ctrl key while clicking **Backup File Two**. Click **Add**.

The two files should show up in the **Select the files and folders to restore** screen.

Click **Next**.

Step 12

The **Where do you want to save the restored files?** screen appears.

Select **In the original location**, and then click **Start restore**.

When the Successfully restored files screen appears, click Finish.

Step 13

Navigate to the Desktop.

Are the two files restored to the Desktop?

Step 14

Open file **Backup File Two**. Add the following text "More text added." to the file. Save the file.

Step 15

Click on the **Backup Status and Configuration** window.

Click **Back Up Files**.

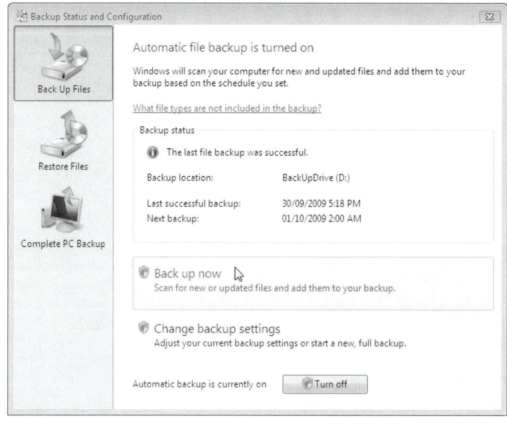

Which files will be backed up?

To where will the files be backed up?

Click **Back up now > Continue**.

The progress bar appears. When the backup is completed click **Close**.

Step 16

Navigate to the Desktop. Delete **Backup File Two**.

Empty the Recycle Bin.

Step 17

Click on the **Backup Status and Configuration** window so it is activated.

Click **Restore Files** icon.

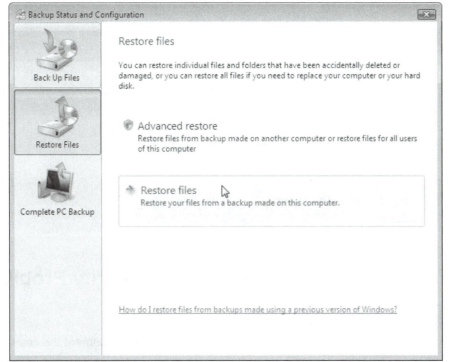

Click **Restore files**.

Restore both **Backup File One** and **Backup File Two**.

Step 18

Navigate to the Desktop. Open file **Backup File Two**.

What text is in the file?

Step 19

Delete the following from the Desktop: **Backup File One,** and **Backup File Two**.

Empty the trash.

16.5.3 Lab: Fix a Security Problem

In this lab, you will gather data from the customer, and then instruct the customer on how to correct a security issue that is preventing connection to the wireless network.

Recommended Equipment

- A computer running Windows XP

- Linksys 300N wireless router

- Ethernet patch cable

Scenario

The computer will not connect to the Internet.

Step 1

Open a command line and use command line tools to determine the ip address, subnet mask, and default gateway of the computer.

Step 2

Use command line tools to attempt to fix the network connection problem.

Step 3

Verify the settings in the wireless router configuration screens.

Step 4

What steps did you perform to fix the network?

16.5.3 Lab: Remote Technician: Fix a Security Problem

(Student Technician Sheet)

Gather data from the customer to begin the troubleshooting process. Document the customer's problem in the work order below.

Work Order

Company Name: Smith Lumber Supply
Contact: James Smith
Company Address: 1234 S. Main Street
Company Phone: 801-555.1212

Generating a New Ticket

Category Security   Closure Code_____   Status Open

Type_____   Escalated_____   Pending_____

Item_____   Pending Until Date_____

Business Impacting?   X Yes   O No

Summary____Customer cannot use laptop wireless connection at work_____
_____

Case ID#_____   Connection Type___Wireless_____
Priority_____   Environment_____
User Platform_____Windows XP Pro_____

Problem Description: Customer's wireless connection does not work in any_____
location at the work place. The customer can use wireless connection at home
and other places._____
_____
_____

Problem Solution: _____
_____
_____
_____
_____
_____
_____
_____
_____

(Student Customer Sheet)

Use the contact information and problem description below to report the following information to your lab partner who will be acting as a level-two technician. Your lab partner will guide you through the process of troubleshooting and fixing your wireless connection remotely. You must perform the tasks your lab partner recommends.

Contact Information

Company Name: Smith Lumber Supply

Contact: James Smith

Company Address: 1234 S. Main Street

Company Phone:801-555-1212

Category: Security

Problem Description

You are unable to use your laptop's wireless connection while at work. The wireless connection works fine at home and the coffee shop downstairs, but for some reason, it will not connect to the wireless anywhere in the office. Since you are unable to access the wireless connection, you have been using the Ethernet cable connection instead. The cable connection is working fine.

(NOTE: Once you have given the problem description, use the Additional Information to answer any follow up questions your lab partner may ask.)

Additional Information

- Windows XP Pro
- XP Wireless Client
- Wireless client can see the wireless network
- My wireless connection worked yesterday at work
- I can connect using an Ethernet cable
- My wireless account is in good standing
- Wireless connection works for other employees
- I have not made any changes to my wireless security settings
- A new wireless router was installed on the network yesterday

16.5.3 Lab: Troubleshooting Access Security with Windows XP

Introduction

In this lab, the instructor will introduce various access security problems. The student will diagnose the causes and solve the problems.

Recommended Equipment

The following equipment is required for this exercise:

- One computer running Windows XP on an NTFS partition

Scenario

Company XYZ has hired Nathan to manage the training department. Natashia was also hired as a temporary employee to replace Ben, who is no longer working for the company. You must solve access security problems for the training department. You might need to access the computers as each user and the administrator. Make sure you document and solve the problems, and then document the solutions.

There are several possible errors. Solve one problem at a time until there are no security breaches and access problems. Use the following tables when solving problems. The user account information is listed in Table 1. Use only the groups shown in Table 2, they are set up with the proper permissions. The instructor will provide the administrator's account information.

Table 1: Accounts

User Name	Password	Group for User
Ben	Cisco2001	Guests
Natashia	Cisco2010	Guests
Nathan	Cisco2100	Academy Student
Administrator user name:	Administrator password:	Administrators

Table 2: Groups

Groups	Group Permissions
Academy Student	Read & Execute, List Folder Contents, Read, Write
Guests	Read & Execute, List Folder Contents, Read
Administrators	Full Control

NOTE: There is a file, with a message, in both the Exploration folder and Discovery folder. The following folder structures are used for the lab:

C:\CiscoCCNA\ Discovery

C:\CiscoCCNA\ Exploration

Step 1

Log on to the computer as Ben and, then try saving text to the both files.

Can Ben log on to the computer?

Can Ben access both files?

If you answered "yes" to either question then there is a security breach in the system.

Can Natashia log on to the computer?

Can Natashia only read both files?

If you answered "no" to either question then there is an access problem in the system.

Can Nathan log on to the computer?

Can Nathan save text to both files?

If you answered "no" to either question then there is an access problem in the system.

Did you encounter any security breaches or access problems?

Log on to the computer with the Administrator account.

Students start by troubleshooting any security breaches or security problems. Answer the following questions after each problem is solved.

Did you encounter any security breaches or access problems?

If there were no security breaches and no access problems, you have successfully solved all security problems.

If there was a security breach or an access problem, continue troubleshooting the problem.

Problem 1

What problem did you find?

What steps did you take to determine the problem?

What is causing the problem?

List the steps taken to fix the problem.

Problem 2

What problem did you find?

What steps did you take to determine the problem?

What is causing the problem?

List the steps taken to fix the problem.

Problem 3

What problem did you find?

What steps did you take to determine the problem?

What is causing the problem?

List the steps taken to fix the problem.

Problem 4

What problem did you find?

What steps did you take to determine the problem?

What is causing the problem?

List the steps taken to fix the problem.

Problem 5

What problem did you find?

What steps did you take to determine the problem?

What is causing the problem?

List the steps taken to fix the problem.

Problem 6

What problem did you find?

What steps did you take to determine the problem?

What is causing the problem?

List the steps taken to fix the problem.

16.5.3 Optional Lab: Troubleshooting Access Security with Windows Vista

Introduction

In this lab, the instructor will introduce various access security problems. The student will diagnose the causes and solve the problems.

Recommended Equipment

The following equipment is required for this exercise:

- One computer running Windows Vista on an NTFS partition

Scenario

Company XYZ has hired Nathan to manage the training department. Natashia was also hired as a temporary employee to replace Ben, who is no longer working for the company. You must solve access security problems for the training department. You might need to access the computers as each user and the administrator. Make sure you document and solve the problems, and then document the solutions.

There are several possible errors. Solve one problem at a time until there are no security breaches and access problems. Use the following tables when solving problems. The user account information is listed in Table 1. Use only the groups shown in Table 2, they are set up with the proper permissions. The instructor will provide the administrator's account information.

Table 1: Accounts

User Name	Password	Group for User
Ben	Cisco2001	Guests
Natashia	Cisco2010	Guests
Nathan	Cisco2100	Academy Student
Administrator user name:	Administrator password:	Administrators

Table 2: Groups

Groups	Group Permissions
Academy Student	Read & Execute, List Folder Contents, Read, Write
Guests	Read & Execute, List Folder Contents, Read
Administrators	Full Control

NOTE: There is a file, with a message, in both the Exploration folder and Discovery folder. The following folder structures are used for the lab:

C:\CiscoCCNA\ Discovery

C:\CiscoCCNA\ Exploration

Step 1

Log on to the computer as Ben and, then try saving text to the both files.

Can Ben log on to the computer?

Can Ben access both files?

If you answered "yes" to either question then there is a security breach in the system.

Can Natashia log on to the computer?

Can Natashia only read both files?

If you answered "no" to either question then there is an access problem in the system.

Can Nathan log on to the computer?

Can Nathan save text to both files?

If you answered "no" to either question then there is an access problem in the system.

Did you encounter any security breaches or access problems?

Log on to the computer with the Administrator account.

Students start by troubleshooting any security breaches or security problems. Answer the following questions after each problem is solved.

Did you encounter any security breaches or access problems?

If there were no security breaches and no access problems, you have successfully solved all security problems.

If there was a security breach or an access problem, continue troubleshooting the problem.

Problem 1

What problem did you find?

What steps did you take to determine the problem?

What is causing the problem?

List the steps taken to fix the problem.

Problem 2

What problem did you find?

What steps did you take to determine the problem?

What is causing the problem?

List the steps taken to fix the problem.

Problem 3

What problem did you find?

What steps did you take to determine the problem?

What is causing the problem?

List the steps taken to fix the problem.

Problem 4

What problem did you find?

What steps did you take to determine the problem?

What is causing the problem?

List the steps taken to fix the problem.

Problem 5

What problem did you find?

What steps did you take to determine the problem?

What is causing the problem?

List the steps taken to fix the problem.

Problem 6

What problem did you find?

What steps did you take to determine the problem?

What is causing the problem?

List the steps taken to fix the problem.